SUBSIDIA BIBLICA

11

subsidia biblica - 11

LUIS ALONSO SCHÖKEL

A Manual of
Hebrew Poetics

EDITRICE PONTIFICIO ISTITUTO BIBLICO — ROMA 1988

This book is a translation and adaptation by the author and by Adrian Graffy of material contained in L. Alonso Schökel, *Hermeneutica de la palabra*. II. *Interpretación literaria de textos bíblicos* (Academia christiana, 38). 542 p. Madrid: Ediciones Cristiandad, 1987. ISBN 87-7057-400-7 [Obra completa]; ISBN 84-7057-413-2 [Tomo II].

ISBN 88-7653-567-5

EDITRICE PONTIFICIA UNIVERSITÀ GREGORIANA
EDITRICE PONTIFICIO ISTITUTO BIBLICO
Piazza della Pilotta 35 - 00187 Roma, Italia

Preface

This *Manual of Hebrew Poetics* closes a circle that began thirty-five years ago with my doctoral dissertation "Studies in Hebrew Poetics". The subject is the same but the genre is quite different. Because the subject is the same, the circle can include various types of work done through the years: commentaries, monographs, articles.

The genre is different, as a dissertation is different from a manual. Thirty-five years have passed since November 1954 when I began writing the doctoral dissertation. The genre of a thesis demands a great deal of reading, including even works which are clearly useless; it requires a show of erudition, wordy analysis, discussion of opinions. It is hoped, or supposed, that the dissertation will contribute something new or personal, a new solution to a long discussed problem, a synthesis of the research of a given period, a new topic not previously treated, a new method. My dissertation had the advantage of taking up a theme relatively new for the exegesis of the time, the poetics of the Hebrew Bible. The method, too, was new, a stylistic analysis according to the models of Leo Spitzer and Dámaso Alonso.

It is inevitable that a dissertation will have the defects inherent in the genre, such as the insecurity of the beginner, naive enthusiasm, exaggerations in one direction or another. My own work had another glaring defect, that of not paying enough attention to source criticism and literary units.

Although I defended the dissertation in April, 1957, it was not published until toward the end of 1962. Because the subject matter was somewhat unusual, and because the dissertation was written in Spanish, it did not reach a wide audience. But it had an extraordinary personal value in that for me it was a thesis that gave me an orientation. In my three decades of teaching and writing, I have always kept an interest in poetics and stylistics. During this time I believe that I have been able to refine my poetic sensibility, to make new exegetical contributions, and, naturally, I have grown in knowledge of the subject. In my articles on Biblical theology, in my exegetical commentaries, and in the books which contain my reflections on inspiration and hermeneutics, this interest has always been manifest.

At the present time a series of fortuitous events has made it possible to integrate the former work with the knowledge since acquired into a new book, this time a manual. The richness of facts and experiences which time has brought does not mean that the present work needs must be thicker and denser than the original thesis of 550 pages. Neither the genre of a manual nor my years would permit it to be so. One learns to economize, to dispense with the accidental, to concentrate on the essential. The baggage we need for our intercontinental trips has wondrously diminished.

The present work contains the substance of the dissertation, "Studies in Hebrew Poetry", as well as many new things, especially about images, figures, and dialogue. And since a good part of this material is taken from my exegetical commentaries, I am obliged to cite these works frequently. Withal, the size of the book justifies the title "manual". In German a book may be called a *"Hand-Atlas"* even when it is 50 cm by 30 cm, fit only for Cyclopean hands. I believe that mine is a manual made for human hands to handle and touch.

The primary purpose of the book is not to serve as a source of information about facts and authors. My intention is, rather, to initiate the reader into the stylistic analysis of poetry. To obtain information, to learn how to identify and classify, the reader can turn to recent works (Watson), earlier works (König, Hempel), or works that have been reprinted (Bullinger). Everything that this manual contains by way of definition, description, or classification is given as a means to doing analysis. For this reason many of the chapters or sections either begin or end with an example of analysis. The manual is not primarily a reference book but rather a book of initiation into the practice of analysis. I believe that when seen this way, the book fills a slot which is empty at the present time. I hope that it will give as much direction and orientation to others' work as the first book gave to mine.

Rome, January 27, 1988

LUIS ALONSO SCHÖKEL, S.J.

Table of Contents

Acknowledgements

Special thanks are due to the Rev. Eduardo Zurro of the Diocese of Valladolid, Spain, and Doctor in Sacred Scripture, for his thorough revision of the original manuscript and to the Rev. Adrian Graffy of the Diocese of Brentwood, England, and Doctor in Sacred Scripture, for his translation of the present work from the original Spanish. And to the Rev. John Welch, S.J., my colleague at the Pontifical Biblical Institute, for his advice on a variety of matters.

Biblical quotations are in part taken from the New English Bible, Second Edition (copyright 1970) by permission of Oxford and Cambridge University Presses. Other quotations are taken from the Revised Standard Version, copyrighted 1971 and 1952 by the Division of Christian Education of the National Council of the Churches of Christ in the USA.

LUIS ALONSO SCHÖKEL, S.J.

CHAPTER I

Historical Survey

The *Israelites* valued their texts and books not only as sacred texts but also as literary or poetic texts: the preservation of legends, epic tales, lyric songs, the imitation of poems and the conscious use of literary techniques show that for the Israelites these texts had not only a religious but also a literary value. In this they are similar to other peoples. What was lacking in their case was theoretical, systematic reflexion, an activity which Aristotle imposed on our Western culture. It is possible that there were in Israel schools of poetry which preserved and handed on practical rules, as happened in other skills. These practical rules would be the nucleus of a poetics formulated by the Hebrews themselves. Such a collection of rules may have existed, but it has left no trace.

As consciousness of the sacred nature of the texts grew, awareness of their literary and poetic value diminished. Thus it happened that, even though the Jews continued composing literary texts (which we call apocryphal) and studied their canonical texts passionately and meticulously, they scarcely considered their literary dimension. Even the living tradition of poetic rhythm was forgotten, and only empirical imitations persisted. In spite of contact with the Greeks they do not produce a Hebrew rhetoric or poetics.

I. Patristic Times

At the beginning of Christianity, when the literary field was occupied exclusively by Greek and Latin writers, the Bible was read simply as a sacred book. Two controversies which might have brought about a new mentality did not have lasting effects. When Julian forbade the Christians from teaching the Greek and Latin "classics" in the year 362, some Christian authors began to compose "Christian classics" by imitation. They took themes and motifs from the Bible and created new literary texts. This was an implicit admission that the Bible as such was not literature. The controversy about Christian *rusticitas* provoked two contrary reactions. On the one hand, the accusation of "rusticity" was accepted and met apologetically with Paul's argument: "The word I spoke, the gospel

I proclaimed, did not sway you with subtle arguments; it carried
conviction by spiritual power, so that your faith might be built not
upon human wisdom but upon the power of God" (1 Cor 2,4-5).
This line was taken by Origen, Chrysostom, etc. On the other hand,
the accusation was denied and it was affirmed that the Bible was
literature. This was demonstrated by compiling lists of tropes and
figures taken from the Bible. This was the approach taken by
Augustine, among others.

These two approaches, the transforming of biblical themes into
western poetry (biblical epic) and the cataloguing of metaphors and
figures of speech from the Bible (biblical rhetoric), dominated the
Middle Ages. Apologetic writers took over the second position and
boldly developed it even to the extent of asserting that the biblical
writers had provided models for the Greeks. Nobody however drew
out the logical conclusion that the Bible should be the object of literary
study and a model of poetic composition. The rhetorical approach was
passed on by Cassiodorus, Isidore, Bede, etc., while Prudentius,
Sedulius and Juvencius developed epic and lyric imitation.

II. The Middle Ages

Special prominence has to be given to the Spanish Jew, Mošé
Ibn 'Ezra (11th century). His starting point was Arabic rhetoric,
which owed so much to Greek rhetoric. He analysed the Hebrew text
directly and composed a kind of Hebrew rhetoric which was superior
to all the works which preceded him. His work and example,
however, had no lasting or extensive effect.

III. The Renaissance

In their polemics against Scholasticism the humanists promoted
the Bible to justify their poetic activity and to exalt the value of
poetry as against speculation (Albertino Mussato, † 1329; Dante;
Boccaccio). The literary value of the Bible was recognised without
drawing out the logical consequences. An unsurpassed exception was
Fray Luis of León (1527-1591), a model of Christian humanism. His
new and refined sensitivity allowed him to savour both biblical and
Latin poetry. His expositions of the Hebrew language, his
commentary on the Song of Songs and Job, and his concept of
poetry, make him a worthy forerunner of Lowth and Herder.

IV. Modern Times

It is the Anglican bishop Robert Lowth (1710-1787), driven
perhaps by the first waves of "pre-romanticism" (van Tieghem),

who inaugurates the systematic study of biblical poetry. Even though he wrote in Latin and used traditional categories, he showed great sensitivity in perceiving the poetic value of the Bible, pointed out and systematized certain poetic techniques such as parallelism, revealed the similarities and differences in respect of classical authors and analyzed individual poems. A new sensitivity was being brought to bear on a new object but with old implements. Lowth's book, *De sacra poesi Hebraeorum* (1753), was widely used in Europe and had great influence (edition annotated by J. D. Michaelis, 1758-1761).

Some years later, in 1782, J. G. Herder published his *Vom Geist der hebräischen Poesie*. The theme is the same, but the approach is very different. Herder wrote in German, and considered poetry as a "creative activity" which reveals the "spirit of a people" (*Volksgeist*). He investigated the direct impact of a poem, drew the connections between poetry and language, delighted in what was primitive or primordial, perceived individuality and difference, and freed himself from formal, conventional rhetoric. He also anticipated the ideas of saga and etiology.

The 19th century produced some works of little importance: the dry rationality of J. G. Wenrich and the pretentious and bombastic work of Plantier. On E. W. Bullinger the reader should refer to the chapter on figures of speech. At the end of the century we find two works of some note. R. C. Moulton published a systematic study of poetic forms, *The Literary Study of the Bible* (1896). E. König composed a most erudite systematic study, *Stilistik, Rhetorik, Poetik in Bezug auf die Biblische Litteratur* (1900): it is a massive attempt to define distinctions, to divide and subdivide, and to catalogue and list tropes and figures of speech. This was a tremendous effort to collect and categorize *more botanico*, but it lacked artistic sensibility.

H. Gunkel inaugurated a new era and had many followers. He considered the Bible as a document of the history of literature and of religion. He displayed both philological rigour and literary sensitivity. His intuitions are abundant, but he is also precise in his formulations. He succeeds not only in the classification and description of literary genres, but also comments acutely on individual texts. He introduces the almost sociological concept of the "setting in life" (*Sitz im Leben*). Among his disciples we should mention H. Gressmann, H. Schmidt, J. Begrich and J. Hempel. Hempel's contribution to a collection directed by O. Walzel is *Die althebräische Literatur und ihr hellenistisch-jüdisches Nachleben* (193). It is one of the best works on the subject.

My *Estudios de poética hebrea* was based on the doctoral thesis I defended in the Pontifical Biblical Institute in Rome in 1957 and was published at the end of 1962. In those days the literary study of the OT was not yet of interest in the academic world and, furthermore, the book was written in Spanish (with the defects of a doctoral thesis and more besides). A full classified bibliography with comments can be found in this book. The central, fundamental part was published in a German translation in 1971, with the unfortunate title *Das Alte Testament als literarisches Kunstwerk*. After the historical introduction the book has two parts: a description and analysis of poetic techniques (or stylemes), and an analysis of individual poems. I have illustrated the stylemes fully in commentaries: the smaller series, *Los Libros Sagrados* (1965-1975), and the larger volumes, *Profetas* (1980), *Job* (1983), and *Proverbios* (1984). The analysis of individual poems prepared me for the writing of *Treinta Salmos: Poesía y oración* (ISJ.EAT 2; Madrid 1981; [2]1986).

In 1971 W. Richter published his work *Exegese als Literaturwissenschaft. Entwurf einer alttestamentlichen Literaturtheorie und Methodologie*. It was intended to be an exposition of principles and methods. It was not very well received.

Recently it seems that interest for the subject is being renewed, as is shown by three very different works.

The work of Wilfred G. E. Watson, *Classical Hebrew Poetry* (1984), is above all a study of literary techniques. It is very clear and systematic with a sectionalized bibliography. Watson introduces comparative material, especially useful indexes. This study reflects the present state of this investigation: very developed, even over-developed in some area, weak and emaciated in others.

Robert Alter in his book *The Art of Biblical Poetry* (1985) studies individual works. He has little concern for bibliography and avoids technical apparatus. He writes in a clear and pleasant style. His influence will be felt in less specialized circles.

Recently the well-known literary critic Northrop Frye published *The Great Code. The Bible and Literature* (1984). In it he displays again his passion for analogy, proportion and structure, and he gives great attention to images and symbols.

The pages which follow this modest history in part bring together already published material which is not readily available and in part is the result of years of reflection on the literature of the OT. My interest is above all stylistic: I examine a particular technique of style, I consider what is its function generally and in the specific poem, I see the technique as a "signifier" linked to a "signified". That is why I avoid long lists and offer analyses of significant texts instead.

Bibliography

I. Patristic Age

P. de Labriolle, *Histoire de la littérature latine chrétienne*. Revue et augmentée par G. Bardy (CEA; Paris ³1947).

P. de Labriolle, *La Réaction païenne: Étude sur la polémique antichrétienne du Ier au VIe siècle* (Paris 1942).

H.-I. Marrou, *Histoire de l'éducation dans l'antiquité* (Paris 1948).

H.-I. Marrou, *Saint Augustin et la fin de la culture antique. "Retractatio"* (BEFAR; Paris ²1949).

J. Bidez, *La vie de l'empereur Julien* (CEA; Paris 1930).

G. Bardy, "L'Église et l'enseignement pendant les trois premiers siècles", *RevSR* 12 (1932) 1-28.

G. Bardy, "L'Église et l'enseignement au IVe siècle", *RevSR* 14 (1934) 525-549; 15 (1935) 1-27.

E. Norden, *Die antike Kuntsprosa vom VI. Jahrhundert v. Chr. bis in die Zeit der Renaissance* (Stuttgart ⁸1981), pp. 521ff.

II. Middle Ages

E. R. Curtius, *Europäische Literatur und lateinisches Mittelalter* (Bern ²1954).

E. de Bruyne, *Études d'esthétique médiévale* (Bruges 1946).

E. Faral, *Les arts poétiques du XIIe et du XIIIe siècle* (Paris 1924).

B. Smalley, *The Study of the Bible in the Middle Ages* (Oxford ³1984).

M. Schreiner, "Le Kitâb al-Mouḥâdara de Moïse B. Ezra et ses sources", *REJ* 21 (1890) 98-117; 22 (1891) 62-81, 236-249.

A. Díez Macho, "Algunas figuras retóricas estudiadas en la 'Poética Hebraica' de Mošé Ibn 'Ezra", *Sef* 4 (1944) 255-274. Cf. also *Sef* 5 (1945) 49-81; 7 (1947) 3-29; 8 (1948) 293-321; 9 (1949) 269-309; 10 (1950) 135-164; 11 (1951) 3-35.

III. Renaissance

J. Toffanin, *Storia del Umanesimo* (Bologna 1950).

Fray Luis de León, *Obras completas castellanas*. Prólogos y notas del Padre F. Garcia (BAC 3; Madrid ³1949).

IV. Modern Scholars

C. Schöttgen, "De exergasia sacra", *Horae hebraicae et talmudicae* (Dresden–Leipzig 1733), pp. 1249-1263.

R. Lowth, *De sacra poesi Hebraeorum* (Oxford 1733) [= *Leçons sur la poésie sacrée des Hébreux*, translated by Suard, Lyons 1812; *Lectures on the Sacred Poetry of the Hebrews*, translated by G. Gregory, London 1787, ³1835; Latin edition edited by J.D. Michaelis, Göttingen 1758-1761, revised by E.F.C. Rosenmüller, Leipzig 1815].

J.G. von Herder, *Vom Geist der ebräischen Poesie* (Dessau 1782-1783).

C.H.A. Plantier, *Études littéraires sur les poètes bibliques* (2 vols.; Nîmes ³1881-1882).

J.G. Wenrich, *De poeseos Hebraicae atque Arabicae origine, indole, mutuoque consensu atque discrimine* (Leipzig 1843).

V. Contemporary Scholars

R.G. Moulton, *The Literary Study of the Bible: An Account of the Leading Forms of Literature Represented in the Sacred Writings* (London 1896).

E.W. Bullinger, *Figures of Speech Used in the Bible Explained and Illustrated* (London 1898; reprinted Grand Rapids 1968ff.).

E. König, *Stilistik, Rhetorik, Poetik in Bezug auf die Biblische Literatur* (Leipzig 1900).

E. König, *Die Poesie des Alten Testaments* (WiB; Leipzig 1907).

A. Wünsche, *Die Schönheit der Bibel. I. Die Schönheit des Alten Testaments* (Leipzig 1906).

H. Gunkel, *Reden und Aufsätze* (Göttingen 1913).

H. Gunkel, *Genesis* (Göttingen ⁹1977).

H. Gunkel, *Die Psalmen* (Göttingen ⁵1968).

H. Gunkel, *Die Urgeschichte und die Patriarchen (Das erste Buch Mosis)* (SAT I/1; Göttingen 1911).

H. Gunkel, "Die israelitische Literatur", *Die orientalischen Literaturen*, P. Hinneberg (ed.) (KGw I/vii; Berlin–Leipzig 1906), pp. 51-102.

G.A. Smith, *The Early Poetry of Israel in its Physical and Social Origins* (The Schweich Lectures 1910; London 1912).

G. Ricciotti, *Dalla Bibbia. Antologia Letteraria* (Bologna 1922).

A. Causse, *Les plus vieux chants de la Bible* (EHPhR 14; Paris 1926).

J. Hempel, *Die althebräische Literatur und ihr hellenistisch-jüdisches Nachleben* (HLW, Lieferung 145; Wildpark–Potsdam 1930).

E. Dhorme, *La poésie biblique* (Paris ⁶1931).

D.B. Macdonald, *The Hebrew Genius: An Interpretation. Being an Introduction to the Reading of the Old Testament* (Princeton 1933).

A. Lods, *Histoire de la littérature hébraïque et juive depuis les origines jusqu'à la ruine de l'état juif* (BH; Paris 1950).

M. Weiss, *The Bible From Within. The Method of Total Interpretation* (Publications of the Perry Foundation for Biblical Research in the Hebrew University of Jerusalem; Jerusalem 1984).

L. Alonso Schökel, *Estudios de poética hebrea* (Barcelona 1963).

S. Gevirtz, *Patterns in the Early Poetry of Israel* (SAOC 32; Chicago 1963).

L. Krinetzki, *Das Hohe Lied. Kommentar zu Gestalt und Kerygma eines alttestamentlichen Liebeslied* (KBANT; Düsseldorf 1964).

W. Bühlmann – K. Scherer, *Stilfiguren der Bibel. Ein kleines Nachschlagewerk* (BiBe 10; Fribourg 1973).

M. Lurker, *Wörterbuch biblischer Bilder und Symbole* (Munich 1973).

L. Ryken, *The Literature of the Bible* (Grand Rapids 1974).

D. Robertson, *The Old Testament and the Literary Critics* (OTSeries; Philadelphia 1977).

D. J. A. Clines – D. M. Gunn – A. J. Hauser, *Art and Meaning: Rhetoric in Biblical Literature* (JSOT, SS 19; Sheffield 1982).

W. G. E. Watson, *Classical Hebrew Poetry. A Guide to its Techniques* (JSOT, SS 26; Sheffield 1984).

N. Frye, *The Great Code. The Bible and Literature* (London 1982).

R. Alter, *The Art of Biblical Poetry* (New York 1985).

CHAPTER II

Poetic Genres

I. According to the Hebrews

The Hebrews show awareness of different literary genres, but they are not clearly differentiated. *Šîr* is a generic term: it is used of an epinicion or victory song (Judg 5) and of some psalms (30; 45; 46; 48; etc.). Sometimes its meaning is restricted by use of an epithet: *šîr yᵉdîdōt* = "nuptial song" (Ps 45), *šîr 'ăgābîm* = "love song" (Ezek 33,32), *šîr ḥādāš* = a "new, original song" (Isa 42,10; Ps 33; 40; 96; 98; 144; 149), *šîr ṣiyyôn* (Ps 137,3), *šîr Yhwh* (Isa 30,29; 2 Chr 29,18), *šîr hamma'ălôt* = "a pilgrimage song" (?) (Pss 120–134). On the other occasions the feminine form *šîrâ* appears: the so-called songs of Moses (Exod 15 and Deut 32); Ps 18; the song of the vineyard (Isa 5); the song of the harlot (Isa 23,15); the song of the wells (Num 21,17). The verb *šyr* is also frequent. It is therefore quite a wide-ranging term, with more specific epithets of place, theme, situation, etc.

The term *mizmôr* is perhaps more restricted, though it is applied to 57 psalms. This disrupts the classifications of Gunkel.

The term *ḥîdâ* also covers a wide range. What appears to predominate is the sense of enigma or riddle. Those of Samson to his guests are famous (Judg 14): they are short, rhythmic, alliterative, ingenious and even malicious. Teachers include this genre too in their catalogue (Prov 1,6). Ezek 17,2 presents *ḥîdâ* and *māšāl* as synonyms. The text given these titles is rather a parable due to its length and style. But it is enigmatic right up to the final explanation. In spite of the literary culture of a prophet like Ezekiel, the distinction of poetic genres is not a major concern. Something similar happens in Pss 49 and 78. The queen of Sheba brings her enigmas to Solomon (1 Kgs 10,1; 2 Chr 9,1). Num 12,8 emphasises the aspect of obscurity by contrasting *ḥîdâ* with the vision "face to face" (cf. 1 Cor 13,12). Habakkuk also combines *ḥîdâ* with *māšāl*, and adds *mᵉlîṣâ*, which seems to mean "satire". Prov 1,6 lists four genres, *māšāl, mᵉlîṣâ, dibrê ḥakāmîm* and *ḥîdōt*, as the intellectual patrimony of the wise and of teachers. Sir 47,17 enumerates among the glories of Solomon his mastery of *šîr, māšāl, ḥîdâ* and *mᵉlîṣâ*.

Māšāl is very frequent. Its usual meanings are "proverb" and "parable". The book of Proverbs with its sayings, aphorisms, axioms and maxims is entitled *mišlê šelōmōh*. It introduces a parable in Ezek 17; 24; etc. Ezekiel receives the derisive title *memaššēl mešālîm* (Ezek 21,5), which might be rendered "purveyor of parables". The narrator of the story of Balaam introduces his oracles with the formula *wayyiśśā' mešālô wayyō'mer* (Num 23,7.18; 24,3.15.23). Balaam twice calls his oracle *ne'um bil'ām* (Num 24,3.15). Another example of vague terminology.

We must not forget the verb *nś'* and the substantive *ne'um*. The substantive *maśśa'*, used to designate the threatening oracles against pagan nations, is derived from the former. The term is used by Isaiah, Habakkuk, Malachi and Zechariah; it is missing in Jeremiah, Ezekiel and Amos 1–2; it is used against one person in 1 Kgs 9,25 and this could be quite an ancient usage of the term.

Qînâ frequently means elegy in our modern sense (different from the Latin). It is used of the funeral lament for one person (2 Chr 35,25), for the people of Israel (Jer 9,9), for pagan nations (Ezek 27,2; 28,11; 32,2). Ezekiel reads in the book which he has to consume *qînîm wāhegeh wāhî* (Ezek 2,10); *hegeh* is a gesture or sign, unarticulated, *hî* is an interjection, *qînâ* is the literary genre. On the other hand, the elegy for Babylon in Isa 14 is called *māšāl*. More indecision regarding the terminology.

Similar to *qînâ* is *nehî*, lamentation. Ezekiel receives the command to raise a lament (*nehēh*, 32,18); in one verse Jeremiah combines the substantives *qînâ, nehî* and *bekî* with the generic verb *nś'* (Jer 9,9); he places *qînâ* and *nehî* as parallels (Jer 9,19); Micah combines *māšāl* with *nehî* (Mic 2,4). The term *nehî* is not so frequent.

Blessing and curses form a clear literary genre: they are usually called *berākâ* and *qelālā*. The blessings in Gen 49 and Deut 33 are called *berākôt*: they are poetic declarations about the tribes and their destinies; the style is concise, rich in enigmatic allusions (enigmatic for us), with emblematic images and very marked rhythm and parallelism. In spite of the general title the content of some is more in the line of curses. Deut 27 presents a series of ritual curses with the formula *'ārûr* = "cursed!" with the choral response *'āmēn*. The parallel series of blessings is found in Deut 28.

Ne'um Yhwh is the name given to the divine oracle. The use of the phrase grows rapidly so that it becomes almost a cliché which punctuates and interrupts oracles.

To sum up, the Israelites knew and used various terms to designate different literary genres. Some cover a wide range, like *šîr* = "song", *māšāl* = "proverb" or "parable", *mizmôr* = "psalm",

$ne'um$ = "oracle". Other terms are more restricted, like $ḥîdâ$ = "enigma", $qînâ$ = "elegy", $maśśa'$ = "threatening oracle", $b^e rāḵâ$ and $q^e lālā$ = "blessing" and "curse". Sometimes they made terms more precise by adding some qualification. Nevertheless, the unstable use of some terms and their free combination in parallelism or in lists show that the Israelites had elaborated no fixed system of literary categories, nor did they give great importance to such classification. The modern commentator ought to bear this in mind so as to moderate his pressing urge to distinguish and classify.

G. Rinaldi, "Alcuni termini ebraici relativi alla letteratura", *Bib* 40 (1959) 267-289.

II. The Concept of Literary Genre

I am not going to explain here in a complete and systematic way the theory of literary genres in the OT. From the point of view of the investigator the literary genre is the object of a typological classification based on differentiated and identifiable characteristics. From the point of view of the author it is a system of formal conventions which are accepted and are useful in literary composition. These conventions of the various literary genres seem to be stronger in literary texts destined for use in specific circumstances, and especially by groups of people.

Literary genres are found in any fairly developed literature and essentially might be organised and described in structural form, according to oppositions. The structures from the different cultures do not coincide, so that it is not possible simply to apply our system to the biblical system. Nevertheless, there are similarities that allow the analogical use of the designations. (Gunkel used the Scandinavian concept of "sagas", and of "Novelle" = short story, a concept applied to Hellenistic texts.)

Gunkel introduced the concept of the "setting in life" (*Sitz im Leben*), the setting to which the genres were directed and in which they were used. The concept stands in contrast to the unrepeatable historical situation, since social situations are repeated.

The importance of literary genres in the OT should not be exaggerated. First, reductionism should be avoided, the effort to reduce any text to a typical form. Secondly, subdivisions should not be multiplied. Thirdly, one should remember that the poet is using the conventions without being dominated by them. Fourthly, in addition to the social context one should remember the literary context of private reading. With these safeguards the classification of the literary genre can be very useful for a first contact with the work: knowledge of the genre orientates the reader. It is also an excellent starting-point for comparing with other texts. When the common elements are realised, the individuality of the text is more clearly perceived. And in the last analysis the literature is made up of individual works, the primary object for contemplation and study.

Beginning with a very comprehensive classification we can say that biblical literature contains an abundance of lyric poetry and that it contains no epic poems and no drama. Nevertheless, we find epic, lyric and dramatic elements (cf. E. Staiger, *Grundbegriffe der Poetik* [Zurich + ²1951]) distributed with freedom and irregularity.

III. Epic

Cf. the article of C. Conroy, "Hebrew Epic: Historical Notes and Critical Reflections", *Bib* 61 (1980) 1-30. An epic poem, in the style of the Iliad, the Odyssey or the Aeneid, cannot be found in the Bible. However, we do find epic tales and heroic songs. The latter (like Exod 15; Judg 5) belong rather to lyric poetry. One might call the final (composite) version of the departure from Egypt an epic tale, Exod 1–15; various tales of the Judges may be compared to our heroic ballads. Some believe that epic traits are to be found in the exploits of David or of Jehu. But all these texts as they are found in the Bible belong to the genre of narrative prose, and not to poetry. (The study of biblical narrative has come alive again with renewed vigour in the last ten years.)

The question thus becomes less ambitious. In the final biblical tales do we have traces of earlier epic poetry which was used by the authors? Is it reasonable to imagine, for example, that an epic poem was handed down orally and in various versions and then transformed into artistic prose and into a finished tale by a later author? Or again, do phrases, citations and traces of epic poems still survive in the present tales? Texts like the following are given as examples: Num 21,14, "the book of the wars of the Lord"; 2 Sam 1,18 and Josh 10,13 (both doubtful); 1 Kgs 8,53 in the Greek. Verses and formulas which show clear rhythm are singled out. The similarity with other near-by cultures is indicated. These pieces of evidence may indicate some probability, but they cannot provide sure texts for literary study.

Cf. the work already cited by W. G. E. Watson, *Classical Hebrew Poetry*, pp. 83-86.

IV. Popular Genres and Learned Genres

This distinction corresponds only partially to the distinction oral/written or preliterary/literary. Anonymity is neither a sufficient nor a reasonable criterion for the distinction. Above all, since nobody now confuses "popular" with "unsophisticated", we must not fall into the trap of thinking about what is "popular" that "nobody wrote it" (as Manuel Machado pointedly said).

What remains of popular poetry in the Bible has been cited, collected or imitated in learned works. Adding to Hempel's list (*Die althebräische Literatur*, pp. 19f.), I would mention: the work song, Num 21,17; imitated and transformed in Isa 5 and 27,2-4; allusions to it in Isa 16,9; Jer 49,33 (on the wine-harvest and wine-press); dance songs, Ezek 15; Ps 149; threatening songs, Gen 4,23-24; elegies, 2 Sam 3,33-34; the song of a watchman, Isa 21,12; of the harlot, Isa 23,16. We should remember also the sayings (Prov) and riddles (Judg 14) to which I have already referred.

Bibliography

R. Robert, "Historique (genre)", *DBS* IV, cols. 7-23.

R. Robert, "Littéraires (genres)", *DBS* V, cols. 405-421.

H. Cazelles, "Le mythe et l'Ancien Testament", *DBS* VI, cols. 246-261.

S. Mowinckel, "Literature", *IDB* K-Q [III], 139-143.

L. Alonso Schökel, "Genera litteraria", *VD* 38 (1960) 3-15.

K.-H. Bernhardt, *Die gattungsgeschichtliche Forschung am Alten Testament als exegetische Methode* (Berlin 1956).

The contribution of Gunkel was decisive. An exemplary application of the method may be found in his posthumous work *Einleitung in die Psalmen. Die Gattungen der religiösen Lyrik Israels* (HK, Ergänzungsband zur II. Abteilung; Göttingen 1933, ⁴1985). See also the series "Die Schriften des Alten Testaments in Auswahl" (Göttingen 1909-1915, 1920-1925), produced by Gunkel and his disciples.

Another ambitious project begun recently, entitled "The Forms of Old Testament Literature" (FOTL). It is directed by R. Knierim and G. M. Tucker. The following volumes have already appeared:

W. G. Coats, *Genesis. With an Introduction to Narrative Literature* (FOTL 1; Grand Rapids 1983).

B. O. Long, *1 Kings. With an Introduction to Historical Literature* (FOTL 9; Grand Rapids 1984).

R. E. Murphy, *Wisdom Literature: Job, Proverbs, Ruth, Canticles, Ecclesiastes, and Esther* (FOTL 13; Grand Rapids 1981), with an introduction to Wisdom literature and a short glossary in which genres and some literary devices are described.

J.J. Collins, *Daniel. With an Introduction to Apocalyptic Literature* (FOTL 20; Grand Rapids 1985), with an introduction to apocalyptic literature and a more detailed glossary, sixteen pages long, accompanied by a select bibliography.

More information may be obtained in the usual volumes of Introduction to the OT, as also in commentaries on books or groups of books.

V. Catalogue of Genres

Leaving previous distinctions to one side, I proceed now to poetic genres. Similar catalogues published already in different works should be borne in mind:

On prophetic genres see the presentation of S. Bretón in L. Alonso Schökel – J.L. Sicre Diaz, *Profetas*. Introducción y comentario ... con la colaboración de S. Bretón y E. Zurro. I. *Isaias. Jeremias* (NBE; Madrid 1980), pp. 76ff.

On wisdom genres see the presentation of J. Vilchez in L. Alonso Schökel – J. Vilchez, con la colaboración de A. Pinto, *Sapienciales*. I. *Proverbios* (NBE; Madrid 1984), pp. 69ff.

See also H. Gunkel, *Einleitung in die Psalmen*.

Drinking song: Isa 22,13, "let us eat and drink; for tomorrow we die!" Allusions in Isa 5,11-13; Am 6,4-6.

Love song: Isa 5,1-7; perhaps Isa 27,2-4; wedding allusions Jer 7,34; the Song of Songs; Ps 45; Isa 62. Cf. F. Horst, "Die Formen des althebräischen Liebesliedes", *Gottes Recht. Gesammelte Studien zum Recht im Alten Testament* (TB 12; Munich 1961), pp. 176-187; R.E. Murphy, "Form-Critical Studies in the Song of Songs", *Inter* 27 (1973) 413-422.

Satire: Isa 14, against the king of Babylon; Isa 37,22-29, against Sennacherib; Isa 28,7-13, against the drunkards. Prophetic oracles against pagan nations and many prophetic denunciations; the five "Woes" in Hab 2. Cf. E. Gerstenberger, "The Woe-Oracles of the Prophets", *JBL* 81 (1962) 249-263.

Elegies: 2 Sam 1,19-27, for Saul and Jonathan; 3,33-34, for Abner; the refrain cited in 1 Mac 9,21; an allusion in 2 Chr 35,25; Lamentations. Cf. H. Jahnow, *Das hebräische Leichenlied im Rahmen der Völkerdichtung* (BZAW 36; Giessen 1923).

Victory songs: Num 21,28; Exod 15; Judg 5; the refrain cited in 1 Sam 18,7; Judg 16,23-24; Jdt 16.

Fables: Judg 8,15; 2 Kgs 14,9.

We should make a distinction between the different genres *Eschatology* and *Apocalypse*. Isa 24–27 and Dan 2–7 cannot be placed in the same category. As regards the content, an eschatology describes the great scene of the final act which inaugurates the final age. An apocalypse, on the other hand, begins by reducing past history (after the exile) to clearly distinguished epochs, and goes on to announce the imminent liberating conclusion of history. As regards the form, an eschatology is like a vision, while an apocalypse has as its starting point an intellectual schematic perception of history which it translates into allegories. As regards the process of composition, an eschatology contrasts extremes, indulges in all-defined fantastic images, and is manneristic. An apocalypse reduces each vision to a clearly articulated image: the parts of a statue, four beasts and a man. Canonical literature has only preserved two works of the apocalyptic genre in prose: Daniel in the OT and the Apocalypse (the Book of Revelation) in the NT. These two biblical apocalypses are exceptional in creating simple and eloquent symbols.

V. Collado Bertomeu, *Escatologías de los profetas. Estudio literario comparativo* (Valencia 1972).

D. S. Russell, *The Method and Message of Jewish Apocalyptic. 200 BC – AD 100* (OTL; Philadelphia 1964).

P. D. Hanson, *The Dawn of Apocalyptic* (Philadelphia 1975).

VI. Descriptive Poetry

The Hebrews did not indulge in descriptive poetry for its own sake. Descriptions of nature are found in liturgical or sapiential praise. Descriptions of customs usually serve a didactic purpose or are used in prophetic preaching.

a) Descriptions of *nature*. The most remarkable texts are Ps 104 and Sir 43. The former depends, perhaps indirectly, on an Egyptian hymn to Aten. Both are not content with describing one particular phenomenon, but rapidly sketch a sequence of phenomena. This requires a rapid characterisation, realistic or metaphorical. Contemplative emotion may permeate the whole poem or show itself explicitly at one particular point. God's dominion is expressed or understood. A realistic description is found in Ps 104: "the birds sing among the leaves... all the beasts of the forest come forth... man comes out to his work, and to his labours until evening" (Ps 104,12.20.23). The realistic description may be made more glorious by a comparison: "He scatters the snow-flakes like birds alighting; they settle like a swarm of locusts...

He spreads frost on the earth like salt, and icicles form like pointed stakes. A cold blast from the north, and ice grows hard on the water, settling on every pool, as though the water were putting on a breastplate" (Sir 43,17-20).

A total imaginative transformation can happen when the poet introduces God in action, for example: "Look at the rainbow... rounding the sky with its gleaming arc, a bow bent by the hands of the Most High" (Sir 43,11-12) (God as a bowman who stretches the heavenly bow). "The stars... at the command of the Holy One stand in their appointed place; they never default at their post" (Sir 43,10) (like soldiers of a squadron). "Wrapped in a robe of light... (thou) takest the clouds for thy chariot, riding on the wings of the wind" (Ps 104,2-3). The emotion of the poet is clearly expressed when the snow falls: "The eye is dazzled by their beautiful whiteness, and as they fall the mind is entranced" (Sir 43,18).

When the storm is seen as a theophany the literary result is a description of a natural phenomenon transformed with great imagination. Pss 18 and 77 are examples.

> The waters saw thee, O God,
> > they saw thee and writhed in anguish;
> > the ocean was troubled to its depth.
> The clouds poured water, the skies thundered,
> > Thy arrows flashed hither and thither.
> The sound of thy thunder was in the whirlwind,
> > thy lightnings lit up the world,
> > earth shook and quaked ... (Ps 77,16-18).

Apart from the two texts just named, the best descriptive passages of the OT are found in the book of Job, put into the mouth of God as a challenge and reproach to Job. Intense imaginative transformation is found in Job 38:

> Who watched over the birth of the sea,
> > when it burst in flood from the womb? —
> > when I wrapped it in a blanket of cloud
> > and cradled it in fog,
> > when I established its bounds,
> > fixing its doors and bars in place. ...
> In all your life have you ever called up the dawn
> > or shown the morning its place?
> Have you taught it to grasp the fringes of the earth
> > and shake the wicked out of it;
> > to give form to the earth as a seal forms clay
> > and to dye it like a garment? (Job 38,8-10.12-14).

> Who is wise enough to marshal the rain-clouds
>   and empty the cisterns of heaven,
>   when the dusty soil sets hard as iron,
>   and the clods of earth cling together? (Job 38,37-38).

There follows a very realistic description of some animals; the most famous is the horse, but I will quote something on the vulture:

> It dwells among the rocks and there it lodges;
>   its station is a crevice in the rock;
>   from there it searches for food,
>   keenly scanning the distance,
>   that its brood may be gorged with blood;
>   and where the slain are, there the vulture is (Job 39,28-30).

Finally, the poet gives two full descriptions of the hippopotamus and the crocodile, seen as incarnations of evil in the world; the second is fantastically transformed into a mythological dragon, a shining fiery creature:

> His sneezing sends out sprays of light,
>   and his eyes gleam like the shimmer of dawn.
> Firebrands shoot from his mouth,
>   and sparks come streaming out;
>   his nostrils pour forth smoke
>   like a cauldron on a fire blown to full heat.
> His breath sets burning coals ablaze,
>   and flames flash from his mouth (Job 41,18-21).

This passage belongs to the genre of imaginative description.

The legend states that Solomon "discoursed" about plants and animals and that he composed three thousand proverbs (1 Kgs 4,12-13). Descriptive poetry may have begun from there, linked with scientific observation, as in the case of Lucretius. The texts we have provide scattered descriptive lines with different functions, which does not strictly amount to "descriptive poetry".

b) On the other hand the Hebrews did use their talent and acuteness of observation in describing *human life*: customs, types of people, ages of life, professions. The poets loved to observe and to reflect on what they observed. They produced proverbs and short didactic poems as a result. The poetry is about daily life and is illuminated by the wisdom and common sense of the teachers. The good wife (Prov 31); seduction (Prov 7); the drunkard, described with condescending irony (Prov 23,29-35); friends: "Accept a greeting from everyone, but advice from only one in a thousand" (Sir 6,5-17); the enemy: "Do not have him at your side, or he will trip you up and supplant you" (Sir 12,8-18); the rich and the poor: "If a rich man staggers, he is held up by his friends; a poor man falls, and his friends disown him as well. ... A rich man speaks, and all are silent; then they praise his speech to the skies. A poor man speaks, and they say, 'Who is this?'" (Sir 13,1-7.15-24); the stingy person: "if ever he does good, it is by mistake" (Sir 14,1-19); the blabber, who does not know how to keep a secret: "A fool with a secret goes through agony like a woman in childbirth. As painful as an arrow through the thigh is a rumour in the heart of a fool" (Sir 19,4-17); the fool: "Teaching a fool is like mending pottery with glue, or like rousing a sleeper from heavy sleep. As well reason with a drowsy man as with a fool; when you have finished, he will say, 'What was that?'" (Sir 22,9-15); slander and calumny (Sir 28,13-23); lending (Sir 29,1-13); the invited guest, wine, the banquet (Sir 31,12 – 32,13); dream (Sir 34,1-8); skills and professions (Sir 38,24-34).

VII. Mythological Poetry

If we take as models the undoubtedly mythological texts of the ancient Near-East — Egyptian, Sumerian, Babylonian and Assyrian — it is clear that the OT has not admitted myths. Neither the religious background, nor the intention, nor the development permit us to identify the biblical stories as myths. To avoid confusion it is better to call the first chapters of Genesis "tales of the origins".

These tales of the origins share with the myths the desire to explain radical cosmic and human situations by going back to the origins, which the OT places at the beginning of time, not outside or beyond time. They also both share the narrative form and the use of certain symbols: the garden of God or "earthly paradise", the tempter serpent, the tree of life, sin "a demon crouching at the door" for Cain (Gen 4), the imperial tower which reaches to the heavens (Gen 11).

The Hebrews do not welcome myths as narratives, but they have no difficulty in incorporating mythical motifs into their lyric texts, with fewer scruples or inhibitions as time goes on. The mythical motif is "historicised" or reduced to its primordial symbolic function.

The most frequent motif is the struggle of God with chaos as he creates or imposes order on the world.

Cf.: H. Gunkel, *Schöpfung und Chaos in Urzeit und Endzeit. Eine religionsgeschichtliche Untersuchung über Gen 1 und Ap Joh 12* (Göttingen 1895); M. K. Wakeman, *God's Battle with the Monster. A Study in Biblical Imagery* (Leiden 1973); J. W. Rogerson, *Myth in Old Testament Interpretation* (BZAW 134; Berlin–New York 1974). The monster may be called *T^{e}hôm* = "Ocean", *Rahab* = the "turbulent one", *Yām* = the "Sea", *Tannîn* = the "monster", "dragon", etc. In poetic texts it is Ps 93 which stands out: "O Lord, the ocean lifts up, the ocean lifts up its clamour; the ocean lifts up its pounding waves. The Lord on high is mightier far than the noise of great waters, mightier than the breakers of the sea" (vv. 3-4). In its historicised version it is applied above all to the crossing of the Red Sea (M. Noth, "Die Historisierung des Mythus", in *Gesammelte Studien zum Alten Testament* II [TB 39; Munich 1969], pp. 29-47). The texts are many:

> By thy power thou didst cleave the sea-monster in two,
> and break the sea-serpent's heads above the waters;
> thou didst crush Leviathan's many heads
> and throw him to the sharks for food (Ps 74,13-14).

> Thou rulest the surging sea,
> calming the turmoil of its waves.
> Thou didst crush the monster Rahab with a mortal blow
> and scatter thy enemies with thy strong arm (Ps 89,10-11).

> He divided the Red Sea in two (Ps 136,13).

> Am I the monster of the deep, am I the sea-serpent,
> that thou settest a watch over me? (Job 7,12).

See also Isa 51,9-10. The motif reappears strongly in the eschatology: "On that day the Lord will punish with his cruel sword, his mighty and powerful sword, Leviathan that twisting sea-serpent, that writhing serpent Leviathan, and slay the monster of the deep" (Isa 27,1).

Other motifs may be of mythical origin: thunder as the voice of God (Ps 29 and others), the stars as armies or squadrons (*ṣ^{e}bā'ôt*) of the Lord, Death personified, Isa 28,15; Ps 49,15: "like sheep they run headlong into Sheol, the land of Death; he is their shepherd and urges them on"; the mountain of the gods, Isa 14,13; Ps 48,3. The great poem of Hab 3 gathers together images applied to the Lord which recall mythical associations.

T. H. Gaster, *Thespis* (New York 1950; 1961).
B. S. Childs, *Myth and Reality in the Old Testament* (Düsseldorf 1960).
A. Ohler, *Mythologische Elemente im Alten Testament* (Düsseldorf 1969).

VIII. Conclusion

The literature of the OT is a developed literature, the result of a long and stable tradition. It is open to foreign influences and well-used to elaborating and re-elaborating earlier or foreign material. For this reason mixed genres are frequent, and many works resist tidy classification. This is why the study of motifs which can transfer to different genres may be just as important as the study of literary genres. And what happens with the myths happens also with folk tales.

IX. Introduction to Poetic Techniques

Just as we cannot distinguish strictly between prose vocabulary and poetic vocabulary, neither can we distinguish techniques which are exclusively poetic. Poetry takes full advantage of and concentrates the resources of a language and widens its possibilities; the techniques of poetry pass then to artistic prose and may descend to ordinary language. Thanks to this alternating movement of descent and ascent the life of a language and of a literature is kept in tension. Purism is a symptom of decadence.

We must speak rather of frequency, predominance, density, intensity. We read a piece of narrative prose, we learn how bad news comes to the king of Judah about an enemy invasion, and the narrator observes: "the heart of the king and the heart of the people were shaken like forest trees in the wind" (Isa 7,2). Suddenly we find a slight poetic trembling, a ripple in the surface of the narrative flow (we find something similar in Herodotus). For its part, poetry may become prosaic and produce sections in verse which we categorise as biblical poetry even though they are more didactic than poetic, as is the case with many of the instructions of Sirach.

Now I intend to examine a series of techniques which are common in biblical poetry while not being absent from artistic prose.

Chapter III

Sounds

The peoples who have preserved the good habit of reciting poetry aloud have also kept alive the sensitivity to listen to and appreciate the phonic, or sound, quality of poetic language. Some literatures or schools have developed great refinement due to long artistic tradition (e.g. Welsh, Gaelic) or due to a special regard for the emotions (symbolism), and give great importance to the sound qualities of a poem. Biblical poetry shares both these qualities: whether it was written or not, it was meant for oral recitation, in public; it developed in a tradition of good craftsmen and great poets. Reading to oneself is a such later development; in Hebrew "to read" is *qārā'*, which means usually "to call, shout". It is notable that the Jews even today call Sacred Scripture *miqrā'* = "reading aloud". Someone who is used to hearing poetry recited can later read to himself and hear in his imagination the effects of the sounds (just as a conductor hears a score when he reads it). However, scholars of the OT generally have a habit of "seeing" the biblical text, without listening to it. This means they are very subjective in their approach, and do not adapt themselves to the object they are studying. A new education and training is needed, to which this exposition hopes to contribute something.

A language develops its phonic techniques of style with the limited store of its phonemes: by combination, by distribution and in relation to the meaning. It may bring out particular characteristics of the phonemes. The principal resources are alliteration, assonance, rhyme, sequences, and dominant sound (*Leitklang*). The uses may be primary — onomatopeia, metaphor of sound, paronomasia, euphony — or they may be subordinated to other effects, like rhythm, antithesis, satire, etc. It is clear that the Hebrews paid more attention to the consonants than to the vowels for these techniques and effects of sound.

I. Repetition of Sound

Let me begin with the binary expression, or verbal pair, *šāmîr wāšāyit* (Isa 5,6), which means "thorns and briars". This kind of twinning is common to all languages: shilly-shally, fiddle-faddle, hugger-mugger are English examples. It simply consists of repeating in a striking way certain elements of sound. An experience is expressed in two parts to give intensity and scope; the two parts are fused together by the similarity of sound. This technique is similar to reduplication in verbs as found in certain languages: *pōlel, pilpel* in Hebrew, the Greek perfect, and the remains of it in Latin: *dedit, stetit*. This simple form of doubling of the sound can be applied also with other techniques, like merismus (various elements represent a complete series), polarised expression (the extremes represent the whole) or any kind of hendiadys. Phonic repetition fuses two elements without destroying the duality: *tōhû bōhû* = "formless chaos", *šēm šᵉ'ār* = "name and descendants", *nîn neked* = "offspring and posterity", *regel rō'š* = "foot and head". Cf. B. Hartmann, *Die nominalen Aufreihungen im Alten Testament* (Zurich 1953).

Poetic language stylizes the technique by using it in contiguous or parallel groups. Once the verbal pair has been stated, it can be developed or extended to whole parallel phrases, in a whole system of corresponding sounds.

The poet usually avoids perfect correspondence, reserving it for very deliberate cases, for example, antithesis:

> *kā'ēt hāri'sôn hēqal ... wᵉhā'aharôn hikbîd...*
> As before he humbled ..., later he exalted (Isa 8,23).

> *mahsᵉbôt saddîqîm mispāt*
> *tahbulôt rᵉsā'îm mirmâ*
> Plans of the righteous, lawful;
> designs of the wicked, deceit (Prov 12,5).

The second example is a sophisticated proverb but fails due to an excess of symmetry.

Another proverbial sentence unites the two verbs by the sound: *rûᵃh yizrā'û wᵉsûpātâ yiqsōrû* = "they sow the wind and reap the whirlwind" (Hos 8,7).

The case of a contiguous verbal pair, where the elements are of different forms, is less obvious. When the sound repetition is due to morphemes of conjugation, gender or number the effect is poor (something like poor rhymes); they arise from the logical articulation of the language and often they are inevitable. But when the two elements giving a similar sound are not grammatically homogeneous the effect is striking: *hôy gôy* = "Woe to a people!" (Isa 1,4); *šānᵉ'â napsî* = "my soul abhors" (Isa 1,14). In the following example there are four inter-related pairs:

šuddad śādeh   *'āb^elâ 'adāmâ*
šuddad dāgān   *hôbîš tîrôš*

the fields are ruined, the parched earth mourns,
the corn is ruined, the new wine is desperate (Joel 1,10).

Alliteration of three words stresses the threefold accentuated
rhythm in Deut 26,5 (the so-called "Credo"): *'arammî 'ōbēd 'ābî* =
"my father was a wandering Aramean". More ingenious is the
twofold and threefold movement in Isa 7,4:

hiššāmēr w^ehašqēṭ 'al-tîrā' ûl^ebāb^ekā 'al-yērak
mišš^enê zanbôt hā'ûdîm hā'ăšēnîm hā'ēlleh

Be on your guard, keep calm; do not be frightened or
      unmanned
by these two smouldering stumps of firewood.

Less striking and more refined is the technique of constructing
a whole poem with words of similar sound. An extraordinary
example is Ps 76, which speaks of God as:

nôdā' (2)   *nā'ôr ... 'addîr* (5)   *nôrā'* (8)
known   radiant ... majestic   to be feared

môrā' (12)   *nôrā'* (13)
terrible   to be feared

Sound can give a solemn quality to an antithesis, as in the
famous case of Isa 5,7:

way^eqaw l^emišpāṭ w^ehinnēh miśpāḥ
      liṣ^edāqâ w^ehinnēh ṣ^e'āqâ

He looked for justice, but behold, bloodshed;
for righteousness, but behold, a cry!

II. Forms

To begin with, a note on the terminology. The term "alliteration" is sometimes used generically, applied to any similarity of
sound. We really have to distinguish the terms according to the
position of the phoneme in question.
     Alliteration is the repetition of a consonantal sound at the
beginning of a word. (The words which we say begin with a vowel
really begin with a phonic utterance which is the same for any

vowel; this is clear in ancient German poetry and Romantic imitations of it.)

Rhyme is repetition of a sound at the end of a word, hemistich or verse.

Chiasmus is the inversion or partial inversion of sounds.

Assonance is similarity of vowel sounds, and is typical of Spanish poetry.

Dominant sound is the reiteration of a sound in any position. It is not essential that the same consonant be repeated; it simply should belong to the same group. Thus the following consonants are closely related: b/m, k/q/g, t/d, '/g, ś/s/š/z, p/b, d/z, l/r.

Let us look at some examples.

Alliteration. When various words begin with aleph (the sound which precedes an initial vowel), this can stress the rhythm of the phrase or even seem like a stutter:

> 'ûlām 'ănî 'edrōš 'el-'ēl
> wᵉ'el-'ĕlōhîm 'āśîm dibrātî

For my part, I would make my petition to God
and lay my cause before him (Job 5,8).

In this text eight of the nine words begin with aleph. The following text is slightly less excessive, with seven out of nine:

> 'ûlām 'ănî 'el-šadday 'ădabbēr
> wᵉhôkēᵃḥ 'el-'ēl 'eḥpāṣ

But for my part I would speak with the Almighty
and am ready to argue with God (Job 13,3).

Ps 46,10: qᵉṣēh ... qešet ... qiṣṣēṣ = "end ... bow ... breaks".
Ps 19,6: yōṣē' ... yāśîś = "comes out ... rejoicing".
Ps 4,3: kābôd ... kᵉlimmâ = "honour ... dishonour".

Rhyme. Poor rhymes are made up by morphemes, but there are rich rhymes too, though these are very rare in Hebrew. Ps 46,10: mašbît ... ḥanît = "stamps out ... spear"; these words come at the beginning of a verse and at the end of a hemistich. Isa 13,12: 'ôqîr ... 'ôpîr = "I will make scarce ... Ophir". This is a consonantal rhyme: Ps 8,3: yōnᵉqîm ... mitnaqqēm = "infants at the breast ... the avenger". Prov 17,11 is very ingenious: 'ak-mᵉrî ... 'akzārî = "rebellious ... cruel".

Poor rhymes produce an effect in Hebrew poetry when they accumulate. A series ending in the vowel -î, suffix of the first person, is both pathetic and dramatic in Job 10,16-17.

Jer 9,16-20 ostentatiously combines the ending of the feminine plural *-nâ* with that of the first person plural *-nû*, and, into the bargain, adds the rhyming noun, *qînâ*, thus giving a rich rhyme produced by the lexeme. In a few verses the following sounds echo:

hitbôn^enû	*t^ebô'ènâ*	*tābô'nâ*	*t^emahērnâ*
consider	make them come	let them come	let them make haste

tiśśenâ 'ālênû		*tēradnâ*		*'ênênû*	*'apappênû*
let them raise for us		let them run down		our eyes	our eyelids

šuddādnû	*bôšnû*	*'āzabnû*	*mišk^enôtênû*	*š^ema'nâ*
we are ruined	we are shamed	we have left	our dwellings	hear

lammednâ	*qînâ*	*ḥallônênû*	*'arm^enôtênû*
teach	lament	our windows	our palaces.

Another example from Jeremiah uses an abundance of first person suffixes:

> *'āzabtî 'et-bêtî nāṭaštî 'et-naḥălātî*
> *nātattî 'et-y^edîdût napšî ...*

I have forsaken my house, I have abandoned my heritage;
I have given the beloved of my soul ... (Jer 12,7).

Six words out of seven end with this suffix. Compare the following texts:

> *'anî nôtartî nābî' la-Yhwh l^ebaddî*
> I am the only prophet of the Lord still left (1 Kgs 18,22).

> *'al-tîr^e'î 'ădāmâ gîlî ûś^emāḥî*
> *kî-higdîl Yhwh la'ăśôt*

Earth, be not afraid, rejoice and be glad;
for the Lord himself has done a great deed (Joel 2,21).

Chiasmus of sound. This is not very frequent. In Isa 40,4 it nicely expresses the change of situation:

w^ehāyâ he'āqōb l^emîšôr	*'qb*	*myšwr*
w^ehār^ekāsîm l^ebiq'â	*rksym*	*bq'*

Rugged places shall be made smooth
and mountain-ranges become a plain.

Isa 61,3 is also worthy of mention:

> *p^e'ēr taḥat 'ēper*
> Garlands instead of ashes.

Assonance, the repetition of vowels, is usually produced by inflection of nouns and verbs and also by some kinds of formation of nouns. It may be more striking by accumulation:

> *qārôb yôm-Yhwh haggādôl*
> *qārôb ûmahēr m^e'ōd*

The great day of the Lord is near,
near and hastening fast (Zeph 1,14).

Here is a selection of verses from Isa 31 which are remarkable for their varied and effective use of sound:

1 *yiššā'enû ... 'al-rekeb kî rāb ... w^elō' šā'û ...*
   they rely ... in chariots many in number ... but do not look.

3b *Yhwh yaṭṭeh yādô*
    w^ekāšal 'ôzēr
    w^enāpal 'āzûr
    w^eyaḥdāw kullām kiklāyûn
8b *w^enās 18 mipp^{e}nê-ḥereb*
    ûbaḥûrāyw lāmas yihyû
9   *... w^eḥattû minnēs śārāyw*
9b *'ăšer-'ûr lô b^{e}ṣiyyôn*
    w^etannûr lô birûšālaim

The Lord will stretch out his hand,
the helper will stumble,
and he who is helped will fall,
and they will all vanish together.
He shall flee before the sword,
and his young warriors shall be put to forced labour.
... his captains too dismayed to flee.
His fire blazes in Zion,
his furnace is set up in Jerusalem.

In v. 1 we find the subtle similarity of sound between the two verbs *š'n* and *š'h*; more clever still is the similarity of consonants in *rkb k-rb*. V. 3b begins with alliteration, three words beginning with *y-*, two phrases follow with very close similarity of sound, and the half-verse concludes with the similarity of *klm* and *yklywn*. In vv. 8b-9a the three words *nās, mas,* and *nēs* stand out. In v. 9b there is a clear rhyme.

Other instances fit better into the following category.

Dominant sound. This is a sound repeated in any position (except rhyme). The same sound appears repeatedly in a group of words without regard for the place it appears. In the Song of Songs the dominant sounds help to create a magical, enchanted atmosphere:

> ... *še'ănî šᵉḥarḥōret*
> *šeššĕzāpatnî haššāmeš*

> ... a little dark I may be
> because I am scorched by the sun (1,6)

> *qûmî lāk ra'yātî*
> *yāpātî ûlᵉkî-lāk*

> Rise up, my darling,
> my fairest, come away (2,10)

In 3,8 the sound *ḥ* dominates: brandish (*'ḥz*), sword (*ḥrb*), war (*mlḥmh*), sword (*ḥrb*), terror (*pḥd*). In 4,1-2 the sound *'ayin* dominates.

A more refined form of this technique consists in bringing together different dominant sounds, especially when they belong to some key word in the text. For example, in the Song of Songs the theme is one of searching in the night. "To search" in Hebrew is *biqqēš*, a verb which is heard four times. The following similar sounding words are also found: *miškāb* = "bed", *šᵉwāqîm* = "streets", and, more softly, *še'ăhăbâ* = "which loves", repeated; there are other techniques using sound also.

The ascent up the mountain in Isa 2 and Mic 4 obtains the effect of a flowing movement by insistence on the sounds *h, n, l* and *r*.

III. Descriptive Function

a) *Onomatopoeia* is an imitation of a sound using the phonic qualities of a language; it is linked to the meaning of the word and the sense of the phrase.

The following are famous: the chirping of the birds in Isa 10,14: *pōṣeh peh ûmᵉṣapṣēp*; the crackle of straw as it is burnt in Isa 5,24: *lākēn ke'ĕkōl qaš lᵉšôn 'ēš*; the buzzing flight of the insects whistled up by the Lord in Isa 7,18:

> *yišrōq Yhwh lazzᵉbûb*
> *'ăšer biqᵉṣê yᵉ'ōrê miṣrāyim*
> *wᵉladdᵉbôrâ 'ăšer bᵉ'ereṣ 'aššûr*

> The Lord will whistle for the fly
> from the distant streams of Egypt
> and for the bee from Assyria;

the work of the smiths in Isa 2,4:

kitt^etû ḥarbôtām le'ittîm
waḥănîtôtêhem l^emazmērôt

They shall beat their swords into mattocks
and their spears into pruning-knives.

A military advance sounds like this in Joel 2,4-5:

k^emar'ēh sûsîm mar'ēhû
ûk^epārāšîm kēn y^erûṣûn
k^eqôl markābôt
    'al-rā'šê h^ehārîm y^eraqqēdûn
k^eqôl lahab 'ēš
    'ōk^elâ qāš

Their appearance is like the appearance of horses,
and like war horses they run.
As with the rumbling of chariots,
they leap on the tops of the mountains,
like the crackling of a flame of fire devouring the stubble.

Nahum 2,5-8 achieves its effect by repeating consonants which are next to each other or near each other: (5) *yithôl^elû ... yištaqš^eqûn ... y^erôṣēṣû* (6) *hukan hassōkēk* (bb) *m^etōp^epōt 'al-libbēhen* (9) *nîn^ewēh kib^erākat-mayim mêmê ...*

The noise of cries and shouts is heard in Jer 51,55:

... qôl gadôl
w^ehāmû gallêhem k^emayim rabbîm
nittan š^e'ôn qôlām

... her mighty voice.
Their waves roar like many waters,
the noise of their voice is raised.

The final, late example gives us verses of great virtuosity of sound. Isa 17,12 compares the advance of an army to the clamour of the ocean:

hôy hămôn 'ammîm rabbîm
kahămôt yammîm yehĕmāyûn
ûš^e'ôn l^e'ummîm kiš^e'ôn
mayim kabbîrîm yiššā'ûn

Listen! it is the thunder of many peoples,
they thunder with the thunder of the sea.
Listen! it is the roar of nations
roaring with the roar of mighty waters.

The eschatology of Isaiah 24–27 (another late text) also takes great pleasure in accumulating mighty effects of sound.

b) The *metaphor of sound* imitates by means of sound sensations derived from the other senses. Hard work is portrayed by reduplication of consonants:

*way^e'azz^{e}qēhû way^{e}saqq^{e}lēhû
wayyiṭṭa'ēhû śōreq*

He trenched it, cleared it of stones,
and planted it with red vines (Isa 5,2).

An easy movement:

l^{e}kû mal'ākîm qallîm

Go, swift messengers (Isa 18,2).

The multitude of invaders, who occupy all the land, like insects:

*b^{e}naḥălê habbattôt ûbin^{e}qîqê hass^e'ālîm
ûb^{e}kôl hanna'ăṣûṣîm ûb^{e}kōl hannaḥălōlîm*

in the steep ravines, and in the clefts of the rocks,
and on all the thornbushes, and on all the pastures
(Isa 17,19).

We might consider Ezek 27,34.26 as the combination of a metaphor of sound and onomatopoeia. The sea is conjured up with the insistence on the consonant *m*, the din and the disaster of the shipwreck by the sounds *k* and *q*:

(34) *'attā! nišberet miyyammîm*   Now you are wrecked by the seas,
b^{e}ma'ămaqqê-māyim   in the depths of the waters;
ma'ărābēk w^{e}kol-q^{e}hālēk   your merchandise and all your crew
b^{e}tôkēk nāpālû   have sunk with you.

(26) *b^{e}mayim rabbîm hĕbî'ûk*   Your rowers have brought you out
haššāṭîm 'ōtāk   into the high seas.
rû^{a}ḥ haqqādîm š^{e}bārēk   The east wind has wrecked you
b^{e}lēb yammîm   in the heart of the seas.

In Ps 98,7 the sea is portrayed with a triple *m*, the land with a triple *b:*

yir'am hayyām ûm^{e}lō'ô
tēbēl w^{e}yōš^{e}bê bāh

Let the sea roar and all that fills it;
the world and those who dwell in it!

IV. Plays on Words. Paronomasia

a) *Plays on words* exploit the polivalence of meaning of one word, or the similarity of sound of various words.

These "plays" on words, or puns, can be quite serious. Prov 30,33 provides us with a remarkable one, which takes advantage of the following words: *'ap/ 'appayim* = "nose, nostrils, anger"; *hem'â* = "curds"; *ḥēmâ* = "anger"; *dām* = "blood (from the nose), homicide":

For pressing milk produces curds,
pressing the nose produces blood,
and pressing anger produces strife.

Job 15,13, *tāšîb 'el-'ēl rûḥekā*, means here "you turn your fury against God", but could also mean "you return your breath to God".

Playing with the sound of *n^{e}bî'îm* = "prophets", Jer 23,9-12 discharges a sarcastic accusation against them: they are "adulterous" (*m^{e}nā'ăpîm*), they are "ungodly" (*ḥānēpû*), and "for this reason" (*mipp^{e}nê*) they will "fall" (*nāp^{e}lû*). A tragic play on words.

In Mic 5,1, *môṣā'ōtāyw miqqedem* means "his origin is from of old", but it could also mean "he emerges from the East". Mic 6,3b-4a plays with the two words: *hel'ētîkā, he'ĕlîtîkā* = "I wearied you, I brought you up".

1 Chr 28,8 show by a play on words the correspondence between behaviour and reward: *diršû ... l^{e}ma'an tîr^{e}šû* = "observe ... so as to possess".

In 1 Kgs 18,21 Elijah makes fun of the people who "hobble on two crutches": *pōs^{e}ḥîm 'al-š^{e}tê hass^e'îpîm*. Such techniques are not exclusive to poetry.

It is probable that many plays on words in the OT escape us; perhaps those which are more ingenious and allusive.

W. G. G. Watson, *Classical Hebrew Poetry,* pp. 237-250.
J. M. Sasson, "Wordplay in the OT", *IDB* Supplementary Volume, pp. 968-970.

b) When, instead of a common noun, the word play concerns a proper name, the technique is called *paronomasia*. It is quite frequent in the OT. Proper names, of persons or places, are used simply to designate the person or place. We are not interested in their meaning. If we know it, we pay no attention to it. We are not aware that Susan means "white lily", Deborah means "bee", Jaffa means "beautiful". The Romans called this literal meaning of a proper name "nomen omen" = "the name signifies the destiny".

A. Strus, *Nomen Omen. La stylistique sonore des noms propres dans le Pentateuque* (AnBib 80; Rome 1978); idem, "Interprétation des noms propres dans les oracles contre les nations", *Congress Volume. Salamanca 1983*. Edited by J. A. Emerton (VTS 36; Leiden 1985), pp. 272-285.

The series in Mic 1,10-16 is a classic example. See also Am 5,5; Zeph 2,4 and Zech 9,3. The poet derives prophetic meaning from the name of the enemy, pagan nation, or from the name of its king. It can be understood as a sarcastic mocking or as an oracle which announces a fate. Some cases are quite clear (at least for those who listen to the text and are not content with seeing it). Other cases are quite exquisite and challenge the acuteness of the listener.

For example, Hos 2,17 says: "the valley of trouble will be the gate of hope". Trouble = *ʿākôr* alludes to the sacrilege of Achan (Josh 7,24). Now *ʿākôr* sounds very similar to "sterile" (*ʿkr/ʿqr*), and *tqwh* is both hope and reservoir; so on a second level we might understand "the valley of the desert will be the gate of the reservoir". In Isa 63,1-6 the toponyms are Edom and the city of Bozrah. Now *ʾedôm* sounds like *ʾādōm* = "red, brown", and like, *dām* = "blood", while *boṣrâ* contains the consonants of *bṣr* = "to gather the vintage". The poet puts together a vision of the wine-harvest and the wine-press, of wine = blood which bespatters the clothes of the wine-presser. Jeremiah addresses Tekoa; this town has the same consonants as the verb *tqʿ* = "to sound, to play an instrument". So the poet can give the order: "Sound the trumpet in Tekoa" (Jer 6,1).

Jer 47,1-7 is interesting not only for the clear cases of paronomasia, but also for some which are *sotto voce,* inserted in a series and which are difficult to catch:

pᵉlištîm "Philistines" — *šôṭēp yišṭᵉpû*

"flood which will inundate" — *ṣāpôn* "north";

ṣōr, ṣîdôn "Tyre, Sidon" — *śārîd* "remaining".

Ashkelon and Gaza are mentioned without paronomasia. But where are the other three cities of the Philistine pentapolis, Gath, Ekron and Ashdod? Gath appears in the verb *(ht)gdd* = "to make incisions"; Ashdod is in the verb *šdd* = "to destroy"; Ekron is in the infinitive *hakrît* = "to cut off".

Jer 48,1-8 is another similar series, rich in paronomasia; the name of the divinity, *kᵉmôš*, sounds quite similar to *kᵉmōṣ* = "like chaff". Jer 51,1ff. is against the Chaldeans, who in Hebrew are called *kaśdîm*; the name sounds like *qešet* = "bow", *qādôš* = "holy" and *mᵉduqqār* = "pierced".

The so-called last of the prophets, Malachi, rebukes the sons of Jacob for having "defrauded" God in his sacrifices (Mal 3,6-9). "To defraud" *(qbʿ)* forms a play on words with "Jacob" *(yaʿăqōb* from the root *ʿqb)*; thus the tradition of Jacob the swindler and crafty trickster, which was already apparent in Genesis and is taken up in Hos 6,7-10; Jer 9,1-7; 12,1-13, is kept alive. (Cf. L. Alonso Schökel, *¿Dónde está tu hermano? Textos de fraternidad en el libro del Génesis* (ISJ 19; Valencia 1985), pp. 239-243.

Zeph 2,4-9 offers another series: "Gaza abandoned", *ʿazzâ ʿăzûbâ*; "Ekron uprooted", *ʿeqrôn tēʿāqēr*; "Amon like Gomorrah", *ʿammôn ka ʿămōrâ*. Hos 14,3-9 is both an invitation and a promise to Israel-Ephraim. The poet takes advantage of the name *'eprayim: pᵉrî* = fruit", *'erpā'* = "I will heal", *yiprah* = "he shall blossom", *bᵉrôš* = "cypress".

Paronomasia is also frequent in narrative prose, applied to important characters in the history of Israel.

V. Sound Configuration

Given the importance of sound and the variety of techniques available to exploit it we can appreciate that a whole poem can show a particular arrangement of sound. Let us look at Isa 6 and Ps 137 as examples.

The narrative of the vocation of Isaiah, 6,1-10, begins with a description of the vision: *yšb ... ks' ... nś'... šlyw ml'ym ... hhykl* (*š/s/ś* and *l*); the appearance of the seraphim achieves its effect by the repetition of *šeš* = "six", *bištayim* = "with two", *yᵉkasseh* = "covered". The chant of the seraphim is striking due to the fulness of the vowels: *qādôš qādôš qādôš Yhwh ṣᵉbā'ôt // mᵉlō' kol-hā'āreṣ kᵉbôdô,* "Holy, holy, holy ...". The shaking of the temple is rendered by reduplicated consonants: *wayyanuʿû 'ammôt hassippîm miqqôl haqqōrē' // wᵉhabbayit yimmālē' 'āšān,* "the foundations of the thresholds shook at the voice of him who called // and the house was filled with smoke". When the prophet speaks, it is with faltering voice: *'ôy-lî kî-nidmêtî kî 'îš // ṭᵉmē'-śᵉpātayim 'ānōkî,* "Woe is me! For I am lost! for I am a man of unclean lips".

     Ps 137 begins with insistent rhythms and an exquisite sound, fit for the lyre:

> *... šām yāšabnû gam-bākînû*
> *bᵉzokrēnû 'et-ṣiyyôn*
> *... tālînû kinnōrôtênû*

> ... there we sat down and wept,
> when we remembered Zion.
> ... we hung up our lyres.

There follows an accumulation of sibilants, emphasising the mockery of the enemies:

> *kî šām šᵉ'ēlûnû šôbênû dibrê-šîr*
>   *wᵉtôlalênû [šôlᵉlênû ?] śimḥâ*
> *šîrû lānû miššîr ṣiyyôn*

> For there our captors required of us songs,
> and our tormentors, mirth, saying,
> "Sing us one of the songs of Zion!"

The reply takes up the sibilants again, but with moderation, and insists on the final sounds *-k, -kî, -q, -î:*

> *'êk nāšîr 'et-šîr-Yhwh ...*
> *'im-'eškāḥēk yᵉrûšālāyim*
>   *tiškaḥ yᵉmînî*
>   *tidbaq-lᵉšônî lᵉḥikkî*
> *'im-lō' 'ezkᵉrēkî*

> How shall we sing the Lord's song ...
> If I forget you, O Jerusalem,
>   let my right hand wither,
> let my tongue cleave to the roof of my mouth,
> if I do not remember you.

At the end the exiles intone their "blessing" and sarcastically dedicate it to Babylon. The sibilants return in a flood:

> *bat-bābel haššᵉdûdâ*
> *'ašrê šeyᵉšallem-lāk*
>   *'et-gᵉmûlēk šeggāmaltᵉ lānû*
> *'ašrê šeyyō'ḥēz wᵉnippēṣ*
>   *'et-ʿōlālayik 'el-hassālaʿ*

O daughter of Babylon, you devastator!
Happy shall he be who requites you
    with what you have done to us!
Happy shall he be who takes your little ones
    and dashes them against the rock!

VI. Translation

The Hebrew poets' conscious, clever and varied use of sound presents great difficulties for the translator. Often they are insoluble. The translator must often give up any idea of reproducing in his own language the styleme of the original. Sometimes he can imitate it. On other occasions, as in the Song of Songs, he can seek some overall compensation, by using the sonority of his own language to recreate the magic of the original. Eduardo Zurro and I spoke about this in the book *La traducción bíblica: Lingüística y estilística* (BiL 3; Madrid 1977); I also considered the problem in the commentary *Proverbios* (Madrid 1984).

CHAPTER IV

Rhythm

I. The Concept

Although rhythm makes use of sound, it ought to be considered in its own right due to its importance and its prominence in biblical investigation.

I will begin by citing two verses in Hebrew, in a simplified transliteration and with an abbreviated translation. The accents are those of the pronunciation normal today.

ṭób lehodót la-Yahwéh //   *lezammér lešimká 'elyón*
Good to praise the Lord   to play to your name Elion (Ps 92,2).

'ašré haggéber 'ašér teyasserénnu //   *Yáh umittoratéka telammedénnu*
Happy the man whom you chasten   Lord and your law you teach
(Ps 94,12).

The first verse is heard as a quite regular rhythm; the second verse perhaps does not sound like verse at all. Leaving aside the problems of ancient pronunciation and simply counting the syllables, we can reproduce the verses thus:

ó ooó ooó // ooó ooó ooó 3 + 3 (accents)

oó oóo oó oooóo // ó oooóo oooóo 4 + 3.

Reading these verses in their respective poems should confirm and clarify this first impression.

It is without doubt that the Hebrews cultivated verse extensively. The investigator and the student quite rightly ask the question: what makes Hebrew verse?

Poetic rhythm stylizes the natural rhythm of the language and of the sentence to produce verse, and, on a lesser scale, artistic prose. Every language has its own rhythm. This rhythm comes about due to the periodical reemergence in a series of a particular significant element. In each language the smallest units of the series are syllables. Syllables can be regularly differentiated due to different characteristics: length, intensity or timbre. I call this differentiating characteristic the constituting factor of the rhythm. If the factor is the length, syllables divide into long and short, and may produce the kind of quantitative rhythm characteristic of Greek verse. If the factor is intensity, there are syllables which have a tonic accent, and others which do not; as is the case with the accentual rhythm of many Western languages. A language with tones might employ one of the diacritical tones to make up its own system of rhythm. Certain mediaeval Saxon languages took the timbre as the constituting factor, seeking alliteration. Silence too may be a constituting factor, since it defines the successive units by the use of pauses and caesuras.

A first kind of stylization takes the smallest units, the syllables, and makes a verse: this is a first level of rhythm. A second level stylization takes the verse as a unit and produces a second level of rhythm, the strophe. When we take the strophes as units we reach the third level of rhythm, the broad rhythm of the poem.

Poetic rhythm is always a question of sound and listening. As Paul said referring to faith, "rhythm comes from hearing". It cannot be seen, although the written signs help; it is not a question of abstract mathematical relations. One either hears it or one does not. And even though anyone should be able to hear the rhythm, the investigator of Hebrew rhythm must have a good ear for rhythm and some degree of training in his own language, and perhaps in others too. Someone who does not have an ear for music cannot be a good musicologist. If an investigator has this kind of training he will know how to avoid theoretical rigidity (cf. L. Alonso Schökel, *Estética y estilística del ritmo poético* [Barcelona 1959]).

II. History of the Investigation

The ancient Jews lost their appreciation of Hebrew rhythm. Synagogue recitation did not abide by its rules. The ancients were influenced by the quantitative rhythm of Greek and Latin poetry (even though in Latin it was quite artificial). Without any detailed analysis or proof they affirmed that the Hebrews wrote in hexameters. When accentuated metre became widely used in Europe and even took over Latin, there were no investigators of the Bible who took advantage of this to give the correct explanation of Hebrew poetry. The great mediaeval Jewish scholar, Mose Ibn 'Ezra (11th century), found no solution; it seems that the Renaissance rabbi Azaria Rossi came closer to a solution, but without positive results. In Ugolino's great *Thesaurus* many theories are put forward, some improbable, none satisfactory, even though Anton (1770) is on the right path, and Leutwein comes close behind. In the nineteenth century, amid the proliferation of theories, J. Ley finds a solution and establishes a series of principles which allow the development of a harmonious theory (1871-1877). Budde's discoveries regarding the *qînâ* = "elegy" (1874; 1882) consolidate the new approach. Finally we should name E. Sievers, the expert in phonetics and rhythm, who provides a strict, systematic account (F. Sievers, *Metrische Studien. I. Studien zur hebräischen Metrik* (ASGW.PH XXI/1-2; Leipzig 1901); II. *Die hebräische Genesis* (ASGW.PH XXIII/1-2; Leipzig 1904, 1905). Even though his approach is rather rigid, he provided teachers with a valid aid which became widely used. We will speak of more recent contributions to the debate later on.

N. Schlögl, *De re metrica veterum Hebraeorum* (Vienna 1899).
S. Euringer, *Die Kunstform der althebräischen Metrik* (BZfr V/9-10; Münster 1912).
J. Begrich, "Zur hebräische Metrik", *TRu* N.F. 4 (1932) 67-89.
L. Alonso Schökel, *Estudios de poética hebrea* (Barcelona 1963), pp. 119-134, with a full chronological catalogue of scholarly works.

III. Hebrew Accentual Rhythm: Description

The Hebrew language was marked by regular tonic accents. In the pronunciation which we have received the accent tends to fall on the last syllable. The constitutive factor of the verse is the tonic accent as it is distributed between pauses and caesuras. A verse, strictly speaking, exists only when repeated (versus < verto), and consequently only a series of verses in a poem allows us to identify the verse. Once tradition has fixed and repeated the forms it is possible to identify one single verse, on its own or immersed within the context of prose.

The shortest psalm in the Psalter consists of two verses:

hal^e lû et-Yhwh kol-gôyīm // šabb^e ḥûhû kol-l^e'ummîm
kî gābar 'ālênû ḥasdô // we'emet-Yhwh l^e'ôlam

Praise the Lord, all nations! Extol him, all peoples!
For great is his steadfast love toward us; and the faithfulness of the Lord endures for ever (Ps 117).

There are two verses with six accents each, and a caesura in the middle of each verse. This can be expressed in the formula: 3 + 3
3 + 3.

A proverb is simply one line but we recognise it as a verse:

dalyû šōqayim mippisēᵃḥ || ûmāšāl bᵉpî kᵉsîlîm

Like a lame man's legs which hang useless, is a proverb in
the mouth of fools (Prov 26,7).

The 3 + 3 verse is the most frequent in Hebrew poetry (perhaps
due to its six accents the ancients took it to be a hexameter). *Qînâ*
rhythm (Budde) is also frequent, 3 + 2:

rᵉ'ēh Yhwh kî-ṣar-lî || mēʿay ḥŏmarmārû
nehpak libbî bᵉqirbî || kî marô marîtî
miḥûṣ šikkᵉlâ ḥereb || babbayit kammāwet

Behold, O Lord, for I am in distress, my soul is in tumult,
my heart is wrung within me, because I have been very rebellious.
In the street the sword bereaves; in the house it is like death
(Lam 1,20).

Other less frequent forms are the symmetrical 2 + 2 and 4 + 4,
the asymmetrical 4 + 3 and 4 + 2, or their inversions 2 + 3, 2 + 4,
3 + 4. It is very rare, and often suspect, to come across a hemistich
with five accents and without a caesura.

Formula 4 + 3:

ḥasdê Yhwh kî lō'-tāmmû || kî lō'-kālû raḥămāyw

The steadfast love of the Lord never ceases, his mercies never
come to an end (Lam 3,2).

Formula 4 + 2:

paḥad wāpaḥat hāyâ lānû || haššē't wᵉhaššāber

Panic and pitfall have come upon us, devastation and
destruction (Lam 3,47).

Formula 2 + 2 2 + 2:

mēḥaṭṭō't nᵉbîèhā || 'ăwōnôt kōhănèhā
haššōpᵉkîm bᵉqirbāh || dam ṣaddîqîm

This was for the sins of her prophets, and the iniquities of
her priests,
who shed in the midst of her the blood of the righteous (Lam
4,13).

Rather infrequent but quite clear are verses of three hemistichs with two caesuras. They stand out quite clearly in the series:

kî ḥillaṣta napšî mimmāwet // *'et-'ênî min-dim'â* //
'et-raglî middeḥî

For thou hast delivered my soul from death, my eyes from tears, my feet from stumbling (Ps 116,8).

Ps 93 uses this kind of verse with great skill, adding further emphasis by the repetition of words and sounds.

nāś^e'û n^ehārôt Yhwh	The floods have lifted up, O Lord,
nāś^e'û n^ehārôt qôlām	the floods have lifted up their voice,
yiś^e'û n^ehārôt dokyām	the floods lift up their roaring.
miqqōlôt mayim rabbîm	Mightier than the thunders of many waters,
'addîrîm mišb^erê-yām	mightier than the waves of the sea,
'addîr bammārôm Yhwh	the Lord on high is mighty!
'ēdōtèkā ne'emnû m^e'ōd	Thy decrees are very sure;
l^ebêt^ekā na'ăwâ qōdeš	holiness befits thy house,
Yhwh l^e'ōrek yāmîm	O Lord, for evermore (Ps 93,3-5).

(Others consider this psalm to be made up of strophes of three short verses, as we will see later.)

We may call each rhythmic unit with its accented and unaccented syllables a "foot". There are various types of foot according to the relation between accented and unaccented syllables. The most frequent types of foot in Hebrew are oó and ooó, which we call iambic and anapaestic. The longer types oooó and ooóo are less frequent, as are the trochaic and dactylic, óo and óoo.

Any departure from what is normal will produce a special effect: an accumulation of iambic feet gives a sense of urgency and speed; anapaestic feet convey a sense of space; where atonic syllables are lacking a jerking syncopation may result. Compare certain verses in Isa 1,10-20:

ḥidlû hārē^a'	oó oó	Cease to do evil,
limdû hêṭeb	oó oó	learn to do good;
diršû mišpāṭ	oó oó	seek justice,
'ašš^erû ḥāmôṣ	ooó oó	correct oppression;
šipṭû yātôm	oó oó	defend the fatherless,
rîbû 'almānâ	óo ooó	plead for the widow (16b-17).
w^e'im t^emā'ănû ûm^erîtem	oó oooó oooó	if you refuse and rebel
ḥereb t^e'ukk^elû	óo oooó	the sword will devour you (20).

The movement of the verse is iambic and anapaestic ("ascending") rather than trochaic and dactylic ("descending"). However, considering the general movement of the poem, the direction of the movement is only really appreciated in exceptional cases suggested by the meaning.

IV. Observations

When we apply the above-mentioned simplified description we must also bear in mind certain techniques and conventions; we must not forget that there are many things we do not know about Hebrew verse.

Firstly, we are unaware of many aspects of ancient pronunciation, some of them rather fundamental. When did the accent move to the final syllable? The ancient forms of the segholates had two syllables and were accented on the first:

malku = "king", *malki* = "of the king", *malka* = "the king" (object). When did the inflexion disappear? Did verse preserve it as a convention? (In many cases such a pronunciation would clearly improve the rhythm.) Some forms of the *wayyiqtōl*, for example *way^{e}qattēl*, may have been pronounced *wayqattēl*, which is what the Masoretic notation seems to indicate. (Thus Sievers.) How many of the unnecessary conjunctions at the beginning of the second hemistich are original, and how many were added later? These doubts and others advise caution in the analysis of the type of foot, and also in determining the number of accents.

On the other hand, poetry has its own rights, and licence. We must consider enclitic and proclitic particles and suffixes, also when a suffix is attached to a preposition. We must not be misled, whether the elements are written together or separately. There are many examples:

Ps 51,12: *lēb ṭāhôr b^{e}rā'-lî 'ĕlōhîm*   ó oó oóo ooó
       14: *hāšîbâ lî š^{e}śôn yišèkā*   oóo oó oóo

Lam 1,2c: *kol-rē'èhā bāg^{e}dû bāh*   ó oóo oóo
        4c: *w^{e}hî' mar-lāh*   oó oó
     2,13c: *mî yirpā'-lāk*   ó oóo

There is also the kind of proclitic particle which affects the whole verse, though it remains outside the verse and is not counted in the series of accents. Robinson called this "anacrusis", but the phenomenon was already observed and described correctly by Sievers in his classic work.

There are some words, especially monosyllables, which may be read with or without an accent, according to the demands of rhythm of the poem: the negation *lō'*, the polysemic particle *kî*. Such words may on the one hand give rise to doubts, and on the other hand may allow the harmonisation of rebel verses. There are instances where the poet adds the conjunction to the negative to obtain one foot more: *wᵉlō' oó*).

A technique of a different nature is the double accent. There are some long words, sometimes with suffixes and prefixes, which can allow two accents, and thus harmonise the verse in the series to which it belongs. We cannot deny to Hebrew poetry those techniques which are normal in other languages, even though they may be exceptional cases.

In Ps 97 hemistichs with three accents dominate so that it is probable that in v. 7 we should read the participle with double accent: *hammithalᵉlîm bā'elōhîm* (oóooó oooó). In Ps 81,13, if we read the word *bᵉmô'aṣôtêhem* with two accents (oóoooó), we hear the expected three accents in the second hemistich.

All these aspects, enclitic and proclitic particles, words with double accent, vowels which may be accented or unaccented, allow in many cases a satisfactory rhythmic reading. They are aspects we experience in other languages and which we apply as a hypothesis to Hebrew verse. The results sufficiently confirm the hypothesis.

V. The Strophe

The second level of rhythm is the strophe, made up of a group of verses. At the turn of the century there was much discussion about the existence and identification of the strophe in Hebrew poetry. Many of the results revealed the great ingenuity of their promotors. The strophe is in fact exceptional in Hebrew poetry. Here are some clear cases.

Lamentations, with the exception of the last, uses strophes of three or two verses; the acrostic layout shows this. In Ecclesiasticus poems combining strophes of six or four verses are frequent. It is probable that Ps 114 is made up of four strophes of two verses each. The presence of a refrain might be the sign of strophic structure as long as the strophes are fairly regular (which is not borne out by our practice or theory). Isa 9,7-21 consists of three strophes marked by the refrain "For all this his anger is not turned away, and his hand is stretched out still". On the other hand the refrain "Shall I not punish them for these things? and shall I not avenge myself on a nation such as this?" in Jer 5,9.29 and 9,8 is not a sign of strophic composition (even if the corresponding fragment in chapter 9 were moved). The refrain in Ps 42–43 gives a quite regular strophic structure. A similar structure is seen in Ps 46 if the refrain is replaced after v. 4. Ps 57 is divided in two strophes of seven verses by the refrain.

Our strict idea of "strophe" requires the repetition of an identical group of verses, for example, triplets or quatrains. When speaking of Hebrew rhythm the term "strophe" is used sometimes in a wider sense, not linked to the rhythm and referring simply to the part of section. Watson proposes a distinction which is perhaps too sophisticated, that of the regular "stanza", and of the irregular "strophe". Some scholars consider the hemistich, or part of a verse, to be a verse, and thus easily discover binary and ternary strophes in Hebrew poetry. From this they go on to what is for them a third level, which they can then call simply "strophe". This distinction comes very close and even overlaps with parallelism.

A. Condamin, *Poèmes de la Bible. Avec une introduction sur la strophique hébraïque* (Paris 1933).

P. van der Lugt, *Strofische structuren in de bijbels-hebreeuwse poëzie. De geschiedenis van het onderzoek en een bijdrage tot de theorievorming omtrent de strofentouw van de Psalmen* (DN.ST; 's-Gravenhage [1980]).

W. G. E. Watson, *Classical Hebrew Poetry*, pp. 160-200.

VI. Regularity of Rhythm

Rhythm is based in the periodical reappearance of the same element or factor. If this is not periodical then there is no rhythm. But what kind of regularity is required? Not a chronometric regularity, but one fitting to language and its perception. In a good recitation a verse with eleven syllables may last double the time without disturbing the rhythm. A trained ear will perceive the underlying regularity. (Just as with music the *ritardando, accelerando* or *rubato* do not disturb the rhythm.) There is the basis of regularity, marked by the metronome, and above it the desired expressive irregularity.

The ideal of rhythmic regularity inflamed and stirred up many controversies in the investigation of the poetry of the OT. Some were champions of absolute regularity (Grimme, Rothstein); others were more tolerant (Haupt, Staerk, Gray, König). Correction of the Hebrew text *metri causa* became fashionable. What was acceptable in exceptional cases, became normal.

These days we are more careful in our treatment of rhythm and of the text. The experience of other languages will help us by comparison to resolve the problems. To preserve the minimum of regularity of rhythm we can consider the following aspects: the pronunciation problems mentioned above, the conjunction of various factors concerning rhythm, the idea of the "rhythmic cell", the distinction between metre and rhythm, and the distinction of different kinds of regularity.

1) Given the role of perception and the importance of recitation we become aware of alternatives of rhythm which allow us to preserve the fundamental regularity. Recitation and perception, however, are not subjective factors which disturb the pure objectivity; they are fundamental to the poetry and the rhythm.

2) Certain factors ensure the regularity, while others introduce variety. Syllabic metre is based on quantity: so many syllables make up the verse (making allowances for hiatuses, synalephas and the law of Musaffia). Now, while it is clear that the quantity of eleven syllables establishes an eleven syllable series, the distribution of accents among these syllables (the intensity factor) produces the necessary variety. There may be different such distributions within the same poem. In Hebrew the number of accents may produce regularity, while the relation between tonic and atonic syllables gives variety.

3) A "rhythmic cell" which is very stressed may give cohesion to a less regular series of syllables. (Some authors cite Hamlet's "to sleep to dream" — oó oó — in this regard.) This technique may be present in the Song of Songs.

4) W. Kayser correctly drew a distinction between metre and rhythm. Metre is the rigorous pattern which underlies the whole poem. It is like the musical 3/4, 6/8, 2/4, etc. In Spanish poetry we could cite the Alexandrian 7 + 7, or the lyric 7 + 11 + 7 + 11 + 11, etc. Rhythm is the free expression which may be in tension with the underlying metre. Beating time is different from conducting an orchestra. Children tend to adopt a mechanical regularity when they recite poetry.

5) The shattering of the rhythm for reasons of expression can be a poetic technique of great effect. Such an effect may be produced by the lengthening of a pause, emphasis on one particular phrase, resonance.

6) A tradition of poetry may be open to different kinds of rhythmic regularity. In Hebrew poetry I have found few poems which are strictly rhythmic, many which are quite rhythmic, and some which I would call free verse. At this stage we are very close to rhythmic prose (Ecclesiastes, prophetic speeches).

Our editions of the Bible during the last decades are printed in such a way that we may distinguish verse from prose. Translators have followed this lead. Nevertheless, there are still texts printed as prose which seem to require a rhythmic reading as with verse; and there are quite a few prophetic texts which might be read and translated as free verse or rhythmic prose.

The new edition of the Biblia Hebraica Stuttgartensia still prints the oracle of Isaiah to king Ahaz as prose. We can say *a priori* that it is not likely that a divine oracle was composed as prose. Furthermore, it is easy to read the oracle as verse and the reading seems convincing:

hinnēh	(anacrusis)	Behold!
hā'almâ hārâ	ooó oó	a young woman shall conceive
wᵉyōledet bēn	ooóo ó	and bear a son,
wᵉqārā't šᵉmô	ooó oó	and shall call his name
'immānû 'ēl	oóo ó	Immanuel.
ḥem'â ûdᵉbaš	oó ooó	Curds and honey
yō'kēl lᵉda'tô	oó ooó	shall he eat until he knows
mā'ôs bārā'	oó oó	how to refuse evil
ûbāḥôr baṭṭôb	ooó oó	and choose good.
kî beṭerem	ó oóo	For before
yēda' hanna'ar	oó oóo	the child knows
mā'ōs bārā'	oó oó	to refuse evil
ûbāḥōr baṭṭôb	ooó oó	and choose good
tē'āzēb hā'ădāmâ	ooó ooó	the land will be deserted
'ăšer 'attâ qāṣ	ooóo ó	of which you dread
mippᵉnê šᵉnê mᵉlākèhā	ooó oó ooóo	the two kings (Isa 7,14-16).

The rhythm runs thus: $2 + 2\ 2 + 2\ 2 + 2\ 2 + 2\ 2 + 2\ 2 + 2\ 2 + 2 + 3$. The particle *kî* must be seen as accentuated. It would be possible to consider "to refuse evil and choose good" as a rhythmic cell (oó oó). One could then on the basis of this see some verses as of the same type, and consider others as diverse, like "for before the child knows", "the land will be deserted...". In any reading the lengthening of final verses will often be encountered.

I would not call the preceding oracle free verse. I would include in that category several pieces from Jeremiah which others consider to be prose. It is possible that the less rhythmic form (free verse or simply prose) is due to secondary elaboration of original poetic oracles of the prophet. If this is true, we must declare that the disciples and followers of the prophet exercised great freedom (and showed a certain lack of respect). I consider the present text of Jer 14,11-16 to be free verse; it contains very rhythmic phrases and even parallels. Chapter 16 also contains various pieces of free verse,

mixed with the prose pieces. Jer 23,25-32 may be considered free
verse; it is very different from the prose which follows it, vv. 33-40. I
consider also that certain pages of Ezekiel may be considered free
verse, even though they may sound like very rhythmic rhetorical
prose: 5,5-17, which contains various instances of parallelism,
though it seems a little overloaded; the same may be said of
chapters 6 and 7; in chapter 13 the rhythmic cell "delusive visions,
lying divinations" $(2+2)$ is repeated; much of chapter 16 employs
poetic language and very rhythmic phrases.

W. E. Barnes, "Hebrew Metre and Text of the Psalms", *JTS* 33 (1932)
374-382, proposes an intermediary form between prose and verse, even
though he does not call it free verse.
L. Alonso Schökel, *Estudios de poética hebrea,* pp. 160-163.

VII. Stylistic Analysis

The descriptions presented hitherto ought naturally to lead in
to the stylistic analysis of the rhythm of various poems. If we stop at
simply establishing rhythmic formulas, we will have reduced the
work of literature to some kind of formal diagram; using Kayser's
terminology, we will have established the metre without perceiving
the rhythm. Once the techniques have been examined as a series of
possibilities, we must proceed to examine their actual expression
and their concrete function. This kind of work is almost
non-existent in Hebrew poetry. I will have to make do with some
examples, allowing some margin of doubt.
Isa 1,2-9 is a passionate poem, a model of prophetic preaching.
Verse 3a shows clearly the formula $3+3$, while v. 4b is $2+2$. With
these two rhythmic formulas we can listen to the whole. To keep
v. 2b within the formula we must accentuate the final *bî,* giving it
special emphasis. Verse 3 contrasts the knowledge shown by the
animals with the lack of understanding shown by Israel: if v. 3b
follows the formula $3+3$, the two negatives both are accentuated:

> The ox knows its owner, and the ass its master's crib;
> but Israel does *not* know, my people does *not* understand.

(But v. 3b could also be read $2+2$, without accentuating the negatives.) V. 4a provides a fearful emphasis by loading accents on two
successive monosyllables which rhyme: *hôy gôy ḥōṭē'* = "Woe to
the sinful people!" V. 4b continues as before but tightens up with
the formula $2+2$. In v. 6b over the basis of an accented rhythm of
$2+2$ we have the internal rhyme and sound repetition in three

words: *peṣaʿ wᵉḥabbûrâ ûmakkâ ṭᵉriyyâ*, "bruises and sores, and bleeding wounds"; the accented 2+2 is in counterpoint with the sound 1+3. Something similar happens in v. 7, which I read 3+3: over this binary rhythm we have the ternary division of sense, brought about by the repetition of the negative: "not pressed out, not bound up, not softened with oil". Something similar again happens in v. 8: the binary rhythm of 2+2 2+2 is overlaid by the triple comparison which produces a sense movement of 1+4. I have said nothing of the initial verse, the solemn exclamation to heavens and earth as God's witnesses: the basic 3+3 is articulated as 2+2+2: "Hear, heavens; give ear, earth; for the Lord speaks".

The book of Job follows the 3+3 metre quite faithfully. Unexpectedly, in 14,4, we come across the following verse: *mî-yittēn ṭāhôr miṭṭāmēʾ lōʾ ʾeḥād* (3+2 or 3+1). Some commentators correct the text to reestablish the regularity. But we can hear the effect of the "broken foot" in the translation: "Who can bring a clean thing out of an unclean? — No one!"

In Ps 5,4 too there are some who would correct the text *metri causa* to harmonise the rhythm, which sounds thus:

bōqer tišmaʿ qôlî	In the morning you hear my voice;
bōqer ʾeʿĕrok-lᵉkā	in the morning I bring my plea,
waʾăṣappeh	and I wait.

This "broken foot" gives dramatic expression to the waiting of the psalmist.

Isa 16,12 is part of a *qînâ*: 3+2 3+2. In violent counterpoint, the sense of the verse contrasts the efforts of Moab, and its downfall. This is reflected in the accentual set-up of 8 accents and then 2. The translation may give the idea:

> And when Moab presents himself,
> when he wearies himself upon the high place,
> when he comes to his sanctuary to pray,
>   he will not prevail.

VIII. Other Theories

I have maintained that the theory based on accentuation is the most convincing to explain and listen to Hebrew poetic rhythm. Comparison with other theories will only reinforce this point.

The theory of the *alternation of accents* was first proposed by Bickel (1890-1900), then by Hölscher (1920); S. Mowinckel defended it tenaciously in a series of articles (1950; 1953); Horst took it up again (1953) and it was continued by S. Segert (1953; 1958; 1969). This theory maintains that Hebrew poetic rhythm is produced by the alternation of atonic and tonic syllables, thus: oóoóoóoó. The theory has to have recourse continually to double accents, even triple accents; far too frequently it must speak of syncopation, or collision of two successive tonic accents; it violates the natural rhythm of the language and produces results which are unacceptable to the ear (cf. *Estudios de poética hebrea*, pp. 139-145, where there are many examples).

The idea of the *short verse* was defended in different ways by E. Balla (1949), G. Fohrer (1952-1955) and Piatti (1950). (Cf. *Estudios...*, pp. 145-152.)

Piatti maintains that the verse or Hebrew metric unit does not have two parts, but one; in other words, he calls verse what I call hemistich. His verses are made up of 3, 2 or 4 accents with no caesura; they combine into minor strophes, and then into larger groups. One of his reasons for this is the alphabetical approach applied to "hemistichs" in Pss 111 and 112. Watson has a similar approach, except that he calls the minor units "colon", and thus speaks of "stanzas" which are bicolon, tricolon, tetracolon, pentacolon, hexacolon, and heptacolon. The obvious difference between pauses and caesuras leads me to prefer the explanation given above, which is still the most popular.

Fohrer applies his theory to texts which I would include in free verse. It seems reasonable but I think he exaggerates the validity of the approach. It has the merit and usefulness of having revealed the rhythm of prophetic pieces which others quickly relegate to prose.

The theory of the *number of syllables* was defended tenaciously by D. N. Freedman, M. Dahood, and by their disciples and others besides. Judging by the results they produce the theory would be that Hebrew metre is made up by the similar number of syllables in a series of verses (for example, between 5 and 11 syllables), and by some kind of equilibrium between two verses or parts of verses (for example, 6+9, 7+8, 9+5). Sometimes there are verses with the same number of syllables on both sides of the caesura (for example, 6+6, 8+8, 9+9). The variations are so enormous that it is not possible to establish any regularity; the occurrence of symmetrical verses is more accidental than fundamental. To see how the theories of accentuation and number of syllables might be applied to the same text the reader may consult my review of D. K. Stuart, *Studies in Early Hebrew Meter* (*Bib* 59 [1978] 421-423).

It is sufficient simply to mention other theories like the "thought unit" theory, and the theory based on the calculation of the number of letters in the Masoretic text. Rhythm comes from hearing!

T. Collins, *Line-Forms in Hebrew Poetry. A Grammatical Approach to the Stylistic Study of the Hebrew Prophets* (SP.SM 7; Rome 1978).

M.P. O'Connor, *Hebrew Verse Structure* (Winona Lake, Indiana 1980).

T. Longman, "A Critique of Two Recent Metrical Systems", *Bib* 63 (1982) 230-254.

CHAPTER V

Parallelism

I. Description and Examples

Parallelism is probably the most frequent and most well-known technique of Hebrew poetry. Since it is so frequent we may judge it monotonous; since it is so well-known we may dispense ourselves from analysing it. Let us begin with some random examples.

> When Israel went forth from Egypt,
>> the house of Jacob from a people of strange language,
> Judah became his sanctuary,
>> Israel his dominion (Ps 114,1-2).

What a curious way of expressing oneself! It is as if when walking one were to go two steps forward with the right foot and then two steps forward with the left. The normal thing in syntax is to give the subordinate clause first and then proceed to the main clause: When Israel went forth from Egypt, Judah became his (God's) sanctuary. The psalm departs from this normal procedure by doubling the subordinate clause and doubling the main clause. It delays the sense so that the first chord may sound and resound before the final chord again sounds and resounds.

In an example like this we are brought face to face with the poetic device of parallelism. The poet could have said:

> When Israel went forth from Egypt,
>> Judah became his sanctuary;
> the house of Jacob from a people of strange language,
>> Israel became his dominion.

In normal syntactical movement the subordinate clause is followed by the main clause. It is however quite abnormal when, after the first clause, a second parallel clause is added. The movement is suspended, the syntactical flow is interrupted, repetition is introduced. If we wanted to show the two cases with a formula, the first would be: AABB, the second: ABAB. (If we wish to use S for subordinate and M for main, the first would be: SSMM, the second

SMSM.) In the first case the parallelism affects an incomplete sentence; in the second it affects the whole sentence.

In both cases we can see a particular preference for parallelism: two lines are taken and placed mentally in parallel position; or one line is announced and another sought for which goes well with the first, a good match; or the same thought is doubled by being announced in two ways.

I take our second example from Ps 124,2-3:

> If it had not been the Lord who was on our side,
>> when men rose up against us,
> then they would have swallowed us up alive,
>> when their anger was kindled against us.

Is there parallelism here? Certainly not of the previous type. The flow of meaning is not arrested, it does not go back to begin again, there are no duplications, no resonating chords. The sentence is complex, but the lines are well distinguished. The clever arrangement of the lines allows us to listen to them as parallels. This is an example of rhythmic parallelism. This is a rather loose use of the term "parallelism". It is nevertheless correct because the ear hears a regular movement, divided into two well-balanced phases; the mind understands the whole as being in two stages.

However, this example from Ps 124 is a bit of a trap. If we had taken the first four biblical verses, we would have seen a broad parallelism, well ordered and emphasised by repetitions:

> If it had not been the Lord who was on our side,
>> — let Israel now say —
> if it had not been the Lord who was on our side,
>> when men rose up against us,
> then they would have swallowed us up alive,
>> when their anger was kindled against us;
> then the flood would have swept us away,
>> the torrent would have gone over us.

The third example is from Ezek 43,1-2:

> After he brought me to the gate, the gate facing east. And behold, the glory of the God of Israel came from the east; and the sound of his coming was like the sound of many waters; and the earth shone with his glory.

Short sentences follow each other, the movement advances: a vision is seen, a sound heard, a reflection is seen. Here there is no parallelism. No matching phrases, no returning back to the beginning, neither the ear nor the mind receives the impression of symmetry or equilibrium. This example serves as a contrast with the organisation of noise and light in Ps 77,18-19:

> Thy arrows flashed on every side,
> the crash of thy thunder was in the whirlwind,
> thy lightnings lighted up the world,
> the earth trembled and shook.

The symmetry is more marked in the original Hebrew.

Finally I am going to present the whole of Ps 114, with which I began. I will write it in parallel columns, A and B. I ask the reader to read first column A, then column B, then read them together as they appear in the original

A	B
When Israel went forth from Egypt,	the house of Jacob from a people of strange language
Judah became his sanctuary.	Israel his dominion.
The sea looked and fled;	Jordan turned back;
the mountains skipped like rams.	the hills like lambs.
What ails you, O sea, that you flee?	O Jordan, that you turn back?
O mountains, that you skip like rams?	O hills, like lambs?
Tremble, O earth, at the presence of the Lord.	at the presence of the God of Jacob.
who turns the rock into a pool of water.	the flint into a spring of water.

The first column is quite self sufficient; column B however lacks some significant elements. Its lines attach themselves to corresponding elements in column A. Column B prolongs, repeats, makes resonant and doubles column A. There will be occasion to return to this example.

II. The Nature of Parallelism

The use of the term "parallelism" is metaphorical. Its proper meaning refers to space, but poetics applies it to a process which is linked more to time than space. It is rather like speaking of the "rhythm" of a diptych of paintings. When we write poetry it is true that we write in parallel lines; but this writing down is simply a lesser substitute for the recited poem, which is real language. (Poems which are "pear-shaped" and calligrams are secondary phenomena.)

I have already said that in parallelism we write two elements symmetrically, or we seek a match for a line already written, or we divide in two halves an already existing unit.

Dámaso Alonso, in his important book written in collaboration with Carlos Bousoño, *Seis calas en la expresión literaria española* (Madrid [2]1956), states that the starting point is the plurality of reality and our perception of this plurality, which is reproduced and stylised by language (pp. 18f.).

Plurality is indeed a frequent element in parallelism but it is not the only one nor is it the most fundamental. We will meet it many times but it is insufficient and does not provide the ultimate foundation of parallelism.

Our initial perception is often of plurality as an undifferentiated mass: a horde, an army, people, a forest. Another case is the initial perception of a continuum in time or space: a day, a circumference, a road. Language seeks to express this plurality or this continuum by dividing and putting together again. It divides the continuum and then rebuilds its unity. Parallelism is part of the most basic operation of language, that of "articulation". There is articulation of sound, syntactic articulation, articulation of semantic fields, of rhythm.

By articulation the continuum is divided into pieces which can be put together again. The continuum is thus more precisely perceived, more genuinely presented, and can be simplified in some of its elements; above all, the elements can be combined in different groups, producing flexibility of language, the great richness of poetic language.

Parallelism is rooted not only in a historical or literary process, but in language itself: it is a basic human fact and raw material for the work of literature.

The simplest kind of articulation is binary parallelism, so common in Hebrew poetry. E. Norden in his classic work *Die Antike Kunstprosa*, p. 814, believes that binary parallelism is the origin of all poetry. Threefold and fourfold parallelism is also frequent, and there are some instances of even more extended parallelism. There are also clever combinations of binary and ternary parallelism.

Various reasons are given for the predominance of binary parallelism. Some give a psychological reason, the fundamental binary nature of the human person in time and space. Others make reference to the popular origins of poetry with its preference for the binary. Such reasons are rather dubious. But what is quite clear is the predominance of binary parallelism in Hebrew poetry.

III. **Classification**

Different criteria are used to classify parallelism:

a) It may be according to the *number* of parallel lines, as already indicated: binary, threefold, fourfold, etc.

b) Classification according to the *quantity of text*. Parallelism may be between two or more hemistichs of a verse, two or more verses, two or more distichs, two or more strophes. Some have called the first instance "internal" and the others "external".

c) Classification according to the *relationship of the contents*. If the meaning of the whole is the same or similar, the parallelism is synonymous. This is the type of parallelism which calls attention to itself. If the meaning contains a contrast it is called antithetic. If the meaning is completed, usually by syntax, Lowth would call it "synthetic", though others have not accepted this designation.

Undoubtedly there are other types of relationship of contents. Individual elements may be correlative: anvil and hammer, water and thirst, fathers and sons, boys and girls. They may form a merismus or an example of polarised expression (see later). They may be an image and explanation, as happens in Proverbs. One may also come across a statement and its explanation, an action and its consequence, a command and the reason for it. We must leave much space for other possible syntactical relationships. To reduce everything to synonymous, antithetic and synthetic parallelism is to create a third category which is far too broad. We must maintain the clearest and simplest divisions, similarity and contrast. But further classification can be left to the analysis of the single cases. Since the first two types, synonymous and antithetic will frequently appear in what follows, I will give a few examples of other types.

> To thee, O Lord, I call;
> my rock, be not deaf to me (Ps 28,1).

The Psalmist's calling, and God's not being deaf are obviously correlative.

> Therefore let every one who is godly offer prayer
>   to thee at a time of distress;
> in the rush of great waters they shall not reach him (Ps 32,6).

There is a relationship between the supplication and the liberation from danger; one may be more precise in speaking of the second verse as consequence of the first.

For the word of the Lord is upright;
and all his work is done in faithfulness (Ps 33,4).

Words and works may be considered as related, or more precisely as a merismus.

The eyes of the Lord are toward the righteous,
and his ears toward their cry (Ps 34,16).

Eyes and ears are both senses and form a merismus.

Like one who binds the stone in the sling
is he who gives honour to a fool (Prov 26,8).

The comparison is followed by the action, in parallel movement. The order may be reversed:

Of no use is eagerness without forethought;
he who walks too quickly will stumble (Prov 19,2).

In my comparative study of the forms of Hebrew sayings and proverbs the reader will be able to find classified examples; cf. L. Alonso Schökel and José Vílchez, *Proverbios*, pp. 117-142.

Even though parallelism is a formal aspect of poetics it is both right and necessary to pay attention to content in order to avoid a sterile formalism.

d) Classification according to the *correspondence of components*. This is the type of classification which has been most studied and refined, perhaps too much so.

I have already spoken of correspondence, both similarities and contrasts. We used capital letters to refer to each member of the parallel structure when we looked at Ps 114. The correspondence there was not complete: verbs were missing in the second column. We can achieve a more precise analysis using small letters and focusing on the component parts of each member:

When Israel went forth from Egypt	a	b	c
the house of Jacob from a people of strange language,	a		c
Judah became his sanctuary	a	b	c
Israel his dominion.	a		c

The more elements there are the more possible permutations and combinations arise. Given the relationships of content, number and disposition the varieties of parallelism when closely examined are very numerous. It is useful to appreciate some differences but it is dangerous to pursue them seeking an exhaustive classification. If the classification is so precise we will often have to cross the boundaries into different categories.

Take me not off with the   wicked and evil-doers,
                                                 who speak peace with their neighbour
                                                 while mischief is in their hearts (Ps 28,3).

The first sentence runs normally until the end, where it divides into two. "Wicked" and "evil-doers" are synonyms, but not placed in parallel lines. They are "twin words": the meaning is delayed; the simple line is divided into two, it might be drawn thus ―――――――――――― ════════════. The two following phrases might have been presented in a parallel line, but this does not happen. They are in fact parallel to "evil-doers" and describe these individuals. If we represent all this by notation we would have: a b c + c // C. The C in its turn is made up of two parallel elements which are antithetic: speak // in their hearts, peace // mischief. Thus in this verse we have both synonymous and antithetic elements. The synonymous elements are found in the first member, and between the first member and the rest. The result is that the description of the "wicked" is more powerful due to the repetition and the description. The antithesis in the final two phrases reveals the profound deviousness of the wicked. Such use of parallelism is not something mechanical or academic.

   Let us analyse certain verses of Ps 31. V. 11a translated in the order of the Hebrew could be rendered thus: "It is spent with sorrow my life, // my years with sighing". The formula would be a b c // c b. V. 11b is slightly different: "It fails in misery my strength, // my bones waste away". The formula here is a b c // c a. V. 11b is in turn parallel to v. 11a: the formula is A // A, A // A. V. 10 was less regular. It might be translated following the Hebrew order: "Be gracious to me, O Lord, for I am in distress; // it is wasted in grief my eye, // my soul and my body also!" The formula here would have to bring in random other letters: k l m // a b c // c c. The second part of v. 10 is in parallel with v. 11. The first part is different except for the phrase "I am in distress", which is like the general announcement which is illustrated in the list which follows. If we count what comes after this general statement, we find four verbs, one of them repeated: "wasted, spent, fails, waste away", and seven words indicating the subjects of these verbs: "eye, soul, body, life, years, strength, bones"; the first three are joined closely together. One might attempt a diagram to illustrate all this:

Be gracious to me, O Lord,   for I am in distress;

> it is wasted in grief my eye,
> > my soul and my body also.
> It is spent with sorrow my life,
> > my years with sighing.
> It fails in misery my strength,
> > my bones waste away.

Translating according to the Hebrew order we can note two chiasms — inversions of position — in the final four lines. These lines attach themselves to the previous line and produce the number seven. The first line of the poem would in fact be enough as an urgent and convincing cry for help. But the psalmist gives full vent to his feelings: what he had said in a brief statement "I am in distress" is developed and explained in a series of details. And all of this enters into the parallelism. He might have simply related the seven descriptions, but he preferred to do it by dividing them three/four, thus breaking the monotony by changing positions and introducing variety. This use of a poetic technique too is neither mechanical nor academic. We can see how parallelism works in the whole poem and in the smallest parts.

It will be very easy now to look at another verse from the same psalm (31,12):

Of all my adversaries I am   the scorn,
  to my neighbours   a horror,
  to my acquaintance   an object of dread.

  Those who see me in the street flee from me.

Three parallel lines followed by one line allows the final line to have more power. If the two central lines are removed the sense will flow logically and will be complete. The poet has provided two synonyms to build up an effective three-line parallel.

The following example, Ps 33,16-17, is four regular lines with the formula A // A, A // A. When we pay closer attention we perceive a subtle arrangement. There are four negatives, parallel and synonymous (though the third is grammatically positive, the sense is negative): "is not saved, is not delivered, is a vain hope, cannot save"; three subjects correspond to these verbs: "a king, a warrior, the war horse", and three qualifying phrases: "by his great army", "by his great strength", "by its great might". The poet is forced to have recourse to some repetitions and the result allows us to see the fatigue in his efforts. It sounds almost like an academic exercise.

I will give a somewhat stilted translation so as to fellow the
original position of the phrases:

> The king does not conquer by his great army,
>> the warrior does not escape because of his great strength
>> of no avail is the cavalry for the victory
>> nor is it the vast army that saves him.

e) *Twofold and threefold articulation*. It happens frequently that
one part of a twofold parallel is doubled to form two parts itself.
There are two possibilities: A is followed by B/B, or B / B are
followed by A. This produces a tension between the formal two-fold
parallel, and the threefold meaning. To explain this there are some
examples from the book of Isaiah:

> The grass withers
>> when the breath of the Lord blows upon it.
> the flower fades
> The grass withers
>> but the word of our God will stand for ever.
> the flower fades (Isa 40,7-8)

> They shall be put be shame,
>> all who are incensed against you.
> they shall be confounded
> They shall be as nothing,
>> those who strive against you.
> they shall perish
> You shall seek
>> those who contend with you.
> but you shall not find them
> They shall be as nothing,
>> those who war against you.
> they shall cease to exist (Isa 41,11-12)

The first example (Isa 40,7-8) gains its effect due to the tension
between the twofold and threefold articulation, due to the
repetition of the first phrases and the contrast in the following
clauses. The second example (Isa 41,11-12) shows Second
Isaiah's great liking for synonyms which he parades before us.
Let us go on:

> There was none who declared it,
>> there was none who heard your words.
> there was none who proclaimed (Isa 41,26b)

He will not cry
                                        or make it heard in the streets.
he will not lift up his voice (Isa 42,2)

I the Lord have called you
                                in righteousness
have taken you by the hand
have kept you
            as a covenant to the people
have given you
            a light to the nations (Isa 42,6).

For a long time   I have held my peace
                   I have kept still
                   I have restrained myself.

Like a woman in travail   I will cry out
                           I will gasp
                           I will pant (Isa 42,14).

In all these examples we have had a view of parallelism as a flexible technique, with a variety of formulations and arrangements according to the different situations. This is where we come across the scholar's determination to divide, subdivide, classify and give a name to each variety. Encouraged by this trend scholars announce as the discovery of a new stylistic technique something which is simply a variation on something well known. I think Watson and those whom he quotes are not free from this passion to classify and give names. The important thing is in fact to develop sensitivity to be able to appreciate the variations in their poetic function. Less classification is needed, and more analysis of style, although I admit that in a manual such as this a certain amount of distinction and classification is necessary. A certain amount, but not too much!

IV. Stylistics of Parallelism

In some of the examples I have given I have already commented on the stylistic function of parallelism.

Parallelism may serve to amplify the picture given, as happens with Isaiah of the exile; it may serve to concentrate the attention, as may happen with the first Isaiah. But the reverse is also possible. Let us imagine that the poet, instead of describing something at length, wants to sum up a situation with a couple of features. In this case parallelism may provide a suitable and reduced mould. If we think about war in those days: one line sounds loud and brutal, the other provides a vivid and pitiable picture:

> Every boot of the tramping warrior in battle tumult,
> and every garment rolled in blood ... (Isa 9,4).

Just the thing for the cinema! Boots, marching boots, which march and advance in great tumult; and then, scattered or in heaps, garments red-black with blood of the wounded and the slain. But I have given in to the temptation of paraphrasing; Isaiah expresses it better. The difference between his version and mine will show the reader the value of parallelism as a mould which compresses and constricts, as a structure which provides greater tension and as a creative poetic technique.

In the same poem the end of oppression is announced: the oppression grows inexorably in three parallel elements, then one verb only resounds and categorically brings an end to it all. One against three. The regular mould of the parallelism must give in, but without disappearing, to stress the contrast:

> For the yoke of his burden,
> and the staff for his shoulder,
> the rod of his oppressor,
> these thou hast broken as on the day of Midian (Isa 9,3).

In the next example we see the poor human being, helpless, threatened on all sides and at every hour. By day and by night, in the darkness and in the light, evil powers are threatening him, powers which are incomprehensible, inexorable; plagues, sickness, weapons, evil spirits. Only the presence of God can help against these terrible threats:

> You will not fear the terror of the night,
> nor the arrow that flies by day,
> nor the pestilence that stalks in darkness,
> nor the destruction that wastes at noonday (Ps 91,5).

No unnecessary amplification. The four lines are a cosmic whole; the regularity of the poetry describes what is inexorable.

No less effective are the following three lines, which transform the final destruction into a watery image in three stages:

> Let not the flood sweep over me,
> or the deep swallow me up,
> or the pit close its mouth over me (Ps 69,16).

I return to Ps 114 to observe the elements which correspond. "Egypt" // "people of strange language": this epithet describing the Egyptians sums up what is strange and alien about the oppressor. "Sanctuary" // "dominion" refer to the cultic presence of God and the political power: this group of slaves seeking liberty are no longer commanded by Pharaoh but by the Lord, who is with them as in his sanctuary. "The (Red) Sea // "the Jordan" are the two great barriers which the people must overcome, miraculously, to leave slavery behind and enter into possession of the land. "Mountains" // "hills" are a common pair, referring to proud obstacles. "Flint" intensifies "rock", while the "spring of water" intensifies the "pool". Due to the clever use of parallelism this fine psalm proceeds with regularity and rapidity evoking great deeds in a fairly short space.

The opening verses of Ps 113 are more formal, with a certain use of counterpoint, marked by repetitions:

> Praise, O servants of the Lord,
> praise the name of the Lord!
> Blessed be the name of the Lord
> from this time forth and for evermore!
> From the rising of the sun to its setting
> the name of the Lord is to be praised! (Ps 113,1-3).

This is a liturgical text, perhaps recited or sung with antiphons. It proceeds slowly, almost not at all, because at the end it takes up the beginning again. The second line adds the "name"; the following four lines are in chiastic arrangement (AB // BA), embracing time and space.

In Jer 5,22 God appeals to his cosmic power which even restless creatures like the sea respect. This is a poetic play on the command and the impotent rebellion of the sea, which is amplified by the parallelism with irregular yet controlled movement. First of all the translation:

> I placed the sand as the bound for the sea,
> a perpetual barrier which it cannot pass;
> though the waves toss, they cannot prevail,
> though they roar, they cannot pass over it.

The second half of the biblical verse develops the idea of "barrier"; the two halves both end with "cannot pass"; but the second half is itself divided, as follows:

they toss   they cannot prevail
they roar   they cannot pass.

The idea of the impotence of the sea is thus very effectively put across.

By way of contrast with these fine examples of parallelism we could give many conventional, academic examples. Every language also has poor rhymes and clichés. Sometimes they have didactic value and help the memory. They also serve by contrast to illustrate how good the good examples are.

I will end with two examples from the wisdom literature, which will show how effectively parallelism can sometimes surprise us. These proverbs make up for so many others which are of lesser worth.

If you have found honey, eat only enough for you,
lest you be surfeited with it and vomit it.
Let your foot be seldom in your neighbour's house,
lest he become surfeited with you and hate you
(Prov 25,16-17).

Answer not a fool according to his folly,
lest you be like him yourself.
Answer a fool according to his folly,
lest he be wise in his own eyes (Prov 26,4-5).

If we had to classify these we would say that they are both "external"; both parallels cover two biblical verses; the first is synonymous and the second is antithetic. Such classifying has limited usefulness.

Bibliography

History

L.I. Newman, *Studies in Old Testament Parallelism* (Berkeley 1918).
J.M. Bover, "Para la historia del paralelismo de la poesía hebrea", *EE* 1 (1922) 62-63.
M. Peinador, "Estudios sobre el paralelismo de la poesía hebrea", *IluCl* 33 (1940) 251-262; 34 (1941) 5-15; 319-328.
L. Alonso Schökel, *Estudios de poética hebrea*, pp. 197-201.
J.L. Kugel, *The Idea of Biblical Poetry. Parallelism and Its History* (New Haven 1981).

Nature

J. F. Schleusner, *Dissertatio de parallelismo membrorum, egregio interpretationis subsidio* (Leipzig 1817).

G. A. Smith, *The Early Poetry of Israel in Its Physical and Social Origins.*

E. Isaacs, "The Origin and Nature of Parallelism", *AJSL* 35 (1919) 113-127.

M. Peinador, "Estudios sobre el paralelismo de la poesía hebrea", *IluCl* 35 (1942) 46-59.

D. Gonzalo Maeso, "Contribución al estudio de la métrica bíblica: Sobre la verdadera significación y alcance del 'paralelismo'", *Sef* 3 (1943) 3-39.

L. Alonso Schökel, *Estudios de poética hebrea*, pp. 205-210.

J. L. Kugel, *The Idea of Biblical Poetry*, pp. 49-58.

W. G. E. Watson, *Classical Hebrew Poetry*, pp. 114-121.

Classification and Stylistics

R. Lowth, *De sacra poesi Hebraeorum.*

R. G. Moulton, *The Literary Study of the Bible: An Account of the Leading Forms of Literature Represented in the Sacred Writings.*

G. B. Gray, *The Forms of Hebrew Poetry. Considered with Special Reference to the Criticism and Interpretation of the Old Testament* (London 1915; reprinted New York 1972 [LBS; Prologomenon by D. N. Freedman]).

J. Begrich, "Der Satzstil in Fünfer", *ZS* 9 (1933-1934) 169-209.

F. Horst, "Die Kennzeichen der hebräischen Poesie", *TRu* 21 (1953) 91-121.

L. Alonso Schökel, *Estudios de poética hebrea*, pp. 195-230.

M. Z. Kaddari, "A Semantic Approach to Biblical Parallelism", *JJS* 24 (1973) 167-175.

A. Berlin, "Grammatical Aspects of Biblical Parallelism", *HUCA* 50 (1979) 17-43.

J. L. Kugel, *The Idea of Biblical Poetry*, pp. 4-7, 18-23, 40-58.

W. G. E. Watson, *Classical Hebrew Poetry*, pp. 123-159.

More bibliographical information can be found in the work by Watson, pp. 121f., 128, 143f., 156.

V. Appendix. Word-Pairs

It is clear that for all the work of development of the poem, especially as regards parallelism, the poet must have at his disposal a store of word pairs: synonyms, antonyms, merismi, related words, etc. The poet does not always invent, rather he uses what is at hand: mountains and hills, girls and boys, the young and the old, city and country, day and night, happiness and joy, sight and hearing...

From where does the poet get this store of word pairs? One might think that the language itself provides them with its lexical and semantic fields. But the fixed nature of many pairs leads us to think that they may already be found in literary form, either in oral tradition or written down. Who was it who invented them? This cannot be answered: but we are aware that Israel gained many from surrounding civilizations.

The actual arrangement of the word pairs is less important, though due to the established usage in Hebrew poetry, they are more likely to be in parallelism. But they may also be found side by side. We have no proof that the side by side position is more ancient and that the position in parallelism was a secondary development. The opposite could happen in a literary tradition: the word pair which is usually found in parallel arrangement is brought side by side by a conscious decision of the poet.

This is why the idea of a "break up of a stereotyped phrase" may be quite incorrect, unless it is quite clear that such a phrase did exist. The example proposed by Watson, *Classical Hebrew Poetry*, p. 329, is quite correct: "innocent blood" is a common expression, which Prov 1,11 distributes in parallel members. This and other examples proposed take as a phrase a noun with an adjective or a construct phrase. On the other hand, when there are two nouns of the same category the case is not so clear: for example, heaven and earth.

W. G. E. Watson, *Classical Hebrew Poetry*, pp. 327-332.
E. Z. Melamed, "Break-up of Stereotype Phrases as an Artistic Device in Biblical Poetry", in S. Rabin (ed.), *Studies in the Bible* (ScrHie 8; Jerusalem 1961), pp. 115-153.

We can also observe that different groups of books have their favourite word pairs: the Prophets, the Psalms, the Proverbs. Word pairs can sometimes overlap: in Proverbs, "wise, prudent", with "honourable, wicked" from the ethical field. The Second Isaiah, the great master of four-line structures, was not content with the already existing repertoire and broadened the lexical and semantic fields.

Lists of word pairs and groups of three or four may be of great interest for the study of the Hebrew lexicon, at a general level or in specific fields. When they are trite they have little artistic value. Because of their obvious usefulness, several lists of such pairs have been compiled:

B. Hartmann, *Die nominalen Aufreihungen im Alten Testament* (Zürich 1953). The lists were published but I do not believe the rest of the thesis was.

M. Dahood – T. Penar, "Ugaritic-Hebrew Parallel Pairs", in L. R. Fisher (ed.), *Ras Shamra Parallels. The Texts from Ugarit and the Hebrew Bible*, Vol. I (AnOr 49; Rome 1972), pp. 71-382; M. Dahood, "Ugaritic-Hebrew Parallel Pairs" and "Ugaritic-Hebrew Parallel Pairs. Supplement", in L. R. Fisher (ed.), *Ras Shamra Parallels. The Texts from Ugarit and the Hebrew Bible*, Vol. II (AnOr 50; Rome 1975), pp. 1-35, 34-39; M. Dahood, "Ugaritic-Hebrew Parallel Pairs" and Ugaritic-Hebrew Parallel Pairs. Supplement", in S. Rummel (ed.), *Ras Shamra Parallels. The Texts from Ugarit and the Hebrew Bible*, Vol. III (AnOr 51; Rome 1981), pp. 1-178, 178-206. The criteria for collection are so ample in this work that in each case one needs to be very selective before using the material.

W. G. E. Watson, *Classical Hebrew Poetry*, pp. 128-144.

CHAPTER VI

Synonymy, Repetition, Merismus

I. Synonymy

A. *Description*

Synonymy in Hebrew poetry has been treated simply as a
variety of parallelism, when in fact it is an autonomous stylistic
technique used on many occasions and with different aims. The
reason why I deal with it here in the same chapter as repetition is
that synonymy is semantic repetition, repetition of the sense, not of
the precise word.

But is the sense really repeated? Do synonymous words and
phrases really exist? A synonymous expression will be all the less
likely when it is made up of a greater number of elements; it would
be almost impossible to find a synonymous phrase for one of three,
four or five words.

In order to deal with the question correctly we must be clear
about the term: poetic synonymy. In linguistics, in studies of the
lexicon, two words which are synonyms would be perfectly
interchangeable on all occasions. One could be substituted for the
other on all possible occasions. In linguistics perfect strict synonymy
supposes that two words are equal in every respect. Perhaps such
pairs of words do not exist, although "commence" and "begin"
may be a good example in English. Linguists accept a broader idea
of synonymy. It is sufficient that two words coincide to some
significant degree.

The idea of the sememe or component with meaning may be of
some use to us. Let us look at a series of words, for example: home,
house, dwelling, palace, apartment, hut, cottage, villa, mansion ...
They all have something in common, and they all have
differentiating features. If I concentrate on what is common to all,
the words may be seen as synonyms; if I concentrate on what
differentiates them, the words may even be seen as antonyms.
Palaces and huts are human constructions where people live, but
they are found at the two extremes of the list. House and apartment
have some things in common, but the first is more generic.
Dictionaries and works like Roget's *Thesaurus* provide lists of

synonyms understood in this way. When a writer or translator consults such lists he does it not to take any word but to find the most precise or expressive word he can. He looks for what is different. But when a poet who uses parallelism consults such lists he may do it to find word pairs with significant common features.

When we speak of synonymy as a poetic technique, we must understand it in the broad sense. We do not take as the criterion our linguistic background, nor our literary tradition, nor again our expertise in the Hebrew lexicon. We observe and respect the sensitivity of the Hebrew poet. For him those two words or those two expressions serve as synonyms in his verses and in his poem.

Repetition will be used in its normal sense. "He worked and worked" is simple repetition; "he went on and continued his speech" is semantic repetition.

Let us begin with a good example:

> The haughty looks of man shall be brought low,
> and the pride of men shall be humbled;
> and the Lord alone will be exalted in that day.
> For the Lord of hosts has a day:
> > against all that is proud and lofty,
> > against all that is lifted up and high;
> > against all the cedars of Lebanon,
> > and against all the oaks of Bashan;
> > against all the high mountains,
> > and against all the lofty hills;
> > against every high tower,
> > and against every fortified wall;
> > against all the ships of Tarshish,
> > and against all the beautiful craft.
> > And the haughtiness of man shall be humbled,
> > and the pride of men shall be brought low;
> > and the Lord alone will be exalted in that day
> > > (Isa 2,11-18).

Nobody will confuse cedars with oaks, nor Lebanon with Bashan; towers and walls are different. We understand *hārîm* = "mountains" to be more generic or higher than *gᵉbā'ôt* = "hills". We could refine the distinction by seeing *gbh* as referring to what is high and *rwm* to what exalts itself. This might warn us against being too clever. The distinction between the Hebrew words for "ships" and "craft" is completely lost to us. The poet has not set out here to differentiate, but to form pairs, to couple together, to arrange symetrically: cedars and oaks, mountains and hills, ships and craft, towers and walls. He wants the pairs to function as synonyms in his poem, even though in other poems they might be in contrast with each other. Furthermore, and going up one stage further, all the pairs must form an ordered group of synonyms: all the elements in the list have something in common and it is this which the poet stresses: all are high, elevated, proud and arrogant. There is a degree of synonymity which is more generic than that which binds each pair together. Before the Lord all is low and will be brought down. So we have a diversified use of synonymy in the poem and it plays a significant poetic role. One ought to declaim the piece aloud to feel its full force.

In the previous piece the synonyms are all found in parallelism, and they are all in phrases which are complements to the principal clause: "the Lord of hosts has a day". In one case the synonyms are side by side with a copula: "all that is proud and lofty... lifted up and high" (v. 12). The position makes no difference to the synonymy. The poet has gathered all the synonyms in a formation like an army which the Lord demolishes. The arrangement may be symetrical, asymetrical, chiasmic, side by side, etc.

Synonyms may also be partial as the following examples shows:

> It is he who established the earth by his craft,
> who stretched out the heavens by his ability (Jer 10,12).

The adverbial element is synonymous: "craft" and "ability" are qualities of the artesan. Both apply to both actions; they are a repetition of sense.

B. *The Reason for Synonymy*

Taken simply we can see in the poetic use of synonymy the tendency to persevere and to prolong. This is an aspect of man's existence in time which finds its expression in language. Emotion persists until it is fully expressed, contemplation remains gazing at the object under consideration.

Language is a temporal thing, it happens in time, just like music. It is thus different from painting, sculpture and architecture. In the same way a dance is a temporal thing, whereas a beautiful garden is static. Rational, discursive knowledge makes progress in time through syllogisms, deductions and inductions. Description proceeds stage by stage, action by action, whether it is of a still object or of an object in action (this famous distinction was put forward by Lessing in his *Laocoön*). On the other hand, emotion tends to remain still and to prolong itself. And contemplation has no wish to depart from the beautiful and loved object.

Synonymy has its privileged place in the genres which are dominated by emotion: the emotion of the subject who expresses himself, or of a person whom the poet wishes to influence. It is thus found in lyric poetry or in rhetoric. Contemplation will often be practised in the face of transcendent realities which are difficult to speak of and resist rigorous description. Emotion and contemplation are two cases, though not the only ones, which help us to understand the use of synonymy.

It is no surprise that we encounter synonymy in the genre of elegy in Lamentations. The poet is more likely to delay over sadness than over joy; it seems that we are more content with feelings of sadness and are not able to free ourselves from them. It is as if joy were always the most passing of feelings. Each one of the Lamentations, with the exception of the fifth, scatters abroad right through the alphabet pathetic descriptions of a situation which gives rise to the painful expression of a contagious sadness. The poet begins with the solitary humiliation of Jerusalem:

> See, Lord, how sorely I am distressed,
>> my bowels writhe in anguish
> and my stomach turns within me,
>> because I wantonly rebelled.
> The sword makes orphans in the streets,
>> as plague does within doors (Lam 1,20).

> How solitary lies the city,
>> once so full of people!
> once great among nations,
>> now become a widow;
> once queen among provinces,
>> now put to forced labour! (Lam 1,1).

Compare this with the following four lines which speak of an action in successive stages:

> My transgressions were bound upon me,
>> his own hand knotted them round me;
> his yoke was lifted on to my neck,
>> my strength failed beneath its weight (Lam 1,14).

Instances of synonymy are not always found in close proximity; they may appear as a refrain:

Lam 1,5a Her adversaries have become her masters,
              her enemies take their ease

7b   when her people fell into the power of the adversary
              and there was no one to help her.
        The adversary saw and mocked
              at her fallen state.

9c   Look, Lord, upon her misery,
              see how the enemy has triumphed.

14c   The Lord abandoned me to its hold,
              and I could not stand.

17b   The Lord gave Jacob's enemy the order
              to beset her on every side.

21b   All my enemies, when they heard of my calamity,
              rejoiced at what thou hadst done.

In another case the synonymy is in the denotation of Jerusalem: it remains before our gaze with a series of three denominations:

What darkness the Lord in his anger
    has brought upon the daughter of Zion!
He hurled down from heaven to earth
    the glory of Israel,
and did not remember in the days of his anger
    that Zion was his footstool (Lam 2,1).

In the following example the poet is seeking a comparison to describe the disgrace Jerusalem has suffered. After the parallel questions in the third line the poet finds a way of expressing the immensity of the disgrace:

How can I cheer you? Whose plight is like yours,
    daughter of Jerusalem!
To what can I compare you for your comfort,
    virgin daughter of Zion?
For your wound gapes wide as the ocean;
    who can heal you? (Lam 2,13).

The following example contains three lines, divided half way through thus breaking the second line; one and a half lines invite weeping, one and a half lines urge persistence in supplication:

Cry with a full heart to the Lord,
    O wall of the daughter of Zion;
let your tears run down like a torrent
    by day and by night.
Give yourself not a moment's rest,
    let your tears never cease (Lam 2,18).

In the next example the synonymy is more subtle, it almost disappears; maybe it should be called metonymy in the strict sense. The speaker sees his affliction as God's punishment, blows from the rod of his wrath (image), delivered by the hand of God. Rod and hand are parallel and broadly speaking synonymous;

Lam 3,1   I am the man who has known affliction,
         I have felt the rod of his wrath.
    3   Against me alone he has turned his hand,
         and so it is all day long.

The following four lines sound similar to the situation of a prisoner who goes round his cell looking for a way out and finds again and again only the four walls which surround him:

Lam 3,5 He has built up walls around me,
        behind and before,
    6 and has cast me into a place of darkness
        like a man long dead.
    7 He has walled me in so that I cannot escape,
        and weighed me down with fetters.
    9 He has barred my road with blocks of stone
        and tangled up my way.

But it is not only sadness which can be prolonged by synonyms. Joy and enthusiasm can also, especially when a prophet wishes to communicate encouragement and hope. Lyric poetry and rhetoric go hand in hand in the flowing poem of Second Isaiah, the great master of Hebrew synonyms, the specialist in four line structures (a good way of learning the Hebrew lexicon). In Isa 41,11-12 the enemy is presented with four designations and suffers disaster with eight verbs. A great parade of words, more rhetorical than lyrical. The theme of the transformed desert is repeated in 41,18:

> I will open rivers on the bare heights,
> and fountains in the midst of the valleys;
> I will make the wilderness a pool of water,
> and the dry land springs of water.

The opposite process is found in 42,15: mountains / herbage / rivers / pools; lay waste / dry up / turn into islands / dry up.

Chapter 35, which in my opinion belongs to the same author or to the same school, might serve as a text for an exercise along the same lines: there are four synonyms for desert, four human disabilities and four synonyms for water.

L. Köhler, *Deuterojesaja (Jesaja 40–55) stilkritisch untersucht* (BZAW 37; Giessen 1923), produced a masterly study of Second Isaiah and comments on the recurrent instances of synonymy: "Abundance replaces exactness" (p. 80); "he has need of volume... the form must say more than the contents" (p. 97); "more rich than vigorous" (p. 128).

The emotion is continued in a kind of pleasant inertia. The prolongation of emotion may be ascending, reaching a climax, or descending, dying out; it cannot remain at the same intensity for any length of time. It may develop in a circular movement, returning to the starting point. As the emotion is expressed in words there will be the need to repeat the same words or words with equivalent meaning.

E. Staiger, *Grundbegriffe der Poetik* (Zürich ²1951), p. 151, says the following about pathos: "Pathos presupposes resistence, a hostility which is open or hidden, and tries to bring them down by its insistence... Pathos is not infused, but engraved, hammered in". Thus pathos is found not only in drama, but also in speech.

Judah will have to follow her sister Samaria by drinking the cup of punishment. The key elements are: the cup, the drinking, the effect. But this is not enough for the poet: he has to repeat himself, to insist on things in order to communicate his strength of feeling and to move his listeners:

> You shall drink from your sister's cup,
>   a cup deep and wide,
> charged with mockery and scorn,
>   more than ever cup can hold.
> It will be full of drunkenness and grief,
>   a cup of ruin and desolation,
> the cup of your sister Samaria;
> and you shall drink it to the dregs.
>   Then you will chew it in pieces
>   and tear out your breasts (Ezek 23,32-34).

Not all synonymy is due to emotion and feeling. It can also be produced by the desire to perceive and formulate. This happens in other poetic cultures also, but attracts attention in Hebrew poetry. Instead of amplifying by dividing, subdividing, doubling and duplicating always on more particular levels, the poet takes a totality and expresses it in a sentence. When he has finished he takes the same totality again and expresses it with another series of words which are similar or equivalent. The morphological or syntactical articulation may be poor. But he presents a contemplation of the same object which reveals new details, new facts. As I have said, synonymy is not complete. Poetic synonymy is a technique for presenting variety in equality.

I wish to spend some time on an example which is exceptional for various reasons. A late author, an essayist rather than a poet, sees reflection as going over things again and again. At the beginning of his short book, made up of notes and jottings, he inserts a kind of poem in prose, in which he reveals his tendency to go over things again and again without making progress. He speaks of man, of the sun, of the wind, of water; and he is speaking of one thing alone. In what another might see as the rich, limitless variety of creation, he contemplates the monotony of existence. The result is that the theme reveals his attitude, and the technique he uses is synonymy. He wants to focus on what is the same and overcome his readers with the fatigue of monotony:

> A generation goes, and a generation comes,
> but the earth remains for ever.
> The sun rises and the sun goes down,
> and hastens to the place where it rises.
> The wind blows to the south,
> and goes round to the north;
> round and round goes the wind,
> and on its circuits the wind returns.
> All streams run to the sea,
> but the sea is not full;
> to the place where the streams flow,
> there they flow again.
> All things are full of weariness;
> a man cannot utter it;
> the eye is not satisfied with seeing,
> nor the ear filled with hearing.
> What has been is what will be,
> and what has been done is what will be done;
> and there is nothing new under the sun (Qoh 1,4-9).

This text ought to be compared with some of the instructions of Ben Sira, who, though he likes synonymy, also allows the exposition to develop.

Let us not forget the formal reason for synonymy: symmetry and proportion, resonance and harmony. It is rather like music and dance. This taste for formality may explain so many cases of conventional synonymy, in works whose lyricism is dull, and in academic exercises. Who could forget what happened in Ps 119? The author takes the twenty-two letters of the alphabet, finds eight synonyms for "law" (precept, decree, command, instruction, etc.) and multiplies them to obtain one hundred and seventy-six verses which all say the same thing. His devotion to God's commands may be praiseworthy, but his poetic achievement is rather questionable.

C. *Stylistic Analysis*

We must take note of the pieces of poetry which take advantage of this technique of synonymy, especially those cases which surprise the trained and attentive reader.

In Jer 13,23 we read: "Can the Ethiopian change his skin, // or the leopard his spots?" Is one meant to conclude that the Ethiopian and the leopard are synonyms? Jeremiah is in fact insulting no-one, but simply rebuking his compatriots who are incapable of changing their lives. Their perversion is as natural to them as the colour of the skin of the Ethiopian or Nubian, and as the spots of the leopard. However, the jump from the Jew to the pagan, and from the pagan to the wild beast, achieves a forceful impact due to synonymy.

A contrasting case is found in the poem about the drought which scorches grass and pastures. These synonyms are very close; the two wild animals, the hind and the wild ass, are rather less so. Listen to the effect of the synonymy due to the arrangement, placing the synonymous phrase as a semantic rhyme at the end of each distich:

> Even the hind in the field forsakes her newborn calf
> because there is no grass.
> The wild asses stand on the bare heights,
> they pant for air like jackals, their eyes fail,
> because there is no herbage (Jer 14,5-6).

We may consider as synonyms the two phrases of Ps 41,9: "A deadly thing has fastened on him; he will not rise again from where he lies". But it is clear that the second line doubles the force of the first. The first might be a medical diagnosis, the second is a sentence of death.

To slay and to slaughter are synonyms; but the latter goes beyond and intensifies the former: "For thy sake we are slain all the day long, and accounted as sheep for the slaughter" (Ps 44,23). The second line builds on the basis of the first and intensifies the force of the expression.

Since synonymy has not been studied on its own, the relevant bibliography is very reduced; it is to be found in treatments of parallelism and repetition. See L. Alonso Schökel, *Estudios de poética hebrea*, pp. 231-250.

D. *Branching Out*

Parallelism is a normal procedure and it develops poetic ideas easily. One particular case is when an element of a preceding line is taken up and repeated or doubled, and this can be done several times. Different elements are repeated and thus the lines "branch out" once or perhaps several times. It may also be compared to a chain in which various links are attached. A fine example can be seen in Isa 30 (called by some the "testament of the prophet"). I will present it first in a diagram, quoting only the decisive words so that the process is clear:

```
rebellious people
lying sons
sons    who will not hear
        who say    to the seers, "See not";
                   to the prophets,    Prophesy not to us what is right;
                                       speak to us smooth things,
                                       prophesy illusions,
                                       leave the way,
                                       turn aside from the path,
                                       let us hear no more of the Holy One
                                           of Israel.


        Thus says            the Holy One of Israel
Because  you despise this word,
              and trust in oppression
                            and perverseness
              and rely on them;

therefore this iniquity shall be to you like a break in a high wall,
                                   and its breaking is like that
                                   of a potter's vessel.
```

Now I will copy out the complete text. The thought of the prophet advances by branching out again and again. The speaker does not pound or hammer away, but everything that he says he rivets and binds to what follows. There is a certain amount of amplification, but there is movement too. The passage is more oratorical than lyrical:

> And now, go, write it before them on a tablet,
> and inscribe it in a book,
> that it may be for the time to come
> as a witness for ever.
> For they are a rebellious people, lying sons,
> sons who will not hear the instruction of the Lord;
> who say to the seers, "See not!";
> and to the prophets, "Prophesy not to us what is right;
> speak to us smooth things, prophesy illusions,
> leave the way, turn aside from the path,
> let us hear no more of the Holy One of Israel".
> Therefore thus says the Holy One of Israel,
> "Because you despise this word
> and trust in oppression and perverseness,
> and rely on them;
> therefore this iniquity shall be to you
> like a break in a high wall,
> bulging out, and about to collapse,
> whose crash comes suddenly, in an instant;
> and its breaking is like that of a potter's vessel
> which is smashed so ruthlessly
> that among its fragments not a sherd is found
> with which to take fire from the hearth
> or to dip up water out of the cistern" (Isa 30,8-14).

Even though the procedure is not applied with rigorous monotony I do not think there is another example as fine as this in Hebrew poetry. What we see here in a great series we can find also separately in many texts: we can call it "branching out".

E. *Synonymy and Conciseness*

The use of synonymy seems quite logically to be the enemy of conciseness. This is true. But we must be clear that this synonymy is conditioned by and itself conditions the limited syntactical articulation of the Hebrew language. Just as in a long Latin sentence there can be a concise and momentous phrase, so in a series of verses dominated by synonymy a concise phrase can stand out, even though there may be other similar phrases which do not show the same conciseness.

An example from Isaiah:

For wickedness burns like a fire,
it consumes briers and thorns;
it kindles the thickets of the forest,
and they roll upward in a column of smoke (Isa 9,17).

It begins with an image which has to be developed. Then there is a hendiadys, "briers and thorns", alliterated in the original Hebrew. The second line resounds in the third, which is synonymous, but which extends the fire to a greater scene, the forest. The final line brings the verse to a magnificent conclusion, with great conciseness. It is as if the final phrase communicates its density to the whole of the distich and absorbs the synonymy.

Second Isaiah, the great master of four-line series, also knows how to construct concise and momentous phrases. I select some examples:

You were sold for nothing, and you shall be redeemed without money (Isa 52,3).

They keep on praying to a god that cannot save (Isa 45,20).

The loss of children and widowhood shall come upon you in full measure (Isa 47,9).

Their fish stink for lack of water, and die of thirst (Isa 50,2).

The bowl of my wrath you shall drink no more (Isa 51,22).

Some of these phrases are part of a synonymous pair.

The poet is in complete control of this technique. He uses it with great variety, sometimes in traditional fashion, sometimes in an original way. He is free to use it or to abandon it. In similar fashion the reader and the critic cannot be content with classifications but must examine each case to see its value.

II. **Repetition**

Having studied synonymy we can proceed to repetition, understood in the strict sense. E. Zurro has produced two studies on the phenomenon of repetition, one short but substantial, the other exhaustive and most erudite.

E. Zurro, "Repetición verbal", in L. Alonso Schökel – E. Zurro, *La traducción bíblica: Lingüística y estilística* (BiL 3; Madrid 1977), pp. 263-277.

E. Zurro, *Procedimientos iterativos en la poesia ugaritica y hebrea* (BibOr 43; Rome 1987).

There is no need to explain what repetition is. But we ought nevertheless to reflect on the literary importance of a phenomenon which seems so trivial and insignificant. The insignificant can often be seen to have great importance. We repeat sounds, words, phrases, feet, verses, strophes; we repeat them in different positions and with different functions.

The chapter on sound was largely dedicated to the repetition of identical and similar sounds. The chapter on rhythm dealt with regular repetition. Now I will speak of verbal repetition, but without getting involved in things already explained.

The great poem of the exile begins thus: "Comfort, comfort my people" (Isa 40,1). Here are three lines from Ps 148:

> Praise him, sun and moon,
> praise him, all you shining stars,
> praise him, you highest heavens! (Ps 148,3-4).

Here are the first and last lines of Psalm 8:

> O Lord, our Lord, how majestic is thy name in all the earth!
> O Lord, our Lord, how majestic is thy name in all the earth!
> (Ps 8,2.10).

In Psalm 42–43 we read the following verses three times:

> Why are you cast down, O my soul,
> and why are you disquieted within me?
> Hope in God; for I shall again praise him,
> my help and my God.

Repetition is such a frequent phenomenon that it needs some kind of classification. To achieve this we must bear in mind four factors: the volume of material repeated, its quality, the arrangement of the repeated elements in the poem, the function of the repetition:

a) quantity or volume: it could be a word, or simply a root or lexeme, or again an incomplete sentence, a completed or more complex sentence, one or various verses.

b) quality: this concerns morphological and syntactical aspects of the language. For example, the repetition of imperatives (from different verbs), of participles, of masculine or feminine plurals (which also produces rhyme); or again, the repetition of temporal or conditional clauses, etc.

c) arrangement: side by side, or at the beginning of sentences, or the end, at the beginning and at the end, regularly or irregularly in a speech, or in an inverted position.

d) The function of the repetition is more difficult to classify and it is better to avoid rigid classifications. Inevitably the criteria overlap.

Here are some examples of side by side repetition of the same word:

> Comfort, comfort my people (Isa 40,1).

> Awake, awake, put on strength, O arm of the Lord (Isa 51,9).

> Rouse yourself, rouse yourself, stand up, O Jerusalem (Isa 51,17).

> Awake, awake, put on your strength, O Zion (Isa 52,1).

> Depart, depart, go out thence (Isa 51,11).

A similar effect may be obtained even when there is an obstacle between the repeated word:

> Set on the pot, set it on (Ezek 24,3).

The "psalm of the seven thunderclaps" (Ps 29) is a classic example of the repetition of a word at the beginning of phrases; seven verses begin with *qôl Yhwh* = the voice of the Lord. In Isa 2, quoted above, the hemistichs began with *'al kol-*, "against all...". This styleme is called an "anaphora". It serves to bind a series together and to lay stress on the list.

> Come with me from Lebanon, my bride,
> come with me from Lebanon, approach (Cant 4,8).

> A garden locked is my sister, my bride,
> a garden locked, a fountain sealed (Cant 4,12).

> You have ravished my heart, my sister, my bride,
> you have ravished my heart with a glance of your eyes
> (Cant 4,9).

Blessings of heaven above,
blessings of the deep that couches beneath,
blessings of the breasts and of the womb.
The blessings of your father are mighty
beyond the blessings of the eternal mountains
    (Gen 49,25-26).

The "epiphora" is the repetition of words at the end of sentences, either hemistichs, or verses or strophes:

When the cares of wealth dismiss sleep,
just as serious illness banishes sleep ... (Sir 31,1-2).

When the word is repeated at the beginning and at the end, in
the first and last verses, this is an *inclusion*. It is a frequent technique
for marking the limits of a poem, the poem is "rounded off".
Sometimes it is used to emphasise an important word. A minor
inclusion is one which does not extend to the whole poem, but
simply to one of its sections. The inclusion is strengthened when
more than one word is repeated.

Ps 58 has an inclusion with two words. Ps 73 puts together
major and minor inclusions with the words "But as for me" in
vv. 2, 23 and 28. The inclusion in Ps 82 repeats two words.

"The day of the Lord" opens and closes Joel 2,1-11. The
technique is very frequent in prophetic literature, as can be seen in
the index of literary themes in our work *Profetas*.

A more refined technique consists in the repetition of the
word in the second member, enriching it with some kind of
qualification:

Many shepherds have destroyed my vineyard,
they have trampled down my portion,
they have made my pleasant portion a desolate wilderness
    (Jer 12,10).

They hewed out cisterns for themselves,
broken cisterns, that can hold no water (Jer 2,13).

It is like the precious oil upon the head,
running down upon the beard,
upon the beard of Aaron (Ps 133,2).

For all these nations are uncircumcised,
and all the house of Israel is uncircumcised in heart
    (Jer 9,25).

The contrary process is to place the qualified word first so that the repetition sounds like a partial resounding:

> He will regard the prayer of the destitute,
> and will not despise their prayer (Ps 102,18).

Repetition of several words. I mentioned this when I spoke about inclusions. When two words are repeated one may have various combinations. As regards the arrangement the most common forms are AB // AB and AB // BA. The latter is called chiasm; it is an X pattern.

The chiasm in Isa 5,20 is very effective because it speaks of the total inversion of values:

> Woe to those who call evil good and good evil,
> who put darkness for light and light for darkness,
> who put bitter for sweet and sweet for bitter!

Cant 6,3, which speaks of the relationship between the lovers, is also very expressive: "I am my beloved's, and my beloved is mine". The following example uses three elements, according to the form ABC // CBA: "He shall open and none shall shut; he shall shut and none shall open" (Isa 22,22).

Gen 9,6 is a similar example: "Whoever sheds the blood of man, by man shall his blood be shed".

Chiasms are normally found in a restricted space; the repeated elements are found near each other. In a broader sense one might call chiasm the chiasmic positioning of elements even at a distance. For example, in Ps 51,3b-4.11 there recur in inverse order, ABC // CBA, the words "cleanse, transgression, sin", forming a minor inclusion.

The chiasm, whether understood strictly or in the broad sense, is a frequent phenomenon in Hebrew poetry. It assists both development and composition. It is no surprise that many studies have been dedicated to it, of which I cite only a few:

R. G. Moulton, *The Literary Study of the Bible: An Account of the Leading Forms of Literature Represented in the Sacred Text.*

N. W. Lund, "The Presence of Chiasmus in the Old Testament", *AJSL* 46 (1929-1930) 104-126.

A. Di Marco, *Il chiasmo nella Bibbia* (RiProp; Turin 1980).

Many articles on biblical books or on particular passages could be added to this list. Given the frequency of the phenomenon the styleme is not always relevant; but the stylistic analysis cannot be content with simply noting its presence.

The *repetition of the root* or the lexeme gives more flexibility to the poet, and provides for more complex combinations. For example, it may hold a poem together by means of a word-lexeme found throughout (somewhat like a *Leitmotiv*); it therefore has a function in the composition.

Let me begin with some minor cases. There is an expression in Hebrew which gives the infinitive of the verb and then the same verb in finite form. It is perhaps best translated into English as: "doing I will do, walking he walked". This is a grammatical rather than a stylistic phenomenon, but the poet may exploit it. The arrangement is always side by side. Something similar is found with what is called the "internal accusative": "he saw sights, he dreamed dreams, he prophesied prophecies...". This too is a grammatical phenomenon, and one more easily exploited by the poet. It too has the side by side position in the repetition.

The lexeme might be found in a verb and a noun: the noun may have different functions — adjectival, adverbial, or nominal; the verb will be in different forms, tenses and conjugations. It is the verb naturally which offers more variety in the repetition:

> Heal me, O Lord, and I shall be healed (Jer 17,14).

> All who devour you shall be devoured (Jer 30,16).

> Rejected silver, they are called,
> for the Lord has rejected them (Jer 6,30).

> He will revive us... he will raise us up,
> that we may live (Hos 6,2).

The examples are extremely abundant and cannot be blamed on the poverty of the Hebrew vocabulary or that of the poets. It is a technique which is more effective in oral recitation where the reader can stress the repeated root; oral repetition also may have a subliminal effect (even though this may not be a point of aesthetics it may have rhetorical value). Let me give a couple of examples which are more complex and more significant. The first is a section from the Song of Songs. The bride expresses her anxiety, the poet plays with this. The technique here is very refined and it sounds as though the anxiety were quite incurable:

> Night after night on my bed
> I have sought my true love;
> I have sought him but not found him,
> I have called him but he has not answered.
> I said, 'I will rise and go the rounds of the city,
>   through the streets and the squares,
> seeking my true love.'
> I sought him but I did not find him,
> I called him but he did not answer.
> The watchmen, going the rounds of the city, met me,
>   and I asked, 'Have you seen my true love?'
> Scarcely had I left them behind me
> when I met my true love.
> I seized him and would not let him go
> until I had brought him to my mother's house,
>   to the room of her who conceived me (Cant 3,1-4).

"To seek" is repeated restlessly, "to meet" is added to it only to be negated, verbs are repeated as subjects are varied, and then again as the beloved is found. If we try to substitute other verbs for the repeated ones the spell of the poem is totally lost. The elegance of the poem depends on the repetition.

Quite different is the great ironical elegy of Ezek 32,18-32 against the Pharaoh. It is as if he is describing a great procession of the illustrious dead who are led to the cemetery and receive solemn burial. In such a situation formulas are repeated with variations at irregular intervals. If the passage is read without listening to its sound it might seem poor and monotonous; if it is read aloud, and slowly with gravity, then it is a most impressive text. And so much more for the listeners of that time, for whom the names represented living peoples.

Repetition of morphemes. The repetition of the form of a verb or of a noun can turn a point of grammar into a point of style. This is especially true when the repetition becomes impressive in its sound due to the reiteration of the morpheme.

Let us take the participle used as a noun: in Ps 136 different verses begin with the participle as a divine title or predicate: *le'ōśēh, lerōqaʿ, le'ōśēh, lemakkēh, leyôṣēʾ, legōzēr, lemôlîk, lemakkēh* = "to him who does, to him who spread out, to him who does, to him who smote, to him who brought out, to him who divided, to him who led, to him who smote". We might call it an anaphora of participles, often with repetition of the morpheme. In Ps 4,4-6 seven imperatives follow each other. It is natural that a rhetorical

piece accumulates imperatives launched against the people as for
example in the ten imperatives of Isa 1,16-18.

The masculine and feminine plurals may seem like a grammatical accident of little importsance. They are clearly differentiated:-
îm for the masculine, and *-ôt* for the feminine. Often a Hebrew poet
will avoid the rhyme by placing in the final positions a masculine
and a feminine, for example *hārîm ... gᵉbā'ôt* = "mountains ...
hills". Isa 3,18-23 mocks the trinkets and ostentation of the rich
women of the capital by listing twenty-one objects. Four words do
not fit the rhyme, but all the rest distribute the morpheme of the
plural in the following order (the exceptions are marked with N):

-îm	-îm	-îm		-ôt	-ôt	-ôt
	-îm	-ôt	-îm			
N — N		-îm		-ôt	N — N	
-ôt	-ôt	-ôt		-îm	-îm	-îm
	-ôt		-îm			

These morphemes are given a stylistic role by this great master of
the poetic art.

The simple repetition of morphemes is not sufficient to be considered a point of style without the presence of some additional factor which underlies it, but this factor may be limited to oratorical
declamation.

A *refrain* is the repetition of one verse or more of a poem,
usually at regular intervals. This regularity is not so important in
Hebrew poetry. We may consider a refrain the exclamation "How
are the mighty fallen!" from David's elegy referred to above (p. 13).
We find one in Pss 42-43; 46 (where we perhaps ought to insert it
also after v. 4); 56; 57; 59; 67; 99 (with expansion at the end); and Ps
107 has a double refrain.

Repetition as in a litany might be considered as a refrain with a
certain sense of urgency. The classic example is Ps 136.

As if the biblical examples were quite few, Slotki suggested that
the copyist may have avoided copying the repetitions, leaving them
to the readers and to the community.

As far as translation is concerned, since the phenomenon is so
frequent and often of little relevance, it is not essential always to
reproduce the repetition in the translation. It may in fact lessen the
effect of another point of style which is more important. We cannot
provide rigid norms here. Much depends on the sensitivity and the
taste of the translator. A simple piece of advice is to treat repetitions

with care! Zurro has demonstrated that repetition comes naturally in Spanish poetry, both ancient and modern (cf. *La traducción bíblica*, pp. 263-277).

Bibliography. Even though E. Zurro absorbs and renders unnecessary almost all the previous studies I will present some here, either due to their importance or because they treat areas not covered by Zurro:

I. Eitan, "La répétition de la racine en hébreu", *JPOS* 1 (1921) 171-186.

J. Muilenburg, "A Study in Hebrew Rhetoric: Repetition and Style", *Congress Volume: Copenhagen* (VTS 1; Leiden 1953), pp. 97-111.

J. Magne, "Répétitions de mots et exégèse dans quelques psaumes et le Pater", *Bib* 39 (1958) 177-197.

M. Kessler, "Inclusio in the Hebrew Bible", *Semitics* 6 (1978) 44-49.

W. G. E. Watson, *Classical Hebrew Poetry*, pp. 274-299.

III. Merismus

Merismus is a special case of synonymy. I distinguish it from polar expression, which I consider to be nearer to antithesis. I am considering it separately because it has received more attention in biblical studies. The most complete study so far is that of J. Krašovec, *Der Merismus im Biblisch-Hebraischen und Nordwest-semitischen* (BibOr 33; Rome 1977).

Merismus reduces a complete series to two of its constituent elements, or it divides a whole into two halves. "Mountains and valleys" represent the whole of the countryside. "Heaven and earth" is the universe. The two elements must represent the totality. We once again come across a phenomenon which shows how (articulate) language is: a plurality is summed up in two elements which represent it, or a totality is divided and put together again from two parts.

The number two is fundamental, so that some speak of "meristic pairs". We should also admit that sometimes there may be three elements. An orange grows ripe and there are eleven segments: I might take two to see what it tastes like. The horizon which we look at is a circumference. How should it be divided? Right, left, forwards, backwards. This is what the Hebrews said. We might say: North, South, East, West. But then we have no difficulty in speaking of NE, NW, SE, SW, and we have eight elements. How many meridians do we need to weave a web that could carry the earth?

In language, at least in poetic language, we tend to simplify. We divide the totality, we select from the plurality. Merismus may appear in series, as we saw in Isa 2,14-16: cedars and oaks, mountains and hills, ships and craft ...

As in any synonymy, the elements of the merismus have common aspects of meaning (sememes): these are what the poet places before the hearer or the reader. He may on the other hand show how they are different: this would mean they would be not longer a merismus and would become an antithesis. Merismus is not an automatic and unchangeable relationship; it depends rather on the specific poetic intention. And there are border-line cases which the scholar will not always be able to distinguish. In Ps 115,15-16 we read: "May you be blessed by the Lord, who made heaven and earth! The heavens are the Lord's heavens, but the earth he has given to the sons of men". Heaven and earth, the universe, the creation of the Lord, form a merismus. But then, as they are assigned to the Lord and to mankind, they are placed in an antithesis.

Krašovec gives a list of 272 words which may introduce a merismus. The list includes many more examples.

I believe that not all the cases which he presents are merismi in the strict sense. Many are conventional, pairs often used so that the text flows easily. Those which are of greater interest show originality or are fine examples. I select some:

"Stone and tree" in Jer 3,9 is a ridiculing reference to idols. Ps 49,3: "low and high, rich and poor". Ps 36,7: "man and beast thou savest, O Lord". Sir 15,3: "She will feed him with the bread of understanding, and give him the water of wisdom to drink". Ps 68,6: "Father of the fatherless and protector of widows". Nah 3,15: "There will the fire devour you..., the sword will cut you off". Hos 9,2: "Threshing floor and winevat shall not feed them". Ps 4,8: "when their grain and wine abound".

Merismus is used to describe a marvellous fertility in Joel 4,18:

> And in that day the mountains shall drip sweet wine,
> and the hills shall flow with milk,
> and all the stream beds of Judah shall flow with water.

Job 29,6 describes the years of abundance:

> My steps were washed with milk,
> and the rock poured out for me streams of oil!

Ben Sira declaims in the style of a proverb:

> Like ruler, like ministers;
> like sovereign, like subjects (Sir 10,2).

> If you do not run, you will not arrive,
> if you do not search you will not find (Sir 11,10).

CHAPTER VII

Antithesis and Polarised Expression

I. Antithesis

A. *The Reason for Antitheses*

Since the time of Lowth the antithesis too has been studied simply as a type of parallelism. Antithesis is a fundamental way of thinking and expressing oneself, a great literary device in both prose and verse. In Hebrew poetry the antithesis is one of the most important stylistic techniques.

This is true however not only for the Hebrews, because the antithesis is something which is used by all peoples. Man lives his life and grows in experience precisely by experiencing opposed forces and polarisations: in front/behind, before/after, power/weakness, work/rest. Ben Sira (in about 180 B.C.) invites us to look at the oppositions in the world as the source of harmony and beauty, and as the design of God:

> Good is the opposite of evil,
> and life the opposite of death;
> so the sinner is the opposite of the godly.
> Look upon all the works of the Most High;
> they likewise are in pairs,
> one the opposite of the other (Sir 33,14-15).

Ben Sira insists on the objectivity of these oppositions. He is right, but he is simplifying the situation, because there are always degrees and intermediary areas: ambiguities in human behaviour, good mixed with evil, dawns and dusks and cloudy days...

Without denying the objective basis of these oppositions, it is in fact man who understands and arranges things by antithesis. He isolates and stresses the opposing aspects of the objective world. This becomes a way of understanding things, of thinking and of expressing oneself.

In doing this he does not deny the intermediary areas, and the degrees of intensity. To compare two good things and declare that one is better than the other is in some way to place them in opposition to each other as regards a certain quality they possess. Hebrew poets continually show this capacity for comparing, and many proverbs begin with the formula "Better ... than ...". Ben Sira has a poem of ten members, in which each member puts forward two things which are similar and a third which is superior. Here are some verses from the passage, Sir 40,18-27:

> Wine and music gladden the heart,
> but better still is the love of wisdom.
> Flute and harp make pleasant melody,
> but better still is a pleasant voice.
> A man likes to see grace and beauty,
> but better still the green shoots in a cornfield (vv. 20-22).

Are there antitheses in God too? Our philosophy tells us that God transcends our created human distinctions: he transcends, he is beyond the before and after, the far and near, the outside and inside. But the Hebrew poets do not reach such philosophical formulations and in fact experience God and present him in polarisations, even in the same poem, but certainly in different texts. Let me quote from Sir 16,11: "Mercy and wrath are with the Lord; he is mighty to forgive and he pours out wrath".

B. *Distinctions*

The ancients defined what they meant by things being contrary as follows: the things belong to the same genre but are at maximum distance from each other, they are found in the same subject but mutually exclude each other, and one may even be proper to the subject. In recent times Greimas has proposed a semiotic square, made of contradictory and contrary elements. For example:

contrary elements	contrary elements	
to speak	*not to speak*	contradictory elements
to be silent	*not to be silent*	contradictory elements

Between contradictory elements there can be no mediation, no middle ground; between contrary elements it is possible to have an intermediate solution.

It is important to note that contrary elements belong to the same sphere: sensible and crippled are not contrary to each other, neither are poor and intelligent. Opposition presupposes a common sphere. This brings us to a first fundamental distinction, which in fact denies the scholastic distinction of *"maxime distant"*. We may place in opposition two elements which are indeed at extremes of a spectrum, but we may also place in opposition two elements which lie close to each other. Literary opposition is a way of focusing on what distinguishes and differentiates two elements.

Fountains and cisterns correspond in providing water and exist side by side. They could function as synonyms of a sort. But Jeremiah places them in opposition:

> They have forsaken me, the fountain of living waters,
> and hewed out cisterns for themselves,
> broken cisterns, that can hold no water (Jer 2,13).

Western thought, with its Greek origins, developed the habit of placing things in opposition to draw distinctions and make them precise. We frequently come across expressions like "not ... but ...". By placing similar concepts together in opposition we search for greater mental precision. Such a process may also enter poetry but without great finesse. Jeremiah draws a distinction between two winds, one gentle and useful, another destructive: "a wind not to winnow or cleanse, a wind too full for this comes for me" (Jer 4,11-12).

In spite of this, use of antithesis to distinguish closely related beings is not frequent in Western poetry, and in Hebrew poetry it is very rare. Even the examples already quoted are more interested in laying particular emphasis on certain aspects than in being precise.

C. *Antithesis in Proverbs*

Many proverbs are made up of an antithesis, usually distributed in two verses. Examination shows that many of them may be the result of later, more sophisticated additions to the original, simple proverb. (See L. Alonso Schökel and J. Vílchez, *Proverbios*, pp. 133ff., and the commentary attached.) Let me offer some varied examples with a few reflexions added.

Prov 13,7: "One man pretends to be rich, yet has nothing". To be rich and to have nothing form an antithesis, here between what appears to be and what is in fact so. The author who brought the proverb into the collection adds another member which announces the contrary antithesis: "another pretends to be poor, yet has great wealth". Two levels of antithesis are placed one above the other: rich/poor // pretence/possession.

In the following example, "flesh and bones" may seem like synonyms, two parts of the body, or like contrary elements though closely related, the flesh outside and the bones inside. More specifically "to give life" is opposed to "to make rot". The proverb not only places tranquillity in opposition to passion, but also emphasises the corrosive and penetrating effect of passion:

> A tranquil mind gives life to the flesh,
> but passion makes the bones rot (Prov 14,30).

Many antitheses are trivial and academic. Prov 15,6: "In the house of the righteous there is much treasure, but trouble befalls the income of the wicked". Prov 15,18: "A hot-tempered man stirs up strife, but he who is slow to anger quiets contention". These are easily forgotten proverbs. Where the antitheses are original and short the proverb is much more distinguished:

> A man's mind plans his way,
> but the Lord directs his steps (Prov 16,9).

> It is better to be of a lowly spirit with the poor
> than to divide the spoil with the proud (Prov 16,19).

This second example is rather refined, since the correspondences cross over. The normal antitheses would be: of lowly spirit/ proud/ to be poor/ to divide the spoil. But the author on the surface of it seems to be contrasting "of lowly spirit/to divide the spoil // to be poor/ to be proud". The contrast between the text and the logic of it, once perceived, deepens the sense.

When someone says "let this happen to me, but not that" it is a way of placing two disasters in opposition; they are placed in opposition to compare them and make one stand out more. This is an emphatic antithesis:

> Let a man meet a she-bear robbed of her cubs,
> rather than a fool in his folly (Prov 17,12).

The following example is also a comparison. The obvious opposition between "man of understanding / fool" is the basis of another more refined contrast between "rebuke" and "blows":

> A rebuke goes deeper into a man of understanding
> than a hundred blows into a fool (Prov 17,10).

The type of proverb which is formulated "Better ... than ...", so common in Hebrew, also presents a comparison and placing in opposition of certain values:

> Better is a dinner of herbs where love is
> than a fatted ox and hatred with it (Prov 15,17).

> Better is a neighbour who is near
> than a brother who is far away (Prov 27,10).

In the book of Proverbs the antitheses belong principally to the spheres of wise/foolish, righteous/evil, happy/wretched, mankind/God. Ben Sira uses opposition and contrast to develop his themes according to the principle of double aspect before he arrives at a conclusion. A typical example, on lending, is found in Sir 29,1-13.

D. *Antithesis Describing a Changing Situation*

Antitheses referring to changes of situation are the most frequent in the prophetic literature and they are also frequent in the psalms. They may be expressing nostalgia for former better times, and presenting a contrast with the present, or threatening a punishment which will bring the present prosperity to an end.

After mocking the ostentation of the women Isaiah delivers the sentence in a series of oppositions:

> Instead of perfume there will be rottenness;
> and instead of a girdle, a rope;
> and instead of well-set hair, baldness;
> and instead of a rich robe, a girding of sackcloth;
> instead of beauty, a scar (Isa 3,24).

In various instances the punishment of the tyrant recurs as a fall from the heights to the depths. The oracle against the king of Babylon is classic. This is the culmination of it:

> You said in your heart,
> 'I will ascend to heaven;
> above the stars of God
> I will set my throne on high;
> I will sit on the mount of assembly in the far north;
> I will ascend above the heights of the clouds,
> I will make myself like the Most High.'
> But you are brought down to Sheol,
> to the depths of the Pit (Isa 14,13-15).

I believe this could have been said more concisely by leaving aside some of the synonyms of the presumed exaltation of the king. The same kind of fall is described in Ezek 31,10.12 with the image of a tree:

> Because it towered high
> and set its top among the clouds,
> and its heart was proud of its height...
> Foreigners, the most terrible of the nations,
> will cut it down and leave it.
> On the mountains and in all the valleys
> its branches will fall,
> and its boughs will lie broken...
> The peoples ... will leave it.

A wisdom text expresses fear in the face of four changes of situation:

> At three things the earth shakes,
>   four things it cannot bear:
>   a slave turned king,
>   a churl gorging himself,
>   a woman unloved when she is married,
>   and a slave-girl displacing her mistress (Prov 30,21-23).

The whole of Psalm 30 is based on a series of oppositions of this type, until the final "Thou hast turned for me my mourning into dancing; thou hast loosed my sackcloth and girded me with gladness" (v. 12).

The antithesis is so common in Hebrew poetry that it is rather strange that the scholars have not examined it. It is true, they have not ruined it by reducing it to minute subdivisions, but attention should have been drawn to it all the same. The reader needs to be made aware of the presence and importance of the antithesis. This is enough, because the antithesis is easy to recognise, understand and appreciate.

God is the master of history, he brings about great changes, which are splendid and glorious. The pride of Babylon is humiliated, Isa 47; the humiliated servant is glorified, Isa 53; the abandoned wife is married again, Isa 49; he exalts the helpless, Ps 113; the rejected stone becomes the corner stone, Ps 11.

- What is infrequent is to find the opposition of contrary elements within the same person and situation, causing a tension which may be resolved. I said that man experiences God in extremes. Does he also experience himself in this way? I think of the experience of love as a tension of two forces, which becomes so topical in the work of Petrarch. Let me quote a beautiful Hebrew proverb which in two verses sums up the contrary elements:

> Even in laughter the heart is sad,
> and the end of joy is grief (Prov 14,13).

A character like Job, who is torn apart between his protest and his loyalty to God, does not express this in separate verses but throughout his speeches.

II. **Polarised Expression**

A. *Description*

Polarised expression can be found rather uncomfortably situated between antithesis and merismus.

Let us look again at the semantic field we saw earlier, that of different places to live: palace, mansion, house... hut, hovel. If I take two of the members as representative of the whole I have a merismus. If the two members are at the extremes of the series, I have a polarised expression. Horace wrote: "Pale death stalks both the hovels of the poor and the towers of the rich". ("*Pallida mors aequo pulsat pede pauperum tabernas regumque turres*".) Between the two extremes Horace wishes to include the totality, all the intermediary stages. Origen explained that, when in the Bible we read "I am the Alpha and the Omega" (first and last letters of the alphabet), this includes the whole series of the letters.

The two extremes must be along the same lines and they must share a common aspect of meaning. Furthermore, they must be extremes. Now, if the poet is presenting them as opposed, then we have an antithesis; if he is emphasising what they have in common, then we have a polarised expression. Polarised expression and merismus coincide in presenting a totality.

In fact, it is not always easy to distinguish between merismus and polarised expression. Perhaps this is not too important since the poet mixes them up without theoretical distinctions. The most difficult case is when the totality divides into two halves: the halves represent and are the totality, and they are also the extremes without intermediary stages. The distinction depends largely on the point of view of the poet or reader. "Heaven and earth" are the Hebrew universe divided into two halves: a merismus. They are also the two extremes of space: polarised expression or antithesis.

When the writer says explicitly "from ... to ...", he is not using polarised expression, but is simply instructing the reader by language to cover the space or the time in between two points.

E. Kemmer, *Die polare Ausdrucksweise in der griechischen Literatur* (BHSGS 15; Wurzburg 1903). This is the basic study on the question.

G. Lambert, "Lier–délier. L'expression de la totalité par l'opposition de deux contraires", *RB* 52 (1945) 91-103.

P. Boccaccio, "Termini contrari come espressioni della totalità in ebraico", *Bib* 33 (1952) 173-190.

L. Alonso Schökel, *Estudios de poética hebrea*, pp. 203f., 211-213.

As can be seen, this technique has been studied little, in spite of its frequency. In Krašovec's list of merismi I find quite a number of cases of polarised expression.

B. *Examples*

To be more precise about the distinction I want to begin with Sir 40,1-4, which places together birth and death, throne and dust, crown and burlap. It could have been a good example of polarised expression, but the author avoids this by using the formula "from ... to ...:

Much labour was created for every man,
and a heavy yoke is upon the sons of Adam,
from the day they come forth from their mother's womb
till the day they return to the mother of all.
Their perplexities and fear of heart —
their anxious thought is the day of death,
from the man who sits on a splendid throne
to the one who is humbled in dust and ashes,
from the man who wears purple and a crown
to the one who is clothed in burlap.

As far as the poetic result is concerned is it really very important whether we have here examples of polarised expression or not? Once more, the aim of stylistic analysis is not to classify.

In many biblical texts man is presented in his natural and unavoidable extremes. One such psalm is Ps 139. Once again, it is not important for the author to keep to one technique. Rather he combines several to produce a fine result. The student may exercise himself in identifying each technique, but the important thing is the coherence, the impressive effect of the whole. We ought to read the whole of the psalm; I will content myself with citing only selected verses:

139,2   Thou knowest when I sit down and when I rise up...
  3   Thou searchest out my path and my lying down ...
  5   Thou dost beset me behind and before ...
  8   If I ascend to heaven, thou art there!
         If I make my bed in Sheol, thou art there!
  9   If I take the wings of the morning
         and dwell in the uttermost parts of the sea,
  10   even there thy hand shall lead me,
         and thy right hand shall hold me.

Above the extremes of human behaviour God arises, who sees and knows and distinguishes and leads. See the related text, Am 9,2-3. Psalm 121 also contemplates human extremes from the point of view of the protecting vigilance of the Lord who does not sleep: "The sun shall not smite you by day, nor the moon by night. ... The Lord will keep your going out and your coming in from this time forth and for evermore" (vv. 6.8).

Ps 95,4-5 combines two extremes and two halves:
    In his hand are the depths of the earth;
    the heights of the mountains are his also.
    The sea is his, for he made it;
    for his hands formed the dry land.

Ps 75,7 covers the four quarters of the horizon:
    For not from the east or from the west,
    nor from the wilderness nor from the mountains,
    it is God alone who executes judgement,
    putting down one and lifting up another.

Prov 30,8 rejects two extremes in order to choose the middle ground. This does not mean that there are only three possibilities. The middle ground lies between and is opposed to whatever lies at the sides:
    Remove far from me falsehood and lying;
    give me neither poverty nor riches;
    feed me with food that is needful for me,
    lest I be full and deny thee,
    and say, "Who is the Lord?"
    or lest I be poor, and steal,
    and profane the name of my God.

The virtuous middle ground in the ethical sense may be expressed thus:

> Do not swerve to the right or to the left;
> turn your foot away from evil (Prov 4,27).

God is above and outside both human and cosmic extremes. However, the poet of the exile can only express this using a series of polarisations: first and last, before and after, near and far, hidden and present. Given the coherence of Isa 40–55 the verses which I am going to select here are in no way out of place and present a unitary vision:

> It is I, the Lord, I am the first,
> and to the last of them I am He (Isa 41,4).

> Before me there was no god fashioned
> nor ever shall be after me (Isa 43,10).

> I am the first and I am the last
> and there is no god but me (Isa 44,6).

> I make the light, I create darkness,
> author alike of prosperity and trouble (Isa 45,7).

> Thou art a god that hidest thyself (Isa 45,15).

> They shall know that it is I who speak:
> here I am (Isa 52,6).

> A load on me from your birth,
> carried by me from the womb:
> till you grow old I am He,
> and when white hairs come,
> I will carry you still (Isa 46,3-4).

> The heavens grow murky as smoke,
> the earth wears into tatters like a garment,...
> but my deliverance is everlasting
> and my saving power shall never wane (Isa 51,6; cf. Ps 102).

> Inquire of the Lord while he is present,
> call upon him when he is close at hand...
> for as the heavens are higher than the earth,
> so are my ways higher than your ways (Isa 55,6.9).

CHAPTER VIII

Images

I. Introduction

We come to the most important, and most difficult, chapter: images. Images are the glory, perhaps the essence of poetry, the enchanted planet of the imagination, a limitless galaxy, ever alive and ever changing. Is it not presumptuous to attempt to explain such a world created for contemplation and surprised delight? Perhaps, in the knowledge that our attempt is condemned to failure, we might first skirt around the subject to decorate it with some peripheral reflexions.

a) The human spirit experiences reality through the senses and then tries to transform its experiences into words by describing the objects perceived. The description may be detailed and leisurely, or it may be limited to a couple of well-chosen and decisive features. b) The human spirit undergoes experiences, makes discoveries and establishes relationships between different things, finding harmony and unity in the plurality it sees. c) The imagination takes over experience and transforms it into a new and coherent system. d) The human spirit goes through what can be perceived with the senses only to go beyond it, it penetrates what can be perceived in order to discover something more. e) The human spirit seeks the help of sense experience in order to approach with it something which is transcendent, in order to express what cannot be expressed.

a) The first section concerns description. I have already dealt with it as a particular genre alongside others. It has its place here too, as a technique, because images always include a certain element of description. But very often the descriptive element is simply a bare outline, so that we cannot speak of description, or it is simply concerned with a couple of features and we may call it a characterisation.

Jeremiah is able to accuse the Lord: "Wilt thou be to me like a deceitful brook, like waters that fail?" (Jer 15,18). The image is not detailed, simply noted and very suggestive in its context. Job on the other hand reproaches his friends for their lack of loyalty:

My brothers have been treacherous
as a mountain stream,
like the channels of streams that run dry,
which turn dark with ice
or are hidden with piled-up snow;
or they vanish the moment they are in spate,
dwindle in the heat and are gone.
Then the caravans, winding hither and thither,
go up into the wilderness and perish;
the caravans of Tema look for their waters,
travelling merchants of Sheba hope for them;
but they are disappointed, for all their confidence.
They reach them only to be balked (Job 6,15-20).

In this case the poet takes advantage of the image to make a short journey contemplating the changing landscape and the people who pass through it.

The concise descriptive note is the more frequent form. While Job 7,6 says: "My days are swifter than a weaver's shuttle", in Isa 38,12 Hezekiah reflects: "Like a weaver I have rolled up my life, he cuts me off from the loom". In the latter text the poet contrasts the regular, cumulative movement of rolling with the brutal and pitiless "he cuts me off".

This is the first stage. In every image the contribution of the senses is seen in the language.

b) No less important is the element of correlation, the relationships found between the two panels of the image. This needs more time to explain. The correlation may be on different levels.

The relationship may be between two perceived sense objects, between the spiritual and the sensed object, between the general and the individual, the abstract and the concrete, the transcendent and the empirical. ...

Let me begin with the easiest case, that of two perceived sense objects. Ben Sira contemplates "the hoarfrost upon the earth like salt", the ice on the pool "like a breastplate" and the snow "like locusts alighting" (Sir 43,19-20). We must bear in mind that the placing together of the two objects does not necessarily put them on the same level. In elements like snow, frost and cold there is clearly something which transcends man, which he cannot control or manipulate. In comparing the two objects the poet domesticates these elements without removing their fascination. There is no exact correspondence between the objects, even though they are both perceived by the senses.

c) Let us turn our attention to human qualities in social life. What about the effect the fool has on others? This is not something which is perceived by the senses, seen or touched. In English we might exclaim: "What a drag he is!" With this expression we compare our experience of the fool with our impression of a great weight to be pulled along. Let us look at a Hebrew proverb:

> Stone is a burden and sand a dead weight,
> but to be vexed by a fool
> is more burdensome than either (Prov 27,3).

The image is very clear, and presents very effectively the feelings we have towards such a person.

d) Let us move on to an example which seems to belie what I am saying:

> A full stomach refuses even honey,
> to a hungry stomach even the bitter is sweet (Prov 27,7).

The descriptive panel is certainly there: the full or hungry stomach. But where is the other panel? This is simply alluded to so that the reader can discover it for himself and thus be just as pleased by his skill at understanding as he is by the poet's cleverness. The object which is sensed, the appetite, leads the reader to think in more general terms of man's cravings and desires.

e) The object of comparison might however be something which transcends man. Something which moves the ordinary mortal and leaves him speechless may be captured by the poet through a comparison and fixed in a poetic image. Let me give two examples of this rather more difficult type. Isn't our consciousness something rather mysterious? How is it that we can be present to ourselves? Who is it who does the perceiving? Is the subject and the object the same? No alien is present in this interior world, which can summon up in a moment things which are absent. Who is it who summons them up? The poet does not ask such questions. This would be to abandon poetic intuition and begin philosophical reflexion. But the poet wonders at the mystery, and does not hesitate to say something about it:

> The spirit of man is a lamp of the Lord,
> searching all his innermost parts (Prov 20,27).

On the sense level, we have a cellar or a store-cupboard within us where we keep what we have experienced; the householder lights a

lamp to go and rummage around, or simply to browse. This lamp
was given by the Lord when he gave man the breath of life (*neˢāmâ*).

In the following example the poet is explicit. He is not speaking
about individual consciousness but about the mysterious relationship
between the sexes, the perpetual enigma about which so much has been
written without ever reaching an explanation. This time the poet does
not say what cannot be said, but says that it cannot be said.
Nevertheless he does not remain silent but generously and calculatingly
he exalts the mystery with a build-up of three images:

> Three things are too wonderful for me;
> four I do not understand:
> the way of an eagle in the sky,
> the way of a serpent on a rock,
> the way of a ship on the high seas,
> and the way of a man with a maiden (Prov 30,18-19).

Whoever wrote these lines is a great poet. Are we now going to try
to explain how he explains what is inexplicable?

f) And what should we say about God? Maybe here the best
thing is to remain silent, as Job 13,5 suggests: "Oh that you would
keep silent, and it would be your wisdom!" Except that the poet is
there to speak, he has to express himself, and the inspired poets had
the task of bequeathing us vocabulary for speaking about God and
to God. God is my rock, my soul is thirsty for God. God is my
rock, and in him I take refuge. God is the light which makes me see
light. The two elements here are the sense object and the One who is
Other and Transcendent. (I will return to this.) If theo-logy is
speaking about God, the biblical poets constructed a proto-
theology. If theology is reflecting on God, then we should think and
rethink these images. The "way of a man with a maiden" was too
difficult for the poet to express; another poet, imagining the
crossing of the Red Sea as a theophany in a storm, ended up by
saying of God:

> Thy way was through the sea,
> thy path through the great waters;
> yet thy footprints were unseen (Ps 77,20).

A poetic image of God's passage through the waters much like
Moses' vision of the Lord's back.

A. Dulles, "Symbol, Myth and the Biblical Revelation", *TS* 27 (1966)
1-26.

As I explained the different cases I have made it clear that the correspondences are always of two panels. And when one of the correlated objects was not stated we have uncovered it. The essential thing about poetic imagery is this placing of two levels alongside each other: it may be the approaching in spirit of what is far away, it may be the fusing of two objects without confusing their diversity, it may be a union which is not simply juxtaposition. It is as if different beings correspond to each other and desire each other's presence (like the northern pine and the southern palm tree in Heine's poem). It is the poet who is the match-maker.

Of course, correspondences between beings are innumerable, and the last verse of poetry therefore will never have been written. When distances are overcome and unexpected similarities discovered, a poetic image is born. It will provoke surprise, joy, recognition. What has war to do with the hearth, an invading army with a boiling pot? Jeremiah replied in 1,13-14:

- I see a boiling pot, its contents spilling out from the north. ...
- Out of the north evil shall break forth upon all the inhabitants of the land.

What do a city being conquered and a pool have in common? Nahum replies in 2,8:

Nineveh is like a pool whose waters run away.
"Halt! Halt!" they cry; but none turns back.

So we have established that the poetic image is not mere juxtaposition of similar objects, not simply the giving of an added meaning to a word. In the poetic image there is in some way the placing together and interchange of certain qualities. That is our conclusion, for the time being.

II. Cautionary Remarks

As we begin the study of biblical images we must beware of certain common errors. They may perhaps be applied to other literatures, but we must denounce their application to biblical literature.

a) Let me begin with what is known as the *oriental imagination* (about which one hears gradually less and less). It has been said that in the Bible the oriental imagination runs riot: this statement can be understood as an accusation of excessive behaviour, or as a condescending assessment. It is therefore either a calumny or a mistake. This false judgement is based on comparing the style proper to the academic professions with poetic style. If in fact we compare Hebrew poetry with others, we will appreciate the moderation of the biblical poets. Fray Luis de León had already made this observation when he compared the Song of Songs to love poems of his time. Commenting on Cant 4,1 — "Your hair is like a flock of goats, moving down the slopes of Gilead" — he writes:

> What causes surprise here is the comparison which seems gross and different from what one is used to. It would be acceptable if the text spoke of locks of gold or said that her hair rivals the rays of the sun in fulness and colour, as our poets say. I would answer that if one thinks of it correctly, the comparison is graceful and quite proper, provided one takes into account the person who is speaking and exactly what it is that he wishes to praise about the hair of the beloved.

After the exaggerations of the baroque, the symbolist movement, creationism and surrealism, all this about the "oriental imagination" makes us laugh. It is only the apocalyptic writers who really let themselves go in using their imagination.

b) The second danger is more insidious, because it comes from a mentality which is firmly rooted and little criticised. It is found in the expression: images serve *to dress up ideas*. The hackneyed image of "dressing up" will help us to analyse this mentality.

The supposition is that first of all comes the idea or concept, which the normal person will enunciate with its corresponding vocabulary. The poet on the other hand, in the interests of decency or fashion, searches around in his imaginative wardrobe, gets out a set of clothes and dresses up his concept or idea. It is the task of the intelligent reader to remove the clothes and understand the idea. If the reader cannot do this alone, the exegete will help him. The biblical text says "the hand, the arm of God"; but it means "the power". The text says "I take refuge in the shadow of your wings"; but it means "I seek the protection of God".

Following this path we can translate the Bible into a language which is more abstract and less expressive, but we will not reach the original meaning. We are dealing with poets, and what comes before the image is not the concept, but the formless experience. The image gave a certain form to the experience; it was the first vision or spiritual reflexion, the first formulation which could be communicated.

By means of the image the author understood what he had experienced and expressed it and it is the image which he intends to put across.

The tragic experience of mortal danger which approaches and increases is expressed in the symbol "the waters have come up to my neck, I sink in deep mire" (Ps 69,2-3); "danger of inevitable death" is a later conceptual translation which we may wish to apply, not a mental formulation of the poet which came before the symbol. The man attacked by his enemies and about to fall feels like "a leaning wall, a tottering fence" (Ps 62,4), and not "like a contingent being exposed to human hostility". Man's deep desire for God is experienced as a thirst: "My soul thirsts for thee; my flesh faints for thee, as in a dry and weary land where no water is" (Ps 63,2). It is a later generation which may wish to speak of "an intense and total desire for God". "Evil talk, false accusation" are precise concepts. Before arriving at this conceptual precision the poet could speak thus of verbal attacks: "... who whet their tongues like swords, who aim bitter words like arrows, shooting from ambush at the blameless, shooting at him suddenly and without fear" (Ps 64,4-5). This may be less precise, but it is more alive, and no less real and authentic.

Conceptual translation is legitimate as long as its working, its function and its limits are recognised. We have seen one way of viewing the process: experience – conceptual formulation – imaginative dressing up – conceptual translation. I proposed another sequence: experience – imaginative formulation – conceptual translation. The first sequence does work in forms which are purely didactic and in certain allegorical exercises. The teacher knows that putting forward ideas in images helps the pupil to understand. But the first sequence cannot be applied to the Psalms or to prophetic poetry in general. Anyone who tries to apply this sequence throughout the biblical material will neither understand nor be able to explain biblical language, but will put something else in its place. The second sequence is legitimate as long as its limitations are realised. Conceptual translation may gain in precision but it loses in richness, it may gain in clarity but it loses in allusiveness, it may be more manageable but it loses its immediate impact. Furthermore, this added conceptual translation must lead us back to the original language. It is simply a passing stage. The symbolic language of the Bible remains always the essential.

c) The image brings together and places alongside two beings. When they cannot be distinguished or when one disappears, the image ceases to work. For such cases we may use the terms *premetaphor* and *lexicalised metaphor*. When the grandson of Victor Hugo (*The Art of Being Grandfather*), visiting the zoo, pointed to a crocodile and said "it's made of handbags", he was not using a poetic image. For him that animal really seemed of the same substance as his mother's handbag. If I did not know that a child had said it, I might read it as an image. It is not an image when a Hebrew says that the sun comes out and goes across the sky; but it certainly is when he says it comes out "like a bridgegroom leaving his chamber" (Ps 19,6). If for the Hebrews the emotions really have bodily organs with which they are associated it is quite logical that by metonymy the emotion may be referred to with the name of the organ. Thus *'ap*, "nostril", may mean "anger" without being an image; a "bad eye" will refer to "meanness".

On the other extreme we find the lexicalised image. This is the image which due to excessive use has lost its reference to the sense object. The lexicon of any language contains very many words of this type: the foot of the page, the head of the department. Not only individual words but also phrases and comparisons: to burn with anger, to grease the palm, like greased lightning. Something similar happens in Hebrew poetry, though it is not so easy to identify. When I come across for the tenth time "numerous as the sand on the seashore" I may begin to think that the image has become part of the lexicon. "Rock" as a title of God may be another case in point. We have no means of being sure, but we must consider the possibility. And we must remember that in biblical exegesis there is a lack of imagination and perception rather than a surfeit. Finally, let us bear in mind that a lexicalised image may regain its sense quality when used by a skilled writer.

d) We must also be wary of something which follows logically from the preceding point, the hasty *spiritualisation* of what is perceived by the senses. Let me explain by referring to the word *nepeš*, the word which perhaps more than any other has suffered from this spiritualisation. Often, too often, it is translated as "soul"; often it means "person", "life"; it also means "breath" and "appetite", and also "neck". When *nepeš* means neck, it must not be translated as "soul" (*anima*).

First, some obvious cases: "the waters reached my neck" (Jon 2,6); "the waters have come up to my neck" (Ps 69,2); "the torrent would have gone over our neck" (Ps 124,4). In the Vulgate we read: "Intraverunt aquae usque ad animam meam". Again, when the text speaks of thirst, it is normal to think of the throat, since we do not feel thirst with our souls. Consequently, Ps 63,2: "my throat thirsts for you" (perhaps a symbolic use of the senses; see the end of this chapter).

Following this line of thought, the phrase *mar nepeš* could mean "to feel bitterness in the throat"; as long as the expression has not been lexicalised to mean simply any interior bitterness, even metaphorical. The frequency of the phrase could lead us to consider it a set phrase: 1 Sam 1,10; 22,2; 2 Sam 17,8; Isa 38,15; Ezek 27,31; Job 3,20; 7,11; 10,1; 21,25, etc. I cannot think the same of the expression *qšr npš bnpš / qšr npš 'l...*, which is usually translated "to love deeply". Read with some imagination it would be "to bid neck to neck", perhaps an image of two animals in the yoke together, walking and working side by side. Since the phrase is found only twice in the whole of the OT, Gen 44,30 and 1 Sam 18,1 (of father and son, and of friends), we cannot affirm that the expression has become lexicalized.

The sense of Ps 105,18 is clear: "his neck was put in a collar of iron", parallel with "his feet were hurt with fetters" (the Vulgate translates: "ferrum pertransiit animam eius"). I have no doubts about the meaning of Jer 4,10: "the sword has reached their necks" (Vulgate: "et ecce pervenit gladius usque ad animam"). If this is true I must be consistent and read Isa 53,12, *he'ĕrâ lammāwet napšô*, in a realistic way, "he bared his neck to die"; this is in clear harmony with the silence and total surrender of the Servant. Also one ought to take in a realistic sense *mitnaqqēš b^enapšî*, 1 Sam 28,9, "putting a noose around my neck", with a metaphorical meaning. Ps 19,8, *m^ešîbat nāpeš*, would mean "restores the breath". Ps 31,8, *b^eṣārôt napšî*, quite apart from "the adversities of my life" could also mean "they are at my very neck", with metaphorical meaning too. In Ps 107,26, which speaks of shipwreck in a violent storm, we are not being told about a generic "evil", but about seasickness in particular; it is not concerned with the soul, but with the body from the neck down: "their stomachs were revolted by seasickness" (Vulgate: "anima eorum deficiebat in malis"). Similarly in Isa 29,8 there is talk of "the dry throat" and "the empty stomach". Isa 1,14 could be "my heart/soul hates" or "I feel nausea".

In our modern languages too we still have expressions which go back to the practice of beheading, and of binding prisoners around the neck. These expressions often have metaphorical value or have become lexicalised. We have the English expressions "to cut someone's throat", "a lump in one's throat". In Spanish: "con el agua al cuello, cortar el cuello, con la soga al cuello". In German: "es kostet ihm den Hals, den Hals abschneiden, brechen". In Italian: "con la corda al collo, prendere per il collo, rompere il collo, piegare il collo". In our modern languages we can sense when the image is still alive and when it has lost its vigour. But in Hebrew it is difficult to make this judgement.

e) I will add a fifth point, a piece of advice. Both the *reader* and the interpreter of the Bible must alert their imagination when they read or study biblical poetry. What has been written with imagination, must also be read with imagination, provided the individual has imagination and it is in working order.

Let me illustrate with examples.

> Set a guard over my mouth, O Lord,
> keep watch over the door of my lips!
> Incline not my heart to any evil (Ps 141,3-4).

Even though for a Hebrew it may not be a metaphor to say that words come out of the mouth, it is a fine image to see a guard at the door of the mouth to prevent undesirable words from leaving. Ben Sira goes further and pleads: "Who would place a captain to guard my thoughts!" (Sir 23,2). On the other hand, I would say that "to turn the heart" is a lexicalised formula, read in similar contexts (Ps 119,112; Prov 2,2; Josh 24,23; 2 Sam 19,15; 1 Kgs 8,48; 11,2.3.4, etc.).

Although the image of the hunt, with nets and traps, is very common, the accumulation and development of the images gives a certain value to Ps 141,9-10:

> Keep me from the trap which they have laid for me,
> and from the snares of evildoers!
> Let the wicked together fall into their own nets,
> while I escape.

The root *ṣrr* originally meant to be narrow, to constrict; it develops its meaning to refer to the objective danger, or the corresponding subjective feeling of being under constraint. The poet may use the lexicalised metaphor with an antonym which makes the spatial quality apparent again: "Thou hast given me room when I was in dire straits" (Ps 4,2).

I have translated Ps 143,3: "He crushes me alive against the ground"; literally it would be "he crushes against the earth my life". How does the ordinary reader understand this? There is more here than is immediately apparent. Man is dust and will return to dust, and when he dies he will return to the earth (cf. Ps 146,4); this dust which was a living being is now crushed and trodden down and becomes part of the ground we walk over. This is how man enters the kingdom of death. Ps 144,4 says: "Man is like a breath, his days are like a passing shadow". These comparisons are repeated in the OT.

One can easily appreciate how deeply cultivation and architecture are valued when one sees the comparisons used in Ps 144,12:

> May our sons in their youth
> Be like plants full grown,
> our daughters like corner pillars
> cut for the structure of a palace.

Without having to imagine caryatids, the vision is still delightful. The Song of Songs has recourse to architecture when the bride describes the lover: "His legs are alabaster columns, set upon bases of gold" (Cant 5,15). Ben Sira affirms: "Children and the building of a city establish a man's name" (Sir 40,19). Of the beautiful woman he says: "Like pillars of gold on a base of silver, so are firm legs over beautiful feet" (Sir 26,18).

The statement that the stars form the army of the Lord can lose its quality as an image due to frequent repetition. In Ps 147,4 we have the image of the chief who recruits an army or summons his servants: "He determines the number of the stars, he gives to all of them their names". Ben Sira also takes pleasure in this image:

> At the command of the Holy One they stand as ordered,
> they never relax in their watches (Sir 43,10).

We do not know whether in ancient times the military function of the stars was taken literally. We read as an image a verse of the so-called Song of Deborah, which seems very ancient:

> From heaven fought the stars,
> from their courses they fought against Sisera (Judg 5,20).

In the following line the Kishon torrent also takes part in the action, a decisive factor in the victory (like the river Scamander against Achilles):

> The torrent Kishon swept them away,
> the onrushing torrent, the torrent Kishon (Judg 5,21).

III. A Beginning of Classification

a) The simplest way of joining two panels is the *comparison*. Various particles can serve as hinges to join the two elements together, like the two pictures of a diptych. They can also be placed

together without any particle between them: similarity holds them
together. They can also be joined together as subject and predicate.
The same effect is achieved and the choice of any of these
techniques is not usually relevant on the stylistic level. Furthermore,
in passing from one language to another one has to bear in mind the
literary conventions of each language. What is still of great
expressive value in the original may turn out to be dull if translated
literally into another language. See *Proverbios*, pp. 128-133.

In the following translations I keep very close to the original so
that the different techniques may be plain.

> Remove the dross from the silver
> and the smith will make a vessel.
> Remove the wicked man from the presence of the king
> and his throne will be established in righteousness
>   (Prov 25,4-5).

The two have simply been placed alongside each other. The
repetition of the verb "remove" serves as the hinge. The two
pictures are very similar in the first half, less so in the second half.
The precious vessel and the royal throne are related.

> Like the freshness of snow in the time of harvest,
> a faithful messenger to those who send him (Prov 25,13).

This example begins with the comparative particle; the verb "to be"
is unnecessary in Hebrew.

> With patience a ruler may be convinced
> and soft tongue breaks a bone (Prov 25,15).

In English the "and" joining the two triple elements seems strange.
Perhaps a colon should replace it.

Prov 25,18 is remarkable for the triple comparison before the
corresponding element is stated: "A war club, and a sword, and a
sharp arrow, a man bearing false witness against his neighbour".
Note that the three elements of comparison come from the same
field.

Job 9,26 simply duplicates the comparison: "My days slip by
like skiffs of reed, like an eagle swooping on the prey".

The final example can serve too to give an important warning
about the so-called *tertium comparationis*. The teaching of rhetorical
principles has supposed that between the two elements under
comparison there is one common point or factor, a third or

mediating element which allows the comparison to be made. The two elements are supposed to have nothing else in common. In fact, this may happen, but usually it is not the case at all. Certainly, the obvious point of comparison serves to bring the two elements together, but once they are together we cannot avoid keeping them together and discovering other similarities and dissimilarities. Mechanical explanations are not appropriate here. In the last example, from Job: his days slip by "like skiffs of reed", without clamour, one after the other, until they are lost from sight, they are the past. Or they group together in the distant future, and suddenly swoop down onto the prey, the poet himself. One future day, whether distant of near, it will be all finished with him. In a case like this the rationalistic explanation of the *tertium comparationis* is quite out of place. It is not insignificant that the poet chose as his points of comparison the water of a calm river or sea, and the air where the birds of prey circle. In between the two is the "third element", poor, suffering Job himself.

Sometimes the comparison intends to contrast two elements, so that some would say this is not true comparison. I think, since two things are placed together, we should also speak of this in this context. Let me take a fairly developed biblical comparison. It frequently happens that human life is compared to a flower, to the grass which dries up (Ps 90,4-6), to the leaves of a tree (Isa 64,5; 1,30): this is due to their frailty. Other comparisons with plants focus on their vitality, like Prov 11,28; Jer 17,8, etc. The really adventurous thing is to take up the well-known comparison in order to challenge it. Man and the tree are not similar: the tree has hope; man does not:

> For there is hope for a tree,
> if it be cut down, that it will sprout again,
> and that its shoots will not cease.
> Though its root grow old in the earth,
> and its stump die in the ground,
> yet at the scent of water it will bud
> and put forth branches like a young plant.
> But man dies, and is laid low;
> man breathes his last, and where is he? (Job 14,7-10).

The slow description of what happens to the tree makes the brief description of human destiny even more tragic. This comparison was designed to bring out the contrasts.

D. F. Payne, "A Perspective on the Use of Simile in the Old Testament", *Semitics* 1 (1970) 111-125.

D. Rosner, "The Simile and its Use in the Old Testament", *Semitics* 4 (1974) 37-46.

b) The *metaphor* is usually distinguished from the comparison at least by two characteristics: it consists of one word or phrase, and it does not give the two elements of comparison, but simply substitutes one for the other. It is as if only one of the elements were given so that the reader could use it to guess the other element. It says one thing, it means another. In this case too some people speak of *tertium comparationis*. We might use the linguistic model of paradigmatic substitution. In the paradigm "grow – develop – grow up – reach adulthood" we could add the expression "shoot up". Instead of saying "he is growing", I could say "he is shooting up", using a metaphorical expressions more commonly used, still in a metaphorical sense, of plants. In this case it is used of a young man.

It is clear that the metaphorical expression occupies the place of the proper expression, in this case "to grow". Thus far the model of the paradigmatic substitution is fine: words with metaphorical meaning can fit into a paradigm *a posteriori*, as it were. But this is not simply a substitution, and nothing more. The metaphorical expression brings in its own world, its own connotations, and it brings them in quite aggressively. It does not simply enter timidly, but brings with it all its range of meaning, and perhaps a whole new context. Only the tips of the toes touch the trampolin, but the full weight of the body is on it.

P. Ricœur, *La métaphore vive* (OrPh; Paris 1975).

The rapid, one word metaphor is not however common in Hebrew poetry. One is surprised by the scarcity of metaphors, though not of images.

The words of the enemy are "words that devour" in Ps 52,6: *dibrê bālaʿ*. In the next verse comes the threat to the wicked man: God "will uproot you"; both in Hebrew and in English this is from the lexical root "root": man is planted in the land of the living, the living earth. In that earth he has his roots and grows; God violently uproots these roots from the life-giving soil. The false language of the wicked is "more slippery than butter", his words are "softer than oil" (Ps 55,22).

An individual prays to God: "Collect my tears in your wine-skin", Ps 56,9. The wine-skin is metaphorical; by using this word the poet transforms the whole phrase, the verb "collect" is altered, and the tears of the man come to represent every aspect of his troubled situation. In Ps 58,7 the Psalmist prays: "Tear out the fangs of the lions", every element of which is a metaphor. Ps 59,13 asks that the wicked "may be trapped in their pride", with the verb *lākad* = "to capture". In Ps 69,10 the Psalmist says: "Zeal for your house devours me"; the metaphorical verb "devour" makes the "zeal" into a person or an animal. Isa 66,14 promises: "Your bones shall flourish".

It is not easy to find pure metaphors in Hebrew poetry. One always has a question about pre-metaphors, and post-metaphors or lexicalised metaphors. When Ps 65,9 says: "The doors of morning and evening you fill with joy", are these doors a metaphor, or are they a proper statement from one who imagines that the sun really comes out from a door? We of course value it as a beautiful metaphor; due to our discoveries, which are already part of our nature, we cannot take it in a literal sense. At the other extreme we have the stereotyped phrase *ḥărôn 'ap* = "burning of the nostrils" = "burning anger". There is perhaps reason for saying that the expression results from a human process: heat comes to the face of an individual, then this is identified with an interior emotion, and finally we have a cliché.

It is arguable that in Hebrew poetic culture there was not yet sufficient imaginative agility to produce the pure metaphor; still less the original and surprising metaphor. The fact is that the poets prefer to delay and widen the metaphor, treating it like a comparison.

We might say "I am full of anger"; the word "full" is in this case a lexicalised metaphor. The poet may feel it is still a metaphor. An old man is "full of years", Jer 6,11; a prince is "full of wisdom", Ezek 28,12. A prophet may feel "full" of the anger of God, just as a cup is full (Ps 75,9); Jeremiah is full, overflowing, with anger:

– I am full of the wrath of the Lord;
I am weary of holding it in.

– Pour it out upon the children in the street,
and upon the gathering of young men, also (Jer 6,11).

c) I distinguish the *allegory* by two qualities. One is general: in its production the conceptual perception comes first and the imaginative transposition follows. The second quality concerns its development: there is strict correspondence, element for element, between the intellectual perception and the imaginative projection of it. A simple concept cannot produce an allegory, a global and continuous perception cannot produce one. The intellectual concept must have several elements and the image must parallel this. If we give small letters to the intellectual perception and capitals to the image, an allegory would have a structure like this:

a = A
b = B
c = C
d = D

The apocalyptic writers are the experts in this technique. History is divided into four epochs, defined by successive empires: Babylonians – Medes – Persians – Macedonians, of lessening prestige and of increasing cruelty. They can be portrayed as a human body: head – chest and arms – stomach and thighs – legs and feet; or as four ferocious beasts: lion – bear – leopard – an unknown animal.

Allegory is in fact a rather poor literary technique, weak poetically (the Daniel examples cited are in prose). In my opinion, it finishes in one of two extremes. A lucky and talented writer will select a suitable image as the basis of his allegory, and such an image may become popular in a particular culture. On the other hand, a less talented writer will become disastrously entangled in the artificial game of working out the corresponding elements. In the eighth chapter of Daniel, for instance, an author begins to allegorize and enters the rather dangerous area of "horns", only to suffer a serious goring. And though we may accept that seven thin cows eat one by one seven fat cows, we cannot accept the same process where ears of grain are concerned. Allegory often takes refuge in dreams.

When a writer has used a series of allegorical elements, the reader has to work them out one by one. One may also come across an allegorical interpretation of a text which is not allegorical. Ezekiel himself allegorizes his magnificent vision of the bones (thereby rendering it less momentous): the bones are the exiles, the tomb is Babylon, the resurrection is the return home.

d) The *symbol* is the highest peak of the imagination. What is essential to the symbol is that it means more than is at first apparent. The symbol is the object perceived plus something else that is revealed in it. While allegory needed the removal of the image to find the sense, the symbol would cease to exist if the image element were lost. The symbol leads us beyond itself without itself retreating from sight. The symbol does not sacrifice its material nature, because only in this is the transcendent element manifest.

The symbol takes the risk of expressing what cannot be expressed in an all-embracing way. The symbol lets itself be seen to allow the reader to catch a glimpse of something more. The symbol is translucent, rather than transparent.

The symbol is rooted in the most profound part of man, at the point where the spirit and the body are not divided as opposing parts. For this reason the symbol appeals to the whole man: imagination, intuition, emotions. The symbol sets vibrating anyone who opens himself to the symbol in an attitude of contemplation. The symbol is open, even expansive.

The poetic symbol, in spite of its name, has nothing to do with the mathematical symbol. It may issue from a metaphor or a comparison, but it hates allegory.

The symbol is the proto-language of transcendent experience, and thus also of religious experience. The symbol does not provide intellectual information, but simply mediates communion. The symbol cannot be reduced to a collection of concepts.

Biblical poetry is a treasure-trove of religious symbols, magnificent or simple. Since the symbol provides material for thought (Ricœur), biblical symbols are the indispensable basis for theological reflexion.

I have attempted to conjure up the symbol and sing its praises, I have not given a definition. I do not think I am able to. I admit that in many cases it is difficult to decide whether an image is working as a symbol or as a simple comparison. Furthermore, by repetition and frequent use a metaphor or an image may be transformed into a symbol. The context in which it is found is usually of decisive importance.

The garden has a symbolic function where the love of a couple is concerned: he goes down to his garden, she is the princess of the gardens; he even courts her with the words: "You are a locked garden". At the other extreme, the desert landscape of Second Isaiah is a symbol of human desolation. This way of using the landscape, so familiar to us in poetry, narrative and cinema, is rare in the Old Testament. But we must not confuse landscape with cosmic elements, which can serve as symbols of the divine presence and action.

e) We can distinguish various types of symbols: archetypal, cultural, historical and literary.

Those which have their root in man's condition, spiritual and bodily, I call *archetypal*. Others call them proto-symbols to avoid seeing the archetype as a conceptual abstraction. We should not consider them to be innate, but they certainly do have some kind of natural matrix which makes them possible. The heavens and the earth, light and darkness, water and fire, home and road, the dream, the mountain ... It is not the objects themselves which are symbols, but our experience of them, which begins as soon as we are born and is deposited even in subliminal form. These examples, even though they may be realised in different forms, are translated easily in time and space. The presence and even abundance of such elemental symbols in the OT make biblical poetry both contemporary and accessible without special difficulty.

Cultural symbols are those which belong to one or more cultures, without being universal. The polarised relationship of man with the animals, wild and domesticated, is universal, because man finds himself surrounded by animals. But the particular relationship of the hunter or fisherman is a cultural realization of this. The juridical institution of the *gō'ēl* is used as a cultural symbol in the Bible.

Historical symbols are those which arise from a historical (or legendary) event, which comes to assume symbolic value for the people. The liberation from Egypt and the crossing of the Red Sea have such a value for Israel.

Literary symbols are those which arise from literature, from fiction, and assume symbolic value. (These days nobody confuses fiction with falsehood.) Cain could perhaps be included in this group.

In the final section one might also include those cosmic and human symbols which have undergone a certain elaboration in myths or stories of the origins (see the chapter on genre).

I am going to present just one example, which ought to be seen in a broader context of symbol. Let us imagine those two humble and serviceable domestic objects: the hand-mill and the oil-lamp. The stone hand-mill has two handles opposite each other which are turned by two women seated on either side, and it continues turning with a grinding noise when the women's hands are removed. The oil-lamp goes out when the wick has no more oil to burn. And now let us turn to a tragic situation: an invasion, a siege, fire, killing, a city and its houses dead. And the poet who sings:

> I will banish from them the voice of mirth and the voice of
>   gladness,
> the voice of the bridegroom and the voice of the bride,
> the grinding of the millstones and the light of the lamp
>   (Jer 25,10).

The mill which comes to a halt, the lamp which goes out, both symbolize the final catastrophe.

f) Should the prophets' *symbolic actions* be included in this chapter? Due to the adjective "symbolic" I would say they should; but the noun 'actions" would go against this. The actions are performed, and when the prophets narrate them they do so in prose. However, we should consider them here. These "pantomimes" are dramatic actions performed in silence before a curious and intrigued audience. They are then interpreted as oracles concerning the future. Here we find again the fundamental relationship of two corresponding panels: the action performed and the future event. The former will always have something of the image, though this will vary considerably.

When Ezekiel makes his bundle of his belongings, puts it on his shoulder and ostentatiously leaves his house, he is presenting the departure for exile before it happens. The correspondence is clear: he does what they will do; he does it like a scene from a mute play, they will do it in all reality (Ezek 12). The same kind of correspondence is there when his wife dies and he does not mourn, except that the correspondence here is partial. His compatriots too will not mourn because they will not be able to; however, it is the destruction of the temple and city which corresponds to the death of the wife (Ezek 24). The correspondence in a symbolic action of Jeremiah is very suggestive: Jeremiah buys an earthen jar, takes with him some reliable witnesses, goes to the Potsherd Gate and there smashes the jar on the ground. In this way God will smash the people and the city (Jer 19). The correspondence is not exact, but the image is very powerful.

The symbolic actions of the prophets do not belong to Hebrew poetry, but they do illustrate well the function of poetic images.

G. Fohrer, *Die symbolischen Handlungen der Propheten* (ATANT 54; Zurich–Stuttgart 1968).

g) The *parable* becomes an allegory with a narrative structure. An event which is articulated with various characters and in various stages is transformed into an image, articulated with corresponding characters and stages. Ezekiel is fond of parables, some of which are derived from traditional metaphors or symbols. The parable of "The eagle and the cedar" (Ezek 17,1-10) is typical; and if the listeners have difficulty in interpreting it, the prophet (or a disciple) adds the interpretation (vv. 11-15). Other examples are "The lioness and the cubs" (Ezek 19,1-9), "The uprooted vine" (Ezek 19,10-14), "The two sisters" (Ezek 23), "The pot on the fire" (Ezek 24,1-8), which has its explanation (vv. 9-14). Ezek 16, "A history of love", can be classified as a parable, with all its additions and expansions. It is based on the great symbol of God's marriage with Jerusalem, or the people of Israel.

When a parable presents a typical (not historical) aspect of human life and uses animals or plants as characters, it is usually called a fable. The classic example in the OT is Judg 9,8-15.

IV. Further Classification. Various Techniques

Let me return to the description of the image as the placing alongside of two panels, at least one of which is perceived by the senses. We leave the previous classifications to one side because the remarks which follow do not coincide with what went before. They can simply be superimposed without rigid rules.

a) I will begin with a rather complex case, which is however quite easy to explain and which will open the way to other instances. The poet stands at the *point of intersection* of the two panels and goes on developing the poem on both panels focusing in turn on one or the other. Some verses may apply to both panels, others apply to one panel. A clear example of this is Ps 23, which begins by comparing the relationship of man to his God with the image of a shepherd and his flock. Ambivalence and indecision produce a curious and allusive vibration in the poem. I will show this by writing some verses at the centre and others at either side:

> The Lord is my shepherd, I shall not want;
> he makes me lie down in green pastures,
> he leads me beside still waters,
>   he restores my strength
> He leads me in right paths,
>   for his name's sake.
> Even though I walk through the valley of the shadow of death,
>   I fear no evil, for thou art with me;
> thy rod and thy staff   they comfort me.

b) An image is given and an *explanation* follows. Often the explanation is not necessary and serves rather to complete the parallelism:

> I would hasten to shelter from the storm,
>   from the hurricane which devours, O Lord,
>   from the torrent of their tongues (Ps 55,9-10).

The mention of tongues clarifies the metaphorical value of the previous elements. This explanation was unnecessary since we already knew from the context and from tradition that the metaphors referred to the enemies.

> Do not deliver the life of thy dove to the wild beasts;
> do not forget the life of thy poor for ever (Ps 74,19).

We knew that the dove represented the oppressed, and we could identify the wild beasts already. However, the final mention of "your poor" intensifies the emotion of the prayer.

Similarly, we find academic proverbs where the second part, the explanation, is unnecessary. Read this example with and without the second part: "The king's heart is a stream of water in the hand of the Lord; he turns it wherever he will" (Prov 21,1). "He who tends a fig tree will eat its fruit, and he who guards his master will be honoured" (Prov 27,18).

c) *Development of the image.* Let us consider new and old friendships. It is just like new and old wine. Let us make these two things, friendships and wine, our two panels. If I do this I have two possibilities. I can develop the comparison at one level or the other. So there are two possibilities I can offer:

> A new friend, new wine: cultivate him and you will gain his affection.

or: A new friend, new wine: when it has aged you will drink it.

In perfect good taste Ben Sira chose the second solution (Sir 9,10).

As a father grows old, the sons he produced when young go out in his name. It is like what happens with the arrows of a hunter or warrior. Once again there are two possibilities:

> Arrows in the hand of a warrior are the sons of one's youth:
> Happy is the man who has many sons!

or: Arrows in the hand of a warrior are the sons of one's youth:
> Happy is the man who has his quiver full of them!

Ps 127,4-5 cleverly chooses the second solution. He offers a delightful surprise, he is less intellectual and less explicit.

d) *Grouping of images.* A series of homogeneous images may be used to develop one panel of imagery alone. We have already seen some examples of proverbs showing such features. This is frequent in the psalms. A good example is the series of metaphorical titles at the beginning of Ps 18 or 144: "Blessed be the Lord, my rock ... my ally, my fortress, my stronghold where I take refuge, my shield, my haven". Ps 133 offers two comparisons: like oil, like dew. We will return to this psalm.

On first reflexion fire and water seem opposites. But as elemental dangers they can represent the same grave risk. This is Ps 124,2-5:

> ... when men rose up against us,
> then they would have swallowed us up alive,
> when their anger was kindled against us;
> then the flood would have swept us away,
> the torrent would have gone over us;
> then over us would have gone
> the raging waters.

The fire consumes with great rapidity; the waters grow higher and higher. The same pair is found in Isa 43,2.

In the world of images, especially if they are symbols, we may even find that two elements which seem to exclude each other may be coupled together. Is the enemy who is tracking me down wild beast or hunter? Ps 57 has no hesitation in combining both images:

> I lie in the midst of lions that greedily devour the sons of men ... (v. 5).
> They set a net for my steps ... (v. 7).

More than a grouping of images we may at times find what we might call a *constellation*, various images or symbols in the same poem. A well-known example is Ps 23: the double image of the shepherd and the host brings forward a series of elemental symbols. Green pastures to rest in, water to restore strength, the path and the dwelling place, food and drink, darkness: all appear in the psalm.

The starting point for Joel 2,1-11 is a plague of locusts: millions of them darken the sky, they swarm down on the crops, they leave them bare. A horrifying and tragic picture, for man is quite unable to oppose this evil and destructive force: a swarm unable to be counted, an irresistible advance, ominous darkness, utter desolation. The advancing multitude is experienced as an army: infantry, cavalry, chariots; they advance, they assault and they plunder. Imagination superimposes images. The army is a plague of voracious insects, the locusts are of gigantic size, and organized in battalions. This is some kind of hallucination: locusts in the form of horses and soldiers. The desolation is experienced as a fire, for this mythical, elemental force needs only to pass by to change the garden into desolate desert, a dream of fruitfulness and vegetation into a chaotic, inhospitable land. The wings crackle like fire. The darkness deepens at the beginning with four adjectives, it is a cloud, a theophany, which both reveals and hides the presence of God. At the end even the sun, moon and stars darken. This plague which man suffers and can do nothing to impede has someone who controls it, like a general his army. The locust-army and the army of fire are in fact a theophany, the day of the Lord. The army is the Lord's and carried out his orders powerfully; it is a holy war. The fire may also be an allusion to the Five Cities, which were like a "garden of the Lord" (Gen 13,10) and were razed by fire (Gen 19).

e) *Diffusion* of an image. This happens when a central or dominant image reappears at different moments in a poem perhaps in new ways. This technique will come in the chapter entitled "Development and Composition", but I refer to it here for convenience.

In Ps 69 danger is presented in the image of waters. It appears at the beginning of the long poem, reappears just before the middle and resounds as a faint echo towards the end. The danger of the waters is threatening at the beginning, is on the point of conquering in the middle of the poem, but at the end they are dominated and recognize God. Let me quote the relevant verses:

> Ps 69,2 Save me, O God,
>   for the waters have risen up to my neck.
>   3 I sink in muddy depths and have no foothold;
>   I am swept into deep water,
>   and the flood carries me away.
>   15 Let no flood carry me away,
>   no abyss swallow me up,
>   no deep close over me.
>   35 Let sky and earth praise him,
>   the seas and all that move in them.

In the great lawsuit of Jer 2–3 the matrimonial image dominates: the people is the bride and young wife, the unfaithful woman, the easy lover, the repudiated wife; in a moment the noble matrimonial image descends to the contrasting level of instinctive animal rutting.

In Ps 62 man's stability and his destiny are seen first in the image of a well-built construction; and then in the contrasting images of weight and lightness.

f) *Total transposition*. This is similar to what preceded, but it differs in the sense that the whole poem is transformed. It is not that the image reappears in different points of the poem, but the whole poem is born out of the imaginative transposition of an experience or a situation.

The famous poem of the mountain in Isa 2,2-5 is a poetic, even a visionary, transformation of a pilgrimage of the nation to Jerusalem at a particular feast: from their various places the different tribes converge on Jerusalem in a spirit of reconciliation and go up to the temple. The scene is transformed: the mountain becomes the eschatological peak rising above the highest mountains; a universal pilgrimage of peoples and nations converge on Jerusalem in a spirit of peace and go to the temple of the Lord.

g) *Visions or inventions*. The poet attempts a description of something in the future, something unknown. He must describe it but he does not know what it will be like. He must proclaim it without precise details. This is when his creative imagination must come into play, combining and transforming known facts.

This is the technique for the prophetic eschatologies, which give way then to the apocalyptic genre. The problem in such cases is to discipline the imagination sufficiently so that a coherent and intelligible picture emerges. Isa 34 is short and achieves unity and coherence in the fantastic vision of a kind of final judgement. This is not the case with Isa 24–27, the unity of which is doubtful; great imaginative blocks follow each other leaving some space for pieces of different types. The imagination hits the mark only in certain sections of this eschatological composition. Too many diverse elements struggle for a place in the vision: the city and the countryside, the cosmos and the elements, heavenly bodies and kings, the royal banquet, the destruction of the dragon.

Chapter 34 of Isaiah describes a catastrophe and its devastating consequences. Perhaps "describes" is not the appropriate word and one ought to say rather "composes" or "creates". The structure of the first part is seen in the four-fold use of the particle *kî* to introduce: the anger of the Lord, the sword of the Lord, the slaughter of the Lord, and the day of vengeance of the Lord. These are not four things, but simply one. Anger is the sentence of condemnation, vengeance is the act of vindicating justice, the sword is the weapon, the slaughter is the execution of the sentence. Such a structure is logical, it presents no difficulties, nor does it baffle or excite the imagination. The poet presents a picture with these elements, using their imaginative value and combining them in a poetic logic and coherence. The slain human corpses are like a slaughter of animals: lambs and goats, rams, oxen, bulls and steers. Their blood reddens the land of Edom, inviting us to hear the assonance *dam – 'ĕdôm*: the sword is sated with blood, the land is soaked with blood, the mountains flow with blood (vv. 6.7.3). But this liquid neither contradicts nor quenches the fire of sulphur and pitch, like some new destruction of the Five Cities. A stench rises from the corpses, smoke from the sulphur and pitch, and this makes the land permanently uninhabitable (vv. 3.10.10b). Edom is seen in a cosmic setting, at the eschatological time. One might consider that the destruction of Edom is transcended in the poetic vision, or that an eschatological vision is being located in the emblematic land of Edom (as happens with Moab in Isa 25). The destruction involves not only mountains and "hills" (correcting v. 3b), but also the very heavens. For, just as men have their armies and retinues and hordes (v. 3), so also do the heavens have their "armies" (v. 4). The heavens, usually stretched like the canvas of a tent, "roll up like a scroll". Does this image suggest that the heavenly book of destiny becomes illegible for man? The stars, like leaves or fruit of a cosmic vine or fig-tree, wither and fall; a plant metaphor to indicate coming to an end, and on a cosmic scale. The sword, before it descends to glut itself on the earth, already "drinks its fill" in the heavens, as if the execution of the powers of the stars was beginning (compare Isa 24,21). Fire, scorching heat, desolation continue "day and night" without rest, "from generation to generation" without end.

What follows in the chapter is a parade of wild-beasts, unwelcome and even fantastic and diabolical, like *lîlît* (v. 14). These will be the new inhabitants of the wilderness of Edom.

I feel I ought to include here the visions of Zechariah. Some, like the flying scroll and, above all, the woman in the great pot carried by two women with wings like the wings of a stork, should certainly be mentioned. These visions are written in prose but deserve special mention in this chapter on imagery. They seem to me like remote ancestors of surrealism. It is of some significance how little influence these images of Zechariah have had in later tradition.

Let me first take Zech 5,1-4 as an example of a "surrealist" image. When an alliance or a covenant is made there are curses associated with in the event of one party not adhering to the agreement. The curse is unleashed against the one who has not been loyal. Curses can also be pronounced outside a pact and have no efficacy, for there are those whose "mouths are filled with cursing" (Ps 10,7). The curse of the covenant is said to settle on the guilty party to exact punishment (Deut 29,20). The curse may be written in the laws of the covenant or in the special book of the rite concerning jealousy (Num 5). In the second version of this rite the curse is written, the book is placed in the water so that the curse may be released and pass into the water, and this water is drunk by the woman suspected of adultery. It will damage her body if she is guilty. (Consult a commentary for the critical discussion of this passage.) From these three elements — the curse, the writing and the efficacy of the curse — the vision of Zechariah takes shape. A scroll comes flying through the sky; it is huge, ten metres by five, and is written on both sides in gigantic letters that the eye manages to read. One side is against those who steal, the other against those who swear falsely, who seem to live on unpunished. The scroll enters the house of the guilty man by the window, sits down there and begins to corrode both timber and stone.

The other vision follows in Zech 5,5-11. The personification of evil — a feminine noun — as a woman is not an unheard of device; but the transportation of this woman from one place to another is. This happens in an act of purification which may recall the ceremony of expiation (Lev 16) in which the goat is led by a man into the wilderness for Azazel. But this "surrealist" vision contains so many realistic features that the image is perceived as rather strange. For here personified evil is trapped in a great pot with a leaden cover so that she cannot escape. She is carried away by two women, angelic or diabolical, on wings like those of a stork, and deposited in the remote and hostile region of Shinar.

This is indeed a new way of dealing with images, which Ezekiel did not anticipate and Daniel did not choose to develop. As a technique it may have some influence on the author of the Apocalypse in the New Testament.

V. Images and Their Subjects

Remembering our model of the diptych, I might analyze and classify images in two columns. What kind of images are used? And what are the subjects transformed into images?

The first question has led to the compilation of *catalogues*. Catalogues of cosmic images, the elements, plants, animals, human beings and human culture. These lists are a useful resource, a kind of concordance of the imagination. But they do not really help because each image has to be analyzed according to its function in the context. They serve only as lists of material classified according to groups. The following works may be regarded as catalogues:

A. Werfer, *Die Poesie der Bibel* (Tübingen 1875).
A. Wünsche, *Die Bildersprache des Alten Testaments. Ein Beitrag zur aesthetischen Würdigung des poetischen Schrifttums im Alten Testament* (Leipzig 1906).
A. Heller, *200 biblische Symbole* (Stuttgart 1962).
M. Lurker, *Wörterbuch biblischer Bilder und Symbole* (Munich 1973).

This last is arranged in alphabetical order with various indices, of authors, themes and biblical citations.

The catalogues provide material for comparative studies. By cataloguing the images used in a book or by an author and studying them I may be able to reconstruct part of the world in which he lived, for example, the world mirrored in Proverbs.

If, on the other hand, instead of producing catalogues, I concentrate on a restricted field, I can produce useful comparative studies. If I focus, for example, on the rich field of the elements, water, or fire, or earth, I will be able to appreciate their persistence in the tradition, and changes in their use according to epochs, authors, books, or genres.

Though I would not place too much importance on the *field* from which the images are taken, I would make exception for two important cases: the Song of Songs and Ps 45. Sense images of taste, smell and touch are rare in biblical poetry. But in the Song of Songs they are frequent: perfumes, aromas, balsam, incense; "my nard gave forth its fragrance", "a bag of myrrh", "the vines are in blossom, they give forth fragrance", "the scent of Lebanon"; together with apples, figs, honey, wine, exquisite fruits, bunches of dates... In a book of love songs such phrases create an all-embracing atmosphere; it envelops the reader invisibly. Feelings have no profile or figure, said A. Brunner. It is an atmosphere of joys brought by the senses, the material accompaniment of an intensely personal love, a love of the person for the person, not purely sensual. All this is counterbalanced by the contemplative attitude of sight and hearing. We might recall the "five lines" of the classical and baroque cultures: see – hear – touch – kiss – come together; smell and taste would be in the third and fourth place. At the same time tastes and scents cannot be easily qualified, a detailed description cannot be made. The poet simply refers them to various delightful objects. In the midst of contemplation, which is the domain of the sense of sight, come allusions to scent and taste. Cant 7,3: "a heap of wheat, encircled with lilies"; 5,13: "his cheeks are like beds of spices, yielding fragrance".

In the wedding song, Ps 45, quite apart from the perfume of the anointing of the king, the robes of the new king "are all fragrant with myrrh, aloes and cassia". The prominence of the senses in narrative texts is also remarkable, even taste and smell as in Gen 27 (see L. Alonso Schökel, ¿Donde está tu hermano?, pp. 135f.).

Ps 133 sings of the delight of life lived in fraternal harmony. It is a joy difficult to describe, perhaps indescribable. It is a blessing which is all-embracing and penetrating, indescribable but sure. The author uses two images which fit together: aroma and freshness.

But let me now turn to something more usefully examined, the subjects transformed into images. This will allow me to bring together certain categories which seem disparate. I will focus on nature, man and God. It will be seen that everything is in some way referred to man.

a) Inanimate beings behave like men, they become human by means of the image: blood cries to the heavens (Gen 4,10); the heavens assist, bear witness, announce; mountains look on with envy (Ps 68,17). Ps 98,8: "Let the floods clap their hands; let the hills sing for joy together". Isa 55,12 concludes: "mountains and hills before you shall break forth into singing, and all the trees of the field shall clap their hands". In the descriptive section of Job this technique is used with skill and originality: the sea is born and grows up like a child; the morning carries out commands like shaking its clothing, giving form, and applying dye; the lightning presents itself and says "Here we are". In Isa 24,20: "The earth staggers like a drunken man". This comparison transforms the earthquake into some kind of living being. The land of desolation "will be married" (Isa 62,4), and "the land of the shades will give birth" (Isa 26,19): both of these examples are "animations" of mythical origin. Hos 2,23-24: just as in a human chain a command can be passed on or a reply can be made to a question or to an action, similarly the chain of fertility is welded together: "I will answer the heavens and they shall answer the earth; and the earth shall answer the grain, the wine and the oil, and they shall answer Jezreel". The earth must "keep silence" in the presence of God, its sovereign (Hab 2,20). Ps 48,12 mentions the gladness of Mount Sion. The mountains see the Lord and tremble (Hab 3,10); they jump like rams (Ps 114,4). The trees will know and understand (Ezek 17,24), they are envious of an exalted tree (Ezek 31,9): these texts present trees as an allegory of princes. Stones "cry out", as in Hab 2,11. The Psalmist calls on his musical instruments: "Awake, harp and lyre!" (Ps 57,9).

Many of the examples given show that the "animation" of inanimate beings is a particular instance of the metaphor or comparison, and may be of mythical origin.

We can therefore call this type of image an *animation*. Many scholars call it a personification, but I prefer to reserve this term for a technique which is very different.

b) *Personification*. I use this term for those cases where an abstract quality acts like a human being, like a person in society. This point of style has not yet been systematically studied in the Bible, in spite of its frequency and importance.

A clear example is Ps 85, which is almost a gathering of ladies on the poetic scene — the qualities personified tend to be denoted by feminine nouns. They meet, they kiss, they salute each other:

> His Salvation is at hand for those who fear him,
> His Glory will dwell in our land.
> Steadfast Love and Faithfulness will meet;
> Righteousness and Peace will kiss each other.
> Faithfulness will spring up from the ground,
> and Righteousness will look down from the sky...
> Righteousness will go before him,
> and make his footsteps a way (Ps 85,10-12.14).

The scene described in Isa 59,14-15 is quite the opposite: the noble ladies are barred from the city which is overrun by injustice:

> Justice is turned back,
> and Righteousness stands afar off;
> for Truth stumbles in the public squares,
> and Uprightness cannot enter.
> Truth is lacking.

These cases and many other similar ones help us to complete the picture given in Isa 35: a caravan of people returning from exile is crossing a desert which is being transformed into thickets and plantations by the abundance of water; the blind and the lame recover, wild beasts depart, the caravan turns into a procession:

> They will come to Sion with singing.
> Everlasting Happiness will be at their head;
> Joy and Happiness will follow;
> Sorrow and Affliction will depart (Isa 35,10).

Cf. L. Alonso Schökel – C. Carniti, "'In testa': Is 35,10", *RivBib* 34 (1986) 397-399.

The study of personification in biblical poetry brings with it the difficulties of perceiving and determining the presence of personification. Personification of qualities or events has become so commonplace in our modern languages that it has almost always been lexicalised and that hinders our perception of it in poetical texts. The poet has to go to great pains to bring alive our lost sense of imagination. As far as the Hebrew poets are concerned, we do have many clear cases and others that are less clear, but we do not have sure criteria for deciding whether the personification in question has not yet been lexicalised. However, since the danger for us is that of not seeing and not listening, it is better to exaggerate the number of personifications than to underestimate them. Let me propose some examples which should appear in any study which might be undertaken.

Ps 23,6: when the psalmist has finished his banquet and is about to depart he is offered a sure escort: "Your Goodness and Kindness follow me." Ps 43,3: the exile hopes that the Lord will send two messengers to announce the good news and to accompany him on the return to the temple: "Send out your Light and your Truth; let them lead me and bring me to your holy hill, to your dwelling!" Along the same lines is Ps 40,12: "Let your Kindness and your Faithfulness ever preserve me!" Probable personification are found in Ps 91,10 (without the article): "Evil shall not befall you, Scourge shall not come near your tent". Along the same lines the evil in Ps 40,13 may also be seen as a personification: "Evils have encompassed me without number, my iniquities have overtaken me". In Ps 22,13.17 the psalmist is hemmed in and surrounded by bulls and dogs. Disaster "looms from the north" in Jer 6,1. In Prov 13,21 "Misfortune pursues sinners"; and in Prov 17,13 "Evil will not depart from his house"; it is like a persistent and unwanted lodger. By contrast the noble dweller in Jerusalem was Justice (Isa 1,21).

In Gen 4,7 Sin (feminine) is crouching (masculine) at the door. In Isa 59,12 "our sins accuse us" like witnesses or prosecutors in a trial. The personification of cities, especially capital cities is very frequent in the feminine figures of young ladies (*bat*) or mothers (as will be seen in marriage symbolism). In Ps 19,3 one night passes information to the next. Job sees the wicked man threatened ceaselessly by hostile forces: "By day Terrors assault him, by night the Whirlwind carries him off". "Darkness" claims possession of a day of misfortune in Job 3,5.

In Isa 58,8 a welcome promise is made to the just and generous man: he will have an illustrious escort before him and behind him:

"Your Righteousness shall go before you, the Glory of the Lord shall be your rear guard". In the great restoration announced in Isa 32,15-17: "The wilderness will become a fruitful field, and the fruitful field will be deemed a forest; Justice will dwell in the wilderness, and Righteousness abide in the fruitful field; and the effect of Righteousness will be peace, and the result of Righteousness quietness and trust for ever". I conclude this catalogue with some verses taken from Ps 89: "Righteousness and Justice are the foundation of your throne, Steadfast Love and Faithfulness go before you. ... My Faithfulness and my Steadfast Love shall be with him" (vv. 15.25).

The biblical personification which has had most success is that of *ḥokmâ*, Lady Wisdom. She parades through the pages of Proverbs, Ecclesiasticus and Wisdom as a courted bride, a hospitable wife, a mother, a rich lady who invites people to a banquet, and as a heavenly character who collaborates in the creation and ordering of the world. She appears in Prov 3 and 9, and again in Sir 4, 6, 14 and 51; and she makes a final appearance in Wis 8. She also appears in two poems of extraordinary worth: Prov 8 and Sir 24. The reader can consult the volume *Proverbios*, pp. 33-35, 76-78, 238-243.

In this section on animation and personification we have to make room for a special group. The reign of death or *šeʾôl* "has enlarged its appetite and opened its mouth beyond measure" in order to devour both nobles and common people (Isa 5,14); or Sheol "is stirred up to meet you" (Isa 14,9); a pact is made with Sheol (Isa 28,15). Death too is personified: "Death enters by the windows" (Jer 9,20); "Death shall be their shepherd" (Ps 49,15); "Death and Perdition say" (Job 28,22); the plague is the "first-born of Death" (Job 18,13).

The sea too is personified: "Sea says: it is not with me" (Job 28,14). Sun and Moon too: "Moon will be confounded, Sun ashamed" (Isa 24,23). We have already seen Sun coming out like a bridegroom (Ps 19,6), the stars come down to fight (Judg 5,20); and we have already heard "the singing of the morning stars" (Job 38,7).

From our point of view these and other examples are to be regarded as animation or personification: inanimate beings are transformed poetically into living or personal beings. In the biblical tradition the movement is different: mythological beings are dethroned and reduced to poetical figures. This is an act of demythologization, which may have a polemical tone: as when the king of Babylon is presented in the figure of Venus, the light of dawn. The star which shines low over the horizon has ambitions to rise to the highest point, the height of the divine heavens; but it is brought down and drowned in the abyss (Isa 14,12-15).

c) *Man*. Since the examples here are so numerous I am going to select a few of the more significant ones.

The *elements* must be mentioned first: water, earth, air, fire. Man is made of earth, he returns to the dust; the air is breath, life; fire is anger and similar passions; water brings fertility. Many of these uses may be premetaphors. The poetic identification of life with the light is frequent, and this has its opposite in the underground of the tomb.

Some scholars interpret as an image of fertility the verses of Balaam in Num 24,7: "Water shall flow from his buckets, and his seed shall be in many waters". The advice given in Prov 5,18.16 corresponds to this: "Let your fountain be blessed, and rejoice in the wife of your youth. ... Should your springs be scattered abroad, streams of water in the streets?" The loved one is a "sealed fountain" in the Song of Songs. In Job 4,19-20 Eliphaz speaks of the earthly condition of man: "They dwell in houses of clay, which are founded in the dust ... between morning and evening they are destroyed".

I have already spoken of plant images used for man. These usually refer to his vitality, or lack of it. The correspondence between plant fertility and human fertility is especially stressed. In some cases this might be viewed as a vestige of mythical representations. In many cases we must proceed in the opposite direction: the symbol is more original than the myth; the symbol appeared and gave rise to the myth. In other words, the biblical text and the foreign myth arise from the same symbolic matrix.

The tree may be reduced to a comparison, as in Ps 37,35: "I have seen a wicked man overbearing, and towering like a cedar of Lebanon". In another instance there is a development:

> The righteous flourish like the palm tree,
> and grow like a cedar in Lebanon.
> They are planted in the house of the Lord,
> they flourish in the courts of our God.
> They still bring forth fruit in old age,
> they are ever full of sap and green (Ps 92,13-15).

Another case, and we find an accumulation of images:

> I will be as the dew to Israel;
> he shall blossom as the lily,
> he shall strike out roots as the poplar;
> his shoots shall spread out;
> his beauty shall be like the olive,

and his fragrance like Lebanon.
They shall return and dwell beneath my shadow,
they shall grow like grain;
they shall blossom as the vine,
their fragrance shall be like the wine of Lebanon...
I am like an evergreen cypress (Hos 14,6-9).

Cf. *Profetas*, p. 920.

The image of a tree is the unifying theme developed in Ezek 31. And seven kinds of trees are found as symbols of the landscape of paradise in Isa 41,19.

What was said earlier, that the function of the image in the poem is as important as the field from which it comes, has been clearly demonstrated.

Man can also be seen as an *animal*. One might say that the biblical poets have a preference for animals when they wish to describe the character of certain types of men, especially when they are speaking of negative characteristics. It is as if the animal image were used to bring out the lower instincts of man, something animal-like in his humanity. This presupposes the superior dignity of man and his calling to subdue the animals.

The most frequent are wild animals, used to describe the hostility of enemies. This is a major topic in the Psalms; Ps 22 takes pleasure in accumulating such images:

Many bulls encompass me,
strong bulls of Bashan surround me;
they open wide their mouths at me,
like a ravening and roaring lion.
Dogs are round about me;
a company of evildoers encircle me (Ps 22,13-14.17).

Leaders of certain foreign countries used to take the names of animals as their proper name or the name of their office. One Ammonite king was called *nāḥāš* = "Serpent"; there were Midianite leaders called Raven and Wolf; another group of officials are called the Bulls. Ezekiel seems to have used such titles in composing his great speeches on the nations, their kings and emperors. Egypt is compared to a crocodile, Ezek 32,1-6; and again in 29,3-5; in 19,1-9 Israel is a lioness with her cubs.

In Isa 11,6-9 peace between domesticated and wild animals becomes a symbol of universal peace. Job 40–41 gives a full description of two wild animals, Leviathan and Behemoth — the crocodile and the hippopotamus, both images of evil forces.

Here are some images of man as an animal taken from the book of Proverbs:

> All at once he follows her,
> as an ox goes to the slaughter,
> or as a stag is caught fast (7,22).

> Like a dog that returns to his vomit
> is a fool that repeats his folly (26,11).

> The dread wrath of a king is like the growling of a lion
>   (20,2).

> The righteous are bold as a lion (28,1).

> Like a bird that strays from its nest
> is a man who strays from his home (27,8).

> The leech has two daughters;
> "Give, give", they cry (30,15).

d) *God*. Biblical poetry is basically religious poetry. It speaks of God through the human experience of God. It sets forth revelation in human form. Its theme is transcendent; its means of expression are human.

In the broad sense everything we say about God is anthropomorphism, for it humanizes God. We experience God in our image and likeness, justified in so doing by the first chapter of the book of Genesis which states that we are made in the image and likeness of God. However, it is possible to make more precise distinctions: we can speak of God in metaphysical terms and in imagery. Alongside the *analogia entis*, we have the analogy of the symbol. And then we can make the distinction of spiritual and abstract qualities, and images perceived by the senses. It is difficult to trace the boundaries of anthropomorphism: roughly speaking it means attributing to God human qualities. Some scholars make another distinction: anthropomorphism gives God a human form: a nose, eyes, arms; while anthropopathism gives God human feelings: anger, pity, repentance.

Let me begin an analysis of some verses from Ps 36:

> Your steadfast love, O Lord, extends to the heavens,
> your faithfulness to the clouds.
> Your righteousness is like the mountains of God,
> your judgements are like the great deep;
> man and beast you save, O Lord.

How precious is your steadfast love, O God!
The children of men take refuge in the shadow of your
    wings.
They feast on the abundance of your house,
and you give them drink from the river of your delights.
For with you is the fountain of life;
in your light do we see light (Ps 36,6-10).

Various qualities known through human experience are
attributed to God: faithfulness, steadfast love, righteousness, just
judgements. God is also said to come to the aid of man and
animals; this too comes from human experience. the poet is
unaware that such statements are analogical, he has no
metaphysical intentions, and we are not usually aware that these
statements are images. Nevertheless, the writer feels that there is
a difference in intensity, as in spiritual qualities. "The dimension
of the spirit is intensity" (Bruno Snell). This intensity is expressed
in a spatial image, which qualifies the simple statement of the
quality: "extends to the heavens, to the clouds, like the
mountains of God, like the great deep". The distinction between
man and the animals begins based on the experience of going to
the temple: a place of refuge, an abundant sacrificial banquet,
with delightful drink. The physical experience is sacramental, a
symbol of the experience of the divine: the temple is "the shadow
of the wings" of God, the feast is offered by God the host at the
banquet, the drink is "from the river of your delights". Note how
the symbolic vision takes off at this point: the small cup that is
drunk becomes a river, not of wine, but of delights, and it is
"yours". At this height of symbolism the two final images of
abundance come: not simply a little water for bodily thirst, but
the fountain of life; and "your light" which gives sight to see the
light, and discover the superior light.

The Hebrew poet attributes human qualities to God, and
human actions, without much of a problem. We also do not really
have a problem with such language, for it is only when we begin to
speak of metaphysics that we apply the fundamental idea of
analogy. Such discourses are quite different from poetic imagery
and can be left to one side here.

Nevertheless, the Hebrew poet also felt that God was
incomprehensible, unattainable, inexhaustible: the source from
which all water flows, the light from which all light comes. One of
the qualities of his God was to be unattainable and undescribable.
This can be stated with or without imagery:

> Such knowledge is beyond my understanding,
>   so high that I cannot reach it ...
> How deep I find your thoughts, O God,
>   how inexhaustible their themes!
> Can I count them? They outnumber the grains of sand;
>   to finish the count, my years must equal thine
>   (Ps 139,6.17.18).

Here we have both affirmation and negation: "beyond my understanding", "high", "I cannot reach it", "deep", "inexhaustible", "outnumber".

> I have not learned wisdom,
> nor have I knowledge of the Holy One.
> Who has ascended to heaven and come down? (Prov 30,3-4).

> He is from eternity to eternity;
> nothing can be added, nothing taken away,
> and he needs no one to give him advice.
> How beautiful is all that he has made,
> down to the smallest spark that can be seen! (Sir 42,21-22).

> However much we say, we cannot exhaust our theme;
> to put it in a word: he is all,
> Where can we find the skill to sing his praises?
> For he is greater than all his works ...
> Summon all your strength to declare his greatness,
> and be untiring, for the most you can do will fall short
>   (Sir 43,27.28.30).

> Lo, these are but the outskirts of his ways;
> and how small a whisper do we hear of him!
> But the thunder of his power who can understand?
>   (Job 26,14; cf. 36,26; 37,5.23).

A later author like Ben Sira (towards 180 B.C.) also uses negatives to affirm the positive, the super-abundance: where shall we find strength, he is greater, he will surpass, you cannot praise him enough. However, he does not use symbolic language.

One of the ways of saying what cannot be said is to use negatives. Often this includes a comparative reference to man and his tasks. The narrator of the book of Kings places on the lips of Solomon the following reflexion precisely when the temple is being consecrated; it is in fact a theological declaration:

But will God indeed dwell on the earth?
Behold, heaven and the highest heaven cannot contain you;
how much less this house which I have built! (1 Kgs 8,27).

God cannot be "contained" either in the temple or in the heavens. This is a spatial concept, used symbolically to express the transcendence of God; and we can understand it as being in opposition to the contemporary idea of heaven as the dwelling place of God ("dwelling place" too is a symbol).

When the exiles complained that God had abandoned them and no longer cared for them, the prophet replied with negatives and comparisons:

He does not faint or grow weary,
his understanding is unsearchable.
He gives power to the faint, ... (Isa 40,28-29).

Work is another image when used of God. The poet affirms that God works, but denies that he grows tired. This is probably a reference to the week's task and rest in Gen 1.

Years, a human temporal category, are applied symbolically to God, with affirmation and negation: Ps 102,28: "your years have no end"; Mal 3,6: "I the Lord do not change".

Alongside these negations the poet also uses the symbol in speaking of God. He uses it not because it is vague and imprecise — it is as if we take concepts and terms as the point of reference or the ideal — but because it is undefined and open.

The *polar-nature* of many symbols is exploited within a certain poem or in the cultural context of different books. God is "a hidden God" (Isa 45,15), "the Lord set the sun in the heavens, but prefers to dwell in thick darkness" (1 Kgs 8,12-13). On the other hand, God is light and shows himself. He shows himself, hiding himself, in the cloud — a frequent symbol.

God does not sleep, "he who keeps you will not slumber", says Ps 121,4. But Ps 44,24 tries to wake up the sleeping God: "Rouse yourself! Why are you sleeping, O Lord?" The same is said in Ps 59,5: "Rouse yourself, come to my help!"; and Ps 78,65 uses a rather daring comparison:

Then the Lord awoke as from sleep,
like a soldier shouting because of wine.

"God is not man, that he should lie, or a son of man, that he should repent" (Num 23,19). Nevertheless, God repented of having made man (Gen 6,6); of having made Saul king (1 Sam 15,11), but he would not repent of having removed him (v. 29). He repents of the threat pronounced against his people (Exod 32,12.14; 2 Sam 24,16b). "I have spoken, I have purposed; I have not relented nor will I turn back" (Jer 4,28). But he does repent if man changes his behaviour (Jer 18,8.10). And the theme could be further developed with other examples.

In Isa 8,14 the polarity is in the change of attitude, and is expressed through the polarity of an image. The Rock is an unassailable place of refuge, a guarantee of security; the stone offers a firm foundation. But God will be "a stone of offence and a rock of stumbling".

This immense God, the synthesis of polarities, is experienced by man positively and negatively, by opposing contrasting qualities. The theme of polarity was first encountered in the chapter on antithesis and will return when I present some concrete symbols.

And so, the hidden God *reveals himself*, but this revelation is expressed in symbols. The Hebrew poet does not proceed with the help of logical reasoning to reach God, but he discovers him in symbolic manifestations. In other words, the poet is very open to what has been called the "symbolic structure of creation", found in nature and in history.

In nature, which becomes translucent, the presence of God is perceived in a kind of overflowing meaning. This does nothing to undervalue God's being and beauty. On the contrary, the urge to praise his God drives the Hebrew poet to describe and sing about nature. We might call it a theophany in the broad sense. In these poems we find the qualities of descriptive poetry to present the reality of creation, and the value of the symbol which goes beyond the empirical reality. The storm is one of the classic theophanies, but not the only one.

The following texts are well known: Pss 18; 29; 77; 104; Hab 3; Job 38–39; Sir 43. Since I must quote from at least one example of this poetry, which is so prominent in biblical literature, I will quote from a less well-known example, even though it is not the best. It is from the speech of Elihu, inserted into the book of Job:

> Hearken to the thunder of his voice
> and the rumbling that comes from his mouth.
> Under the whole heaven he lets it go,
> and his lightning to the corners of the earth.
>
> For to the snow he says, 'Fall on the earth';
> and to the shower and the rain, 'Be strong'.

From its chamber comes the whirlwind,
and cold from the scattered winds.
By the breath of God ice is given,
and the broad waters are frozen fast.
He loads the thick cloud with moisture;
the clouds scatter his lightning.
They turn round and round by his guidance,
to accomplish all that he commands them
on the face of the habitable world.

Do you know how God lays his command upon them,
and causes the lightning of his cloud to shine?
Do you know the balancings of the clouds,
the wondrous works of him who is perfect in knowledge,
you whose garments are hot
when the earth is still because of the south wind?
Can you, like him, spread out the skies,
hard as a molten mirror?

And now men cannot look on the light
when it is bright in the skies,
when the wind has passed and cleared them.
Out of the north comes golden splendour;
God is clothed with terrible majesty.
The Almighty — we cannot find him;
he is great in power and justice,
and abundant righteousness he will not violate.
Therefore men fear him;
he does not regard any who are wise in their own conceit
(Job 37,2-3.6.9-12.15-18.21-24).

See also the theophany of judgement in Isa 30,27-30; and other shorter ones, like that in Mic 1,3-4.

A. Causse, "Sentiment de la nature et symbolisme chez les lyriques hébreux", *RHPhilRel* 1 (1921) 387-408.
H. Fisch, "The Analogy of Nature, a Note on the structure of the Old Testament Imagery", *JTS* 6 (1955) 161-173.

History too is a theophany of divine action in the OT, and in this sense it too has symbolic value. Within this history some events are more important than others, like the departure from Egypt with the crossing of the Red Sea. Poets have abundantly exploited this in the Psalms and prophetic oracles.

I have already cited Ps 77. The instances where the crossing is transformed poetically into the struggle of God with chaos or the primordial dragon are quite remarkable (see what was said earlier about motifs).

God may sometimes complain of the people's blindness to the sense of their history:

> But you did not look to him who did it,
> or have regard for him who planned it long ago (Isa 22,11).

> You saw many things without observing,
> your ears were open, but you did not hear (Isa 42,20).

Just as creation is bringing something from non-being into existence, similarly in history what did not exist begins to be; and God is its creator. It does not suddenly appear, but progresses gradually, and one has to concentrate to realise it is the action of God. The poet uses an image to express this: "Behold, I am doing a new thing; now it springs forth, do you not perceive it?" (Isa 43,19).

In this section what interests us is the history of Israel in its symbolic value, as interpreted by the poets. The figure of Cyrus and the anonymous Servant are relevant here; and, on the other hand, aggressive empires, vanquished by the Lord of history.

We might examine also other particular manifestations of God, for example: the temple and the capital city:

> Walk about Sion, go round about her,
> number her towers,
> consider well her ramparts,
> go through her citadels;
> that you may tell the next generation
> that this is God,
> our God for ever and ever,
> He will be our guide for ever (Ps 48,13-15).

The face of a reconciled brother might also be a theophany: "like seeing the face of God", in the prose narrative of Gen 33,10 (¿-Dónde está tu hermano?, pp. 214-215).

And so we have manifestation with hiddenness, a veiled revelation, both ambiguous and ambivalent. Man must open himself to it, he can also reject it. It is what S. Terrien calls "the elusive presence" (The Elusive Presence: Toward a New Biblical Theology [RPS 26; San Francisco 1978]).

For this reason the manifestation of God will be qualified in some way. One could apply to many texts what is stated in Isa 28,21:

> For the Lord will rise up as on Mount Perazim,
> he will be wroth as in the valley of Gibeon;
> to do his deed — strange is his deed!
> and to work his work — alien is his work!

In one case the strangeness is disconcerting:

> I will again do marvellous things with this people,
>   wonderful and marvellous;
> and the wisdom of their wise men shall perish (Isa 29,14).

In another case the strangeness will be the great sign of revelation: "Kings shall shut their mouths because of him; for that which has been told them they shall see; and that which they have not heard they shall understand" (Isa 52,15).

I will now go through some of the more common symbols used for God. Let me begin with *anthropomorphism* in general. The poet imagines God in human form, with eyes and ears, arms and hands, and the corresponding activities: "He who planted the ear, does he not hear? He who formed the eye, does he not see?" (Ps 94,9). Ezekiel goes to great pains to make clear that this is a figure, only a vision: "a likeness as it were of a human form. And upward from what had the appearance of his loins... and downward from what had the appearance of his loins. ... Such was the appearance of the likeness of the glory of the Lord" (Ezek 1,26-28). These human comparisons can become monstrous: "Smoke went up from his nostrils, and devouring fire from his mouth" (Ps 18,9). Is this a human figure or an imagery dragon?

Anthropomorphism may seem quite harmless, because we are used to it. On occasion due to its originality or strangeness it may provoke the reader to reject it and then accept it on a higher level. By surprise and strangeness what cannot be expressed is put into words. The reader must make the mental adjustment. But on occasion the poet himself does this.

One way is by attributing to the human figure or activity superhuman dimensions:

> He who moves mountains without knowing it
> when he overturns them in his anger (Job 9,5).

> By your strength you have established the mountains,
> being girded with might (Ps 65,7).

> As wax melts before fire,
> let the wicked perish before God (Ps 68,3).

> At your rebuke, O God of Jacob,
> both rider and horse lay stunned (Ps 76,7).

Superhuman dimensions reappear in some of the following anthropomorphic symbols too.

There are two or three from the sphere of family life: God as father, and mother also, and God as spouse. The paternal image is less frequent than the conjugal image, but it is expressed with great intensity. The classic texts are these:

> It was I who taught Ephraim to walk,
> I took them up in my arms;

> How can I give you up, O Ephraim!
> How can I hand you over, O Israel! ...
> My heart recoils within me,
> my compassion grows warm and tender (Hos 11,3.8).

> Is Ephraim my dear son?
> Is he my darling child?
> For as often as I speak against him,
> I do remember him still.
> Therefore my heart yearns for him;
> I will surely have mercy on him (Jer 31,20).

> As a father pities his children,
> so the Lord pities those who fear him.
> For he knows our frame;
> he remembers that we are dust (Ps 103,13-14).

The conjugal symbol is more frequent in the prophets; as frequent or more so than the symbol of political alliance. I do not think it is right to consider this conjugal symbolism as a secondary expression of the covenant. I believe it is autonomous. The principal texts are: Hos 2; Isa 1,21-26; Ezek 16; 23; Isa 49; 51–52; 54; 62; 66; Bar 4–5. They alone form a fine poetic anthology. We ought to read the whole of the poems so I will quote only two verses:

> For, as a young man weds a maiden,
> so you shall wed him who rebuilds you,
> and as the bridegroom rejoices over the bride,
> so shall your God rejoice over you (Isa 62,5).

The bride is usually the personified capital city, representing the community.

Let me now list some offices and occupations used symbolically of God.

King. In the vocation of Isaiah, chapter 6. Certain Psalms, especially 93; 96–99; 47. In the eschatology of Isa 24–27 God is a king who inaugurates a new reign and offers a universal banquet.

Sovereign. This is implicit in the symbol of the covenant. The suzerain dictates terms for the vassal king. This is not found frequently in poetry.

Warrior. It may be found in a short reference, or it may fill a whole poem. In Ps 18 God struggles with the arms of the storm; Exod 15 sings of the military victory of the Lord: "The Lord is a warrior" (v. 3); he is defiant and incites battle in Ezek 39; Hab 3 displays great imagination. Ps 35 can even request of God:

> Take hold of shield and buckler,
> and rise for my help!
> Draw the spear and javelin
> against my pursuers! (Ps 35,2-3).

Craftsman. This is implicit in many poems of creation, when God's skill is mentioned. Gen 1 mixes the image of the Lord who gives commands which are carried out with that of the craftsman who performs the task. Ps 8 speaks of "the work of your fingers" (v. 4). The Hebrew verb *yṣr* = "to form", which is applied to God, comes from the world of crafts and skills. Prov 8 and Job 38 are two other good examples.

Judge or someone taking part in a trial. This can be linked with the symbols of King or Sovereign. The king judges his subjects, which are all the kingdoms and empires. The sovereign accuses his vassal who has been unfaithful to the covenant. This can be explicit or implicit in penitential liturgies (Ps 50–51); and in many prophetic accusations against the people. "The Lord judges the peoples" (Ps 7,9).

Avenger. The Lord is the *gō'ēl* who, in solidarity, ransoms his people from slavery. The son, though born free, must be redeemed. This symbol recurs in Second Isaiah.

Shepherd. The classic text is of course Ps 23. See also Ezek 34, and the title in Ps 80,2.

Farmer. God is portrayed as farmer in the second part of Ps 65; he plants and cares for his vine, which is Israel, in Ps 80.

Animals. Finding God compared to an animal, especially if it is a wild one, perhaps seems more strange to us. He is a protecting eagle (Deut 32,11); a lion and a bird (Isa 31,4f.); a bear (Hos 13,8); a moth (Ps 39,12).

W. Pangritz, *Das Tier in der Bibel* (Basel–Munich 1963).

The elements. I have already mentioned *light*, symbol of the divinity in many cultures. The light may come from the "radiant" face of God: Pss 31,17; 67,2, etc.

Fire too is an element of divinity, a symbol, or an accompanying element. It is inaccessible, can purify or destroy:

> Who among us can dwell with the devouring fire?
> Who among us can dwell with everlasting burnings?
> (Isa 33,14).

> Behold, the name of the Lord comes from far,
> burning with his anger, and in thick rising smoke;
> his lips are full of indignation,
> and his tongue is like a devouring fire;

> For a burning place has long been prepared;
> yea, for the king it is made ready,
> its pyre made deep and wide,
> with fire and wood in abundance;
> the breath of the Lord, like a stream of brimstone, kindles
>   it (Isa 30,27.33).

Water too is a frequent symbol of the divinity. We have seen this already in Ps 36. It appears ambivalently in Ps 42: God is the water which quenches thirst and gives life, and the water which brings sweeping floods.

P. Reymond, *L'eau, sa vie et sa signification dans l'Ancien Testament* (VTS 6; Leiden 1958).

Many of these symbols have been studied in monographs, which usually focus on the doctrinal aspect and neglect or presuppose poetic analysis.

e) *Experience*. When man perceives the presence or action of God intellectually or spiritually, the poets do not seem to use images. However, when the poet uses the senses to express an experience of God, he uses them as symbols of another kind of experience, a transcendent experience, which cannot be described adequately. Using the senses the poet communicates the immediate, concrete character of the spiritual experience and the aspect of calm prolongation. The most frequently used sense is that of hearing: when the object is the word of God it seems to be used in a proper sense. But here too we must be aware of the analogy, for what the individual hears is a prophetic oracle, words of man, or images in his imagination. The sense of sight, with God as the object, is both used and denied in the OT; this ambiguity allows us to appreciate the analogical value of this idea. Man sees God, but it is a type of seeing which might be better described as not seeing. Less frequently we find the sense of taste, smell and touch. For this reason the instances where these senses appear are of some significance.

In Christian tradition the symbolic use of the senses as the expression of a transcendent experience, or perhaps as the initiation to this, has been prominent above all due to the influence of Bonaventure and Ignatius of Loyola in his *Spiritual Exercises*, where this is referred to as "application of the senses". The starting point is found in the OT, as the following examples show:

> Look to him and be radiant. ...
> Taste and see that the Lord is good ... (Ps 34,6.9).

The first verse may allude to the brightness on the face of Moses when he was exposed to the splendour of the Glory of God (Exod 34,29-35); that unique experience is offered by the psalmist to all people. The second verse refers to the sense of taste: taste how sweet and pleasing to the taste is the Lord. The sense of touch is referred to less explicitly; especially if the verb *dbq* = "to stick to" is already lexicalised to mean support for a cause or a person. Other uses, even in the Psalms, show its material sense. In conclusion we can read some verses of Ps 63, where this symbolism of the senses is proposed again, or suggested:

> My throat thirsts for you. ...
> So I have looked upon you in the sanctuary,
> beholding your power and glory. ...
> I am feasted as with marrow and fat. ...
> My being clings to you,
> your right hand upholds me (Ps 63,2-3.6-9).

God "holds man by the right hand" in Ps 73,23 (*'ḥz*); Isa 41,13; 42,6; 45,1 (*ḥzq*).

VI. The Analysis of Symbols

When they have not been reduced to pure concept, despoiled of their imaginative quality, biblical symbols have been analyzed in different ways. And what we say here of symbols is valid also for imagery in general.

The interpretation based on *comparative religions* has been one of the most frequent approaches, especially where myths are concerned. Even biblical prayer has been compared to that in other religions. Since archetypal symbols are of necessity universal and since all people share many common experiences, it is not strange that other similar images in other nations correspond to the biblical images. The study of these corresponding images can be mutually illuminating and could be useful also in what is called these days inculturation.

The *psychoanalytical interpretation* runs the well-known risk of exaggerating sexual significance. See the studies edited by Yorick Spiegel, *Psychoanalitische Interpretationen biblischer Texte* (Munich 1972). Jung's approach is less limited, but has not had supporters in the biblical world.

G. Cope, *Symbolism in the Bible and the Church* (London 1959).
M. Kassel, *Biblische Urbilder. Tiefenpsychologische Auslegung nach C. G. Jung* (Munich 1982²).
E. Drewermann, *Tiefenpsychologie und Exegese.* I. *Die Wahrheit der Formen.* (Olten–Frankfurt 1985).

If we concentrate on the Bible itself *comparative* analysis is very useful, if possible diachronic, following the development of an image. This is very difficult since we know too little about the dating of the texts of the OT. Synchronic comparison is possible. It has in its favour the fact that the world of images and symbols is less dated than other aspects; it can be separated more easily from the original context. The kingdom of the imagination is less "historical", symbols are open and expansive. The persistence of conjugal symbolism through eight centuries, from Hosea to the book of Wisdom, is one fine example.

One very useful area would be the study of symbols in their post-biblical life, and practically nothing has been produced so far on this aspect. It would be an interesting chapter of the history of interpretation. The symbolic reading of the OT has dominated Christian exegesis right up to the 17th century.

Of fundamental importance is the analysis of images and symbols *within the work* to which they belong. One might say that this is the most important point of all. But in practice the better procedure is an alternating or circular movement, going back and forth from the study of the text to a comparative analysis.

What is always essential, as I said at the very beginning, is to use one's imagination as the natural way to consider poetry. It is not right to say that understanding is objective and imagination is subjective. Both understanding and imagination are operations of the subject who contemplates or analyzes. The important thing is to use the faculty which is right for the object. I could confirm this point with some practical examples; but this chapter has already gone on long enough.

Bibliography

L. Alonso Schökel, *Estudios de poética hebrea*, pp. 269-307.

W. G. E. Watson, *Classical Hebrew Poetry*, pp. 251-272.

D. Buzy, *Les Symboles de l'Ancien Testament* (Paris 1923).

S. J. Brown, *Images and Truth: Studies in the Imagery of the Bible* (Rome 1955).

A. Brunner, *Die Religion. Eine philosophische Untersuchung auf geschichtlicher Grundlage* (Freiburg 1956). The chapter entitled "Gestalt, Bild und Archetypen" (pp. 154-170) is particularly important.

J. Hempel, *Das Bild in Bibel und Gottesdienst* (SGV 212; Tübingen 1957).

W. Stählin, "Das Bild der Natur in der Heiligen Schrift", in W. Stählin, *Symbolon. Vom gleichnishaften Denken* (edited by A. Köberle; Stuttgart 1958), pp. 127-134. Even though this essay focuses more on the New Testament, the exposition of general principles is important.

E. Biser, *Theologische Sprachtheorie und Hermeneutik* (Munich 1970).

O. Keel, *The Symbolism of the Biblical World. Ancient Near Eastern Iconography and the Book of Psalms*. Translated by T. J. Hallett (New York 1978). Interesting as a comparative study of cultures, and of literature and sculpture. In later works Keel continued this type of study: on Job and the Song of Songs.

R. Lack, *La Symbolique du Livre d'Isaïe. Essai sur l'Image littéraire comme élément de structuration* (AnBib 59; Rome 1973). Even though this considers one biblical book, the author offers much material of general value and a good annotated bibliography.

G. B. Caird. *The Language and Imagery of the Bible*.

K. H. Schelkle, "Auslegung als Symbolverständnis", *TQ* 132 (1952) 129-151.

H. de Lubac, *Exégèse médiévale. Les quatre sens de l'Écriture* (Theol[P] 41: I/1 and I/2 [1959]; Theol[P] 42: II/1 [1961]; Theol[P] 59: II/1 [1964]. Fundamental for the history of interpretation.

Many other articles consider a particular image, a particular book or passage.

CHAPTER IX

Figures of Speech

I. Introduction

I want now to give a brief presentation of other points of style which for the sake of convenience I will call "figures of speech", following the classic denomination, even though not all the points considered belong to this category. I am not going to consider them all, far from it, so as not to present a stylistics so complex as to resemble botanical classifications.

The work is both simplified and complicated by the fact that these days we have three works of consultation, three classified collections of tropes and figures of speech with quotations from the Old Testament or from the whole Bible. These works are, in chronological order:

E. W. Bullinger, *Figures of Speech Used in the Bible.*

E. König, *Stilistik, Rhetorik, Poetik in Bezug auf die biblische Litteratur.*

W. Bühlmann – K. Scherer, *Stilfiguren der Bibel. Ein kleines Nachschlagewerk.*

The first is a volume of 1104 pages, organised in 210 categories or "figures", with abundant subdivisions. The presentation is excellent, planned for the convenient use of the reader. It includes the whole Bible, Old and New Testaments, both prose and poetry.

The second volume contains 421 pages, with highly condensed data. The presentation is designed to use every space available in the book, so that the reader will waste a certain amount of time finding his way round. There is a great desire to systematize the categories and references to Greek and Latin classical works abound.

The third is a manual of 113 pages. There are more than two-hundred categories, short and clear definitions and selected examples.

The great mass of data given in the first two works and the very careful differentiation of categories at first sight would seem to help whoever consults these works. But these works hinder the reader for another reason: the authors do not distinguish sufficiently what is stylistic and what is simply grammatical. Many of the examples given are simply illustrations of Hebrew grammatical usage. Furthermore, these authors do not give sufficient attention to the phenomenon of lexicalization (which we encountered in metaphors): what in the past may have been a point of style has become simply normal usage. So anyone who is interested in poetic or stylistic analysis must first check each example.

Finally, it is rather curious that in this kind of study we are going back in a rather more refined way to the first attempts of the Fathers to demonstrate the literary worth of the Bible.

I am going to select certain techniques which from experience seem the most interesting or most useful for an appreciation of Hebrew biblical poetry.

II. Citations, Allusions, Reminiscences

The *citation* repeats a sentence spoken by another author, giving or remaining silent about the source; in biblical poetry the source is not usually given. The *allusion* points from a distance to a known fact, a shared tradition, a well-known text; the allusion makes these things present in a discrete kind of way. More so than with the citation, the allusion needs the intelligent collaboration of the reader; sometimes it can be a showing off of culture, on other occasions a challenge to the sharpness of the reader. *Reminiscences* can be unconscious, brought about by association.

Reminiscences and allusions are more probable at the end of a period of development, when a tradition has been built up. The dividing lines between the three categories are not rigid. Let me begin by commenting on a late Psalm, which illustrates these techniques and perhaps thereby is rather poor in inspiration, Ps 144:

Ps 144,1:   He trains my hands for war,
            and my fingers for battle.

            He trains my hands for war (Ps 18,35).

Through this sentence and through the predicates given to the Lord the psalm begins as if it were Davidic, or at least royal.

Ps 144,3:   O Lord, what is man that you regard him,
            or the son of man that you think of him?

            What is man that you are mindful of him,
            and the son of man that you care for him? (Ps 8,5).

One might call this a citation *ad sensum*, with a change of verbs and slight variation of the nouns (see the Hebrew); the context is profoundly different. More different still is what Job says in citing this verse:

> What is man, that you make so much of him,
> and that you set your mind upon him,
> visit him every morning,
> and test him every moment? (Job 7,17-18).

Job cites the psalm in order to twist its meaning: it would be better if God was not so preoccupied with man and left him in peace. Citing in order to change the meaning, to turn the citation against someone, is a polemical device, even more surprising when used against God. Let us return to Ps 144:

Ps 144,4a: Man is like a breath.

> Every man is a breath (Ps 39,6).

> Men are a breath (Ps 62,10).

Ps 144,4b: His days are like a passing shadow.

> Our days on earth are a shadow (Job 8,9).

Breath and shadow are two easily recognisable images; the verse is a conscious citation or a reminiscence. The same image which was used in a painful supplication is used later in an act of thanksgiving.

Ps 144,5b: Touch the mountains and they will smoke.

> He touches the mountains and they smoke (Ps 104,32).

Ps 144,6: Flash forth the lightning and scatter them,
send out your arrows and rout them!

> He sent out his arrows, and scattered them;
> he flashed forth lightnings, and routed them (Ps 18,15).

The author of Ps 144 returns to Ps 18, which he quoted at the outset. The smoke of the mountains (which is referred to the nostrils of God in Ps 18) may be a tacit allusion to the Sinai theophany.

Exod 19,18: "Mount Sinai was wrapped in smoke".

Ps 144,7: Stretch forth your hand from on high, rescue me,
and deliver me from the many waters.

> He reached me from on high, he took me,
> he drew me out of many waters (Ps 18,17).

Due to the change of synonyms this seems a quotation from memory, *ad sensum*. The "new song" referred to in v. 9 is a phrase which occurs six times in the Psalter.

As is now clear, the first part of this psalm uses motifs, phrases and images from earlier sources. It alludes to David, perhaps also to Sinai. Some have called this an "anthological style" (Robert), which does not seem a very useful expression. Neither is it a cento in the strict sense of a collection of pieces from other authors. For in the new context the elements cited or alluded to take on new significance and connotations. The reader will feel at home, but will also discover something new. This is a rather special approach, very faithful to traditional ways of thinking. But when we reach v. 12 we find that the Psalm changes style and theme. It speaks about social well-being — a Davidic theme — in a series of concrete petitions, clearly expressed. We ought to compare the first part of the Psalm with the second in order to appreciate more fully the style of citations and allusions:

Ps 144,12: May our sons in their youth
            be like plants full grown,
            our daughters like corner pillars
            cut for the structure of a palace;

      13:   may our garners be full,
            providing all manner of store;
            may our sheep bring forth thousands
            and ten thousands in our fields;

      14:   may our cattle be heavy with young,
            suffering no mischance or failure in bearing;
            may there be no cry of distress in our streets!

Let me now quote from another late psalm:

            I remember the days of old,
            I meditate on all that you have done;
            I muse on what your hands have wrought.
            I stretch out my hands to you;
            I thirst for you like a parched land (Ps 143,5-6).

There are clear reminiscences of Ps 77,6: "I consider the days of old ... I remember", and of Ps 63,2: "My throat thirsts for you ... like a dry land". Something similar happens in Ps 145,15: "The eyes of all look to you, and you give them their food in due season", an unmistakable allusion to Ps 104,27: "These all look to you, to give them their food in due season".

Allusions are not always easy to discover, to identify and to prove. The means we have at our disposal are in fact a very restricted collection of literary texts which extend across many centuries. We have no knowledge of the oral material which did not pass into the official, canonical texts, whether they were legends or popular songs, or such like material; we are ignorant of many facts and situations. This means that we are unable to grasp many allusions. What is sure is that when we read we fail to recognise the vast majority of allusions and thus we impoverish our reading. In our concern not to lose an allusion, we may exaggerate and confuse allusions with reminiscences. However, this is better than failing to recognize such aspects at all. These cross references abound in our commentaries; I will give some examples here, indicating their literary origin, of allusions as a poetic technique:

Ps 147,4: "He determines the number of the stars, he gives to all of them their names". Is there an allusion here to the narrative of Gen 15? God commands the patriarch Abraham to count the stars; what Abraham is unable to do, God can do. And is there a polemical allusion to the astronomers of Babylon, who claim to give names to stars and constellations in practising divination (cf. Isa 47,13)?

Ps 149,9: "To execute the judgement written is an honour for all his faithful ones". This text betrays a Maccabean tone and perhaps belonged to the circles of the ḥasîdîm. It might allude to the sentence against king Agag, not carried out by Saul (1 Sam 15). The execution of a sentence decreed by God is an obligation for man, an honour for his chosen ones (Judg 8,20-21).

Isa 24,18b is part of the great eschatology: "The windows of heaven open". One can be sure here of an allusion to the flood (Gen 7,11); the rare word 'ărubbôt confirms this.

Jer 50,3: An enemy from the North will come and destroy Babylon. Even if this text is not of Jeremiah, it is included in his book and it reminds us that the enemy of Israel who destroyed nation, city and temple also came from the North and was Babylon. Babylon will suffer what she inflicted on others; roles are reversed, and the poet says so with this allusion.

Jer 51,13 is also against Babylon: "O you who dwell by many waters, rich in treasures, your end has come, the thread of your life is cut". This image of the loom is already known from the prayer of Hezekiah (Isa 38,12). It is possible that the poet is alluding to this, or that it was a common expression: death seen as a cutting off of the thread of life which is woven on the loom.

Jer 51,27 compares horses to locusts; Joel compares a plague of locusts to an attack of calvary. What relation is there between the two? We cannot date them with certainty. We do not know whether there is any dependence or whether this is a pure coincidence of poetic intuition.

III. Questions, Exclamations, Apostrophes, Aphorisms

Among the more "rhetorical" of rhetorical figures of speech are the question, the exclamation and the apostrophe. The aphorism or maxim on the other hand belongs rather to the essay, to some kind of didactic work.

In much of Hebrew poetry these figures of speech are abundant and mixed together, adding great movement and liveliness to the development of the poem. This happens above all in the prophetic literature. This is no surprise for the prophets are for the most part preachers: in the name of God they address the people to get them to understand and change their ways. For this end they use the normal tools of the orator, techniques which were identified, described and classified by the classical rhetoricians. One might say that the aphorism, as it becomes general and even universal, loses immediate contact with the listeners. But this is not so. The aphorisms are inserted without being immersed in the flow of the speech, but they elevate it and make it more profound, like a sky reflected in a flowing stream.

A. *An Example*

An important way of appreciating biblical poetry is to be aware of the free combination of different figures of speech. I will be looking at different figures separately, but before we do so I will present one text as an example of this free combination of figures of speech. We see Jer 2 as a trial against his people by God in which both sides take active part in the dispute. The speech of the offended party attempts to bring about recognition and repentance in the offending party, in order to reach a reconciliation. It is therefore a very personal rhetorical piece, for the speaker is not a lawyer dealing with the case or a judge who weighs up the evidence and dispassionately pronounces the sentence (*Profetas*, pp. 426-433).

The chapter begins with personal memories, directed to Jerusalem in the second person — Jerusalem is personified as the bride, symbolizing the community. The speaker speaks in the first person: he tells of how his love has been cheated:

Jer 2,2:   I remember the devotion of your youth,
your love as a bride,
how you followed me in the wilderness,
in a land not sown.

Then he addresses the community: "Listen, house of Jacob!"
He begins with a defiant rhetorical question: "What wrong did your
fathers find in me that they went far from me?" (v. 5) The question
contains within itself the negative reply: it is a clear denial, it defies
the listener to find a satisfactory answer, thus making him admit the
guilt of his fathers. In v. 6, staying with the fore-fathers, there is a
slight digression: the speaker cites what they did not say, what they
should have said and never did. After the digression, he continues
(vv. 7-8) in an antithesis of what he did for them and what they did
or did not do. Then comes an apostrophe in an imperative form:
"cross... see..." (v. 10). Then immediately, a rhetorical question
and an exclamation:

Jer 2,11: Does a nation change its gods? And these are no gods...

12: Be appalled, O heavens, at this! Be shocked! Be utterly
desolate!

This exclamation is to a person, a personification, who had not
been introduced before, but whose presence could be presumed in
the lawsuit. In v. 14 rhetorical questions return but with some
variation: God does not address the people in the second person,
but speaks of them in the third person, but in a loud voice in
order to be heard. This is a refined way of addressing someone
without addressing them, as if those addressed were a third person whose situation provokes some degree of surprise. The two
rhetorical questions express strangeness and curiosity, put on in
rhetorical style:

Jer 2,14: Is Israel a slave? Is he a homeborn servant?
Why then has he become a prey?

15: The lions have roared against him, they have roared loudly.

In v. 16b we return to the second person: what was repressed
by the speaker in his digression in the third person now pours
forth. Vv. 17-18 are a series of questions: some are simply rhetorical, with a positive reply implied; others pretend to await a reply
so that the listeners may see and confess, or at least understand
their errors:

Jer 2,17: Have you not brought this upon yourself
by forsaking the Lord your God,
when he led you in the way?

18: And now what do you gain by going to Egypt?
to drink the waters of the Nile?
Or what do you gain by going to Assyria?
to drink the waters of the Euphrates?

There follows a new apostrophe in the imperative: "Know and see!" (v. 19); this introduces an aphorism, a general principle: "It is evil and bitter to forsake the Lord"; this principle becomes more relevant by the addition of "your God".

The text continues in the second person and cites the words of the accused in accusation: "I will not serve" (v. 20). In v. 23 a rhetorical question introduces the reply of the accused, which is negative: "How can you say, 'I am not defiled'?" There is another question in v. 24, with a negative reply included. A further apostrophe in the imperative comes in v. 25, and a citation of the reply: "Certainly not!" In v. 26 we return to the third person, as if the offended party were telling others — the jury? — what the offending party had done; further words of the accused are used in accusation.

In vv. 28-29 there is a new development of questions and exclamations:

But where are your gods that you made for yourself?
Let them arise, if they can save you, in your time of
trouble!
For as many as your cities are your gods, O Judah.
Why do you complain against me since you have all
rebelled?

Further questions follow in vv. 31-32a, exclamations in v. 33, and citation of the words of the accused in v. 35. After the exclamation in v. 36 the sentence of condemnation finally comes.

This is a speech of two of three pages. I have not given a complete literary commentary, but have concentrated on the rhetorical movement of rhetorical questions with different functions, exclamations, apostrophes to the accused and to those present. It is always the offended party who speaks: of himself, in the first person; of the offender in the third person; to the offender in the second person. He quotes old and new words of the offender; he also makes a general statement, the aphorism. This is the kind of movement which König observed ("Bewegheit", *Stilistik, Rhetorik, Poetik*, pp. 228-232). In other cases one might also encounter changes in the person speaking and elements of dialogue and monologue.

B. *Questions*

I wish to distinguish the rhetorical question in the strict sense from the wisdom question. They both share a fictitious character and a common stylistic function. They are not "true" questions. The question means something else: an affirmation or negation, a doubt, encouragement, strangeness or indignation. It is a frequent and flexible literary technique.

a) Bullinger is a maximalist and finds 329 rhetorical questions in Job and 195 in Jeremiah. Often they come in series, a kind of cascade of rhetorical questions, like those which God bombards against Job in Job 38. Here is an example from Ps 30,10:

> What profit is there in my death,
> if I go down to the Pit?
> Will the dust praise you?
> Will it tell of your faithfulness?

It is as if the psalmist wishes to convince God by his reasoning.

> O Lord, who is like you ...? (Ps 35,10).

> Rouse yourself! Why are you sleeping, Lord?
> Awake! Do not cast us off for ever!
> Why do you hide your face? ...
> Rise up, come to our help! ... (Ps 44,24-25.27).

As in Jer 2, there is here an effective combination of rhetorical questions and apostrophes. Ps 50 is a lawsuit much like Jer 2; We find both questions and apostrophes there (*Treinta Salmos*, pp. 209-214). Ps 52 and Ps 58 open quite abruptly with rhetorical questions. Ps 59,8 cites the defiant questions of the wicked: "Who will hear us?"; the same happens in Ps 64,6: "Who can see us?"

> How long, O Lord? Will you be angry for ever?
> Will your jealous wrath burn like fire? ...
> Why should the nations say, "Where is their God?"?
>   (Ps 79,5.10).

The question within the question is interesting. The second is made in mockery, the first is in rebuff.

Isa 40,12ff. begins with three questions composed of various members, and places a further three in vv. 18, 21 and 25. All of them aim to establish the incomparable nature of God and to exalt him. Similarly Isa 44,6-8 has four questions concentrated in little space, and of three varying types: "Who...? Have I not...?" The same concentration and variety are found in Isa 50,1-2:

> Where is your mother's bill of divorce,
> with which I put her away?
> Or which of my creditors is it
> to whom I have sold you?...
> Why, when I came, was there no man?
> When I called, was there no one to answer?
> Is my hand shortened, that it cannot redeem?
> Or have I no power to deliver?

In Isa 58 it is the people who reproach God, and God responds with his questions:

> Why have we fasted, and you do not see it?
> Why have we humbled ourselves, and you take no notice?
>
> Is this the fast that I choose...?
> Do you call this a fast...? (Isa 58,3.5).

b) I call *wisdom questions* those which the teacher puts to his students to arouse their interest and provoke their collaboration. The professor puts the question, and shows that his teaching is the result of a search. It is logical that this type of question is more frequent in the wisdom texts, so I will begin with Sirach:

> A worthy race? — The human race.
> A worthy race? — Those who fear God.
> An unworthy race? — The human race.
> An unworthy race? — Those who transgress the commandments
> (Sir 10,19).

Repeated questions are coupled with responses which correspond and oppose each other. Man is seen in his polarized reactions and ambivalence, the difference being in his religious and ethical behaviour.

> Who will pity a snake charmer bitten by a serpent,
> or any who go near wild beasts?
> So no one will pity a man who associates with a sinner...
> (Sir 12,13-14).

> How can the clay pot associate with the iron kettle?
> The pot will strike against it, and will itself be broken
>   (Sir 13,2)

> What is brighter than the sun?
> Yet it too has its eclipses (Sir 17,31).

> What is heavier than lead?
> And what is its name except "Fool"? (Sir 22,14).

Questions may serve to introduce a comparison; the explanation is given in the reply. In the last example it served as a kind of riddle.

We find this type of question in certain psalms called wisdom psalms:

> Who is the man that fears the Lord?
> Him will he instruct in the way that he should choose
>   (Ps 25,12).

> What man is there who desires life,
> And covets many days that he may enjoy good?
> Keep your tongue from evil,
> and your lips from speaking deceit (Ps 34,13-14).

The question is an emphatic substitution for what would normally be a conditional clause. In Job we find the rhetorical question more frequently than the wisdom question. The wisdom question is not lacking even in the prophetic literature. The question in Jer 13,23 is similar to those in Sirach: "Can the Ethiopian change his skin, or the leopard his spots?" Isa 63,1 begins a fictitious dialogue with questions which pretend ignorance.

C. *Exclamations. Epiphonemes*

a) Your name is wonderful. How wonderful is your name! The *exclamation* adds feeling to the simple piece of information. The statement simply proposes something, the exclamation expresses it forcefully. It is a basic form of language which literary style can exploit. It really has little variety for language does not distinguish between the different feelings which are being expressed. The same linguistic sign expresses admiration, enthusiasm, joy, sadness, discouragement. The exclamation expresses only the dimensions of the object, the intensity of the feeling. It may open or close a poem, and is even more effective when it interrupts the poem unexpectedly. It can easily be combined with questions, as we have seen. It is usually quite short, it cannot carry with it complex syntactical structures, and it is not found in series.

Ps 133 begins: "Behold, how good and pleasant it is when brothers dwell in unity!" Ps 3,2 ponders on a number: "Lord, how many are my foes!" Ps 31,20 interrupts the prayer by exclaiming: "How abundant is your goodness, which you have laid up for those who fear you!" Similarly, Ps 21,2, which brings together exclamation and statement. Other examples: 36,8; 66,3; 84,2; 92,6; 119,103; 139,17. It is no surprise that exclamations abound in the Song of Songs.

Elegy too is a suitable genre for the exclamation:

How the faithful city has become a harlot! (Isa 1,21).

How lonely sits the city that was full of people! (Lam 1,1).

How the Lord in his anger has set the daughter of Sion under a cloud! (Lam 2,1).

How the gold has grown dim, how the pure gold is changed! (Lam 4,1).

How you are fallen from heaven! (Isa 14,12).

How the hammer of the whole earth is cut down and broken! (Jer 50,23).

There is one literary genre which always begins with an exclamation: the woe speech. Habakkuk makes a group of people intone a poem with five woes: (*Profetas*, pp. 1104-1105):

Woe to him who heaps up what is not his own ...!
Woe to him who gets evil gain for his house ...!
Woe to him who builds a town with blood ...!
Woe to him who makes his neighbours drink ... to gaze on their shame!
Woe to him who says to a wooden thing, Awake!
(Hab 2,6.9.12.15.19).

The first prophecy of the book of Isaiah begins with an apostrophe to heaven and earth, a statement of the crime and an exclamation. Isa 45,9-11 launches two woes. The exclamation is even more effective when it interrupts a speech, as in Ezek 16,22-23:

And in all your abominations and your harlotries
you did not remember the days of your youth,
when you were naked and bare,
Weltering in your blood.
And after all your wickedness, woe, woe to you!
you built yourself a vaulted chamber ... in every square.

The rhetorical exclamation stylizes a normal phenomenon of language.

b) When the exclamation comes at the end, as a final cadence, we might call it an epiphoneme; indeed some use this term for any final reflexion. Ps 3 ends with an epiphoneme, which is an apostrophe rather than an exclamation:

> Deliverance comes from you, O Lord
> and blessing for your people (Ps 3,9; *Treinta Salmos*, p. 56).

Ps 66 develops with rapid movement: it is addressed to the assembly, to all the people, to God, and again to the assembly; and it closes with the exclamation:

> Blessed be God, because he has not rejected my prayer,
> or removed his steadfast love from me! (Ps 66,20).

In this broad sense we may consider an (Ps 66,20) epiphoneme the conclusion of one of the interventions of Job. After polemically describing the luck and the well-being of evil men he closes the speech:

> How then will you comfort me with empty nothings?
> There is nothing left of your answers but falsehood
>   (Job 21,34).

By contrast in Sir 13,15-24, an instruction on the treatment of rich and poor, the epiphoneme is a maxim or aphorism:

> Riches are good if they are free from sin,
> and poverty is evil in the opinion of the ungodly (Sir 13,24).

D. *The Apostrophe*

Apostrophe is not the simple fact of directing speech to others, for this is the very essence of oratory. By an apostrophe I mean suddenly directing the speech at someone, thereby interrupting the course of the exposition.

Isa 49,1-13 is considered to be the second song of the Servant. The Servant speaks first to his audience, then the Lord speaks to the Servant, explaining his mission and announcing the return of the exiles: "they shall feed ... they shall not hunger or thirst ... for he who has pity on them will lead them .... I will make the mountains a way ...". Suddenly the announcement is interrupted: the Lord addresses an anonymous audience to witness the return, and then the heavens and the earth:

Look at them coming from afar,
look at them coming from north and west....
Sing for joy, O heavens, and exult, O earth;
break forth, O mountains, into singing! (Isa 49,12-13).

The apostrophe in Zech 2,17 is also at the end. After the solemn announcement of restoration this call sounds forth:

Be silent, all flesh, before the Lord;
for he has roused himself from his holy dwelling
(cf. Hab 2,20).

In Nah 2,9 the apostrophe is very effective, interrupting the presentation of an image of Nineveh with shouts of command: "Nineveh is like a pool whose waters run away. Halt! Halt! But none turns back". Something similar occurs in Jer 12,9:

My heritage has become a leopard
and the birds of prey circle over her:
Come, wild beasts, approach and eat!

In the Psalms the words are normally directed to God, or to the assembly, inviting them to praise. It is not abnormal that the psalmist should suddenly turn his words to God in an apostrophe. What is strange is when he turns away to address others: "Depart from me, all you workers of evil..." (Ps 6,9).

The same feature is found in the "prophetic" beginning of Ps 58 (*Treinta Salmos*, 242).

E. *Aphorisms*

A maxim or an aphorism in the middle of a speech or a poem is quite different from the last figures of speech considered. It calms the emotions, quietens the movement, makes the flow more gentle. This does not mean that the poetry is less effective, for still waters run deep. We do not therefore include in this category the separate proverbs found in the collection known as the Book of Proverbs. But aphorism abound in wisdom instructions, for example in Sirach; this is not surprising and it is sufficient to give a couple of examples:

For "gold is tested in the fire",
and acceptable men in the furnace of humiliation (Sir 2,5).

Water wears away stones...
and you destroy the hope of man (Job 14,19).

Perhaps more significant is the general aphorism in prophetic oracles. In Isa 40,31: "Those who wait for the Lord renew their strength"; Isa 45,20b: "They have no knowledge, those who carry about their wooden idols"; Isa 57,13: "He who takes refuge in me shall possess the land". Ezekiel cites a couple of proverbs: "The fathers have eaten sour grapes, and the children's teeth are set on edge" (Ezek 18,2); "Like mother, like daughter" (Ezek 16,44).

Hosea is always concerned with concrete events, whether past or present, without turning to universal reflexions. This is why many suspect the authenticity of the final lines:

> The ways of the Lord are right,
> and the upright walk in them,
> but transgressors stumble in them (Hos 14,10; *Profetas*, p. 921).

One of the most intense moments in the Song of Songs is when, towards the end, the lovers take on a more universal tone, singing of love, its mysterious power, its inestimable value, its inextinguishable life:

> Love is strong as death,
> jealousy is cruel as the grave;
> its flashes are flashes of fire, a divine flame;
> many waters cannot quench love,
> neither can floods drown it ... (Cant 8,6-7).

III. Irony, Sarcasm and Humour

A. *Distinction of Terms*

These three terms, without further precision, belong to the sphere of laughter and of the ridiculous. When this sphere comes into the literary work we speak of what is comical, in a general sense. A person, an event or a situation may be ridiculous; but an author can also make the object seem ridiculous, he can laugh disdainfully at a situation, he can despise a person. In short, the author laughs at someone or something. Furthermore, the author can also create a character or a literary situation in order to laugh at them and to share his laughter with the reader. This activity supposes normally a certain distance. The author is situated outside or above his object, whether it is real or created by him. In an extreme case the author distances himself and laughs at himself.

In modern usage the term "irony" is used with a certain freedom. We should distinguish at least: dramatic irony, rhetorical irony and narrative irony. The distinction will become clear as we go on.

I will begin with another distinction which is both more traditional and more modern: irony, sarcasm and humour. In all three there is some kind of mockery, all three laugh at someone or something. In all three there is also a substantial distance. Laughing at something with a neutral distance we can call simply irony. Laughter which keeps a certain distance so as to poke fun and at the same time draws near its object to hurt it, is sarcasm. Laughter at sufficient distance but nevertheless a laughter which is sympathetic — this we would call simply humour. Dramatic irony in plays or narratives also has its distance, and narrative irony requires distance of the theme or of the narrator. And, finally, there is rhetorical irony.

Narrative and dramatic irony are obviously found in drama and narrative. Neutral irony and sarcasm find plenty of scope in satire. Humour can be found anywhere.

The Greek and Latin classics left us two basic forms of irony: rhetorical irony, which consists in saying the opposite of what one intends, but allowing this to be understood; and dramatic irony (also called "sophoclean" from *Oedipus Rex*), which consists in making a character say something which he does not understand or the implications of which he has not grasped. Humour as an aesthetical category has only been considered in the last few centuries, even though it is a very ancient practice.

I am not giving all these distinctions simply for the fun of it, but rather to give us some signs along the way once we begin our journey through the biblical text. Even though we have formulated these distinctions they can always be adapted if it is necessary. Moreover, they have heuristic value in helping the reader to discover aspects of the biblical text which he has not hitherto noticed.

B. *Rhetorical Irony*

By oral intonation or through the written context the author lets us know that one should not take seriously, literally, what is said, but understand the opposite. "Nero, with characteristic goodness, sent a hundred citizens to be burnt as torches". It is quite clear that "goodness" here really means "cruelty", and this is intended to mock.

In the midst of a lawsuit with his people in exile, recalling past infidelity — "I have not burdened you with sacrifices.... You have burdened me with your sins" —, the Lord gives this invitation:

> Remind me, and we can discuss it;
> set forth your case, and you will be absolved (Isa 43,26).

This really means: you do not have to remind me, I know it already, and do not think you will be able to justify yourself and be absolved. The imperative form is frequent in this kind of biblical irony. Later on he argues again: "Listen to me, you valiant ones, who are so far from victory" (Isa 46,12). "Valiant" ones or champions, who do not know how to win — this too is ironical. Returning to the imperative, here are two examples from a satire — most of the oracles against pagans in the prophetic literature are satires:

> Advance, horses, and rage, chariots!
> Let the warriors go forth....
> The sword devours, is sated, and drinks its fill....
> Go up to Gilead, and take balm... (Jer 46,9-11).

It begins with an ironical invitation to a bloody defeat; it ends with another ironical invitation to an impossible cure.

When Am 4,11 calls the women of Samaria "cows of Bashan", this is an ironical title. What is in fact an insult is being presented as a title of honour. The chiefs of a town gave themselves the honorific title of "bulls of Bashan"; but when the wives are called "cows" it is no honour, but an insult due to their animal fatness.

We read in Zeph 1,7: "The Lord has prepared a banquet/sacrifice, he has purified/consecrated his guests". This is a sacred banquet or sacrifice with a rite of purification, offered by the Lord; it is a sign of friendship. Ironically, however, another meaning of the word *zebah* is slaughter, which is what is intended here. The irony is based on the desired ambiguity and ambivalence of the word. Similarly Ezekiel speaks of a colossal banquet: the irony lies in the inversion of roles. It is not men who are being invited to eat the flesh of birds and animals, but animals invited to devour human corpses:

> Speak to the birds of every sort and to all beasts of the field: Assemble, and come, gather from all sides to the sacrificial feast which I am preparing for you, a great sacrificial feast upon the mountains of Israel, and you shall eat flesh and drink blood. You shall eat the flesh of the mighty, and drink the blood of the princes of the earth; they will be the rams, lambs, goats, bulls, and fatlings of Bashan. And you shall eat fat until you are filled, and drink blood till you are drunk, at the sacrificial feast which I am preparing for you. And you shall be filled at my table... (Ezek 39,17-20).

Without realising it we have entered the realms of sarcasm, for this
detailed description, this profusion of foods, gives expression to a
certain degree of cruelty which is here combined with the simple
distancing of irony.

Another ironic invitation is found in the song of the harlot:

> Take a harp, go about the city,
> O forgotten harlot!
> Make sweet melody, sing many songs,
> that you may be remembered (Isa 23,16).

The title given by the Lord to the city/community is ironical in
Jer 11,15:

> What right has my beloved in my house,
> when she has done vile deeds?

In Lam 4,21 the invitation to joy is ironical:

> Rejoice and be glad, capital of Edom,
> that to you also the cup shall pass.

Ezekiel bestows an ironical title on the prince of Tyre:

> You are indeed wiser than Daniel;
> no secret is hidden from you! (Ezek 28,3).

In Job's dialogue with his friends, which gradually becomes
more polemical, ironical expressions are not rare:

> You are such important people!
> And wisdom will no doubt die with you (Job 12,2).

> Bear with me and I will speak,
> and after I have spoken, you will be able to mock (Job 21,3).

> How you have helped him who has no power!
> How you have saved the arm that has no strength!
> How you have counselled him who has no wisdom,
> and plentifully declared sound knowledge! (Job 26,2-3).

Sometimes it is the characters within the poem who express
themselves ironically; like the enemies in Ps 22,9. "He committed his
cause to the Lord; let him deliver him, let him rescue him, for he
delights in him!" In Isa 5,19 the unbelievers defy the Lord: "Let him
make haste, let him speed his work that we may see it". In Jer 20,10
the enemies turn against the prophet the name which he had given
to Pashhur: "I hear many whispering: Terror is on every side!"

We can consider finally the invitation of Isa 8,10: "Take counsel together, but it will come to naught; speak a word, but it will not stand". And the name given to Assyria in Isa 30,7: "The beast who roars and does nothing" (*Profetas*, p. 230).

C. *Sarcasm*

Sarcasm vents fury on the enemy, it "devours his flesh" (sarcasm comes from *sárx* = flesh). It is of no importance that this may happen in order to cure him of faults. A scalpel rends the flesh just as effectively as a razor. Furthermore, when mockery is pronounced by a friend it is more penetrating, more painful, more heart-breaking. It is no surprise that we hear it on the lips of God, directed to his people. Am 4,4-5 closes a lawsuit with a series of fierce imperatives:

> Go to Bethel and sin; to Gilgal and multiply transgressions:
> bring your sacrifices every morning,
> your tithes every three days;
> burn your thank-offering without leaven,
> proclaim freewill offerings, publish them;
> for this is what pleases you, Israelites.

Similarly God gives an invitation in Ezek 20,39: "Let every one go and serve his idols, if he does not wish to obey me!" Jer 7,21 declares with some violence: "Add your burnt offerings to your sacrifices and eat the flesh!"

The mockery in Am 2,13 is less obvious, as God threatens Israel:

> Behold, I will press you down in your place,
> as a cart full of sheaves presses down.

To press down with a lowly cart and under the weight of an abundant harvest adds sarcasm to the threat.

Chapter 47 of Isaiah is a satire against Babylon, in which the capital is personified as a woman. Mocking imperatives are frequent to describe her humiliation; as the text proceeds the imperatives become more sarcastic, because they invite the city to have recourse to her usual ways of protecting herself:

> Carry on with your enchantments and your many sorceries,
> with which you have laboured since your youth;
> perhaps you will succeed, perhaps you will inspire terror.

> You are wearied with your many counsels;
> let them stand forth and save you,
> those who divide the heavens,
> who gaze at the stars,
> who at the new moons predict
> what shall befall you (Isa 47,12-13).

Maybe we should consider Ezek 15,1-8 sarcasm in spite of the restrained tone. The prophet takes the traditional honoured image of Israel as the vine of the Lord and violently twists it round: they will throw it in the fire as fuel.

D. *Oxymoron, Paradox, and Double Meaning*

a) One of the linguistic techniques used to express irony is to place together two incongruous words so that one invalidates the other (*òxý – mōron* = "sharp – dull"). As far as double meaning is concerned the public must be aware of it. It is quite possible that many expressions with ironical double meaning in Hebrew poetry are lost to us. Here are some biblical examples of oxymoron, which we might also call paradoxes.

> The Lord applies the measuring-line of chaos
> and the level of nothingness (Isa 34,11).

> He will be buried with the funeral of an ass (Jer 22,19).

> They stored up treasures of violence and robbery in their palaces (Am 3,10).

We have already seen the first example as an image. The chaos of destruction and the measuring-line for construction are contradictory ideas. God the architect uses his tools carefully to turn Edom into chaos. The second example puts together funeral and ass: this is no funeral at all. The text goes on to explain: "He will be dragged out and cast forth beyond the gates of Jerusalem". The third example shows what are the "treasures" of the wicked.

b) The verb *pqd* has a double meaning in Ezek 38,8: to "review a parade" and to "take into account", and it is directed to Gog. In one sense, the troops will be reviewed in preparation for a march against Israel; in the other sense, you will be brought to account for your pride and your cruelty. The two meanings are condensed into the ambivalence of one ironical verb. See also the double meaning of *bōšet* = "shame/idol" in Jer 7,19.

Isa 21,11 is complicated: we find the people's question and the reply of the watchman. The reply is open, ambiguous; the watchman — the prophet — seems to be mocking those who question him. We almost slip into an enigma, except that the intention seems to be ironical:

> – Watchman, what of the night?
> Watchman, what of the night?
> – The morning will come, and the night.
> If you inquire, inquire; come, return.

E. *Humour. Burlesque*

a) In the sense proposed above, of sympathetic laughter, both distant and close, I think we find true humour in the book of Job. I have already quoted a couple of ironical passages from this book and I will have cause to quote other aspects too. The whole book is a masterly work of pathos and irony in the broad sense. Job sings a hymn of praise... to the destructive God (9,5-10); this is almost sarcasm. God will use sarcasm when he invites Job to occupy his place to arrange the world (40,7-14). Before this moment of climax, when God has accepted Job's challenge and has come down to answer him, he speaks ironically with him in a series of questions and observations: "Tell me, if you know so much..." (38,4); "Explain it to me, if you know all this..." (38,18); "You must know this, since you were already born then and you have lived so many years..." (38,21). Nevertheless, this cascade of rhetorical questions, this parade of ignorance uncovered and wonders disclosed proceeds with a feeling of indulgence, understanding, and even affection. God does not annihilate Job with lightning, nor does he crush him with a refutation; he takes him by the hand, and, gently mocking him, leads him towards his final discovery and confession. I believe that it is thus that we must understand this passage for it to make sense within the book. If we accept this, it would be the most distinguished example of humour in the OT. I have no problem in saying this of an author who, among all biblical writers, gives the clearest demonstration of genius (*Iob*, pp. 537, 553, 557, 577, 595).

The humour in this case is internal to the text: one character uses humour with the other, God with Job.

b) In quite a separate place from humour we find the genre of burlesque, which I only mention here. This is found in narrative prose so should not concern us here. A comic tale makes a character seem ridiculous so that we can laugh at him, as happens very clearly in the Greek additions to the book of Daniel. The two short tales of Bel and the dragon both ridicule idolatry.

F. *Dramatic and Narrative Irony*

Both presuppose the author–character–reader triangle. The technique is clearest in dramatic irony. The author takes his distance from a character and denies him a piece of information which he then shares with the reader. There is thus a complicity between author and reader at the expense of the character. Let us consider a clear and simple example, within a lyric poem — Judg 5 — which many scholars consider to be ancient. As the reader reads the book he knows quite well, from chapter 4, what has happened: Sisera has been killed by a bedouin woman. If the reader only reads the poem in Judg 5 he will be aware of this fact from vv. 25-27. But then the poet takes us off to another scene, in a clever montage we find a character who does not know of the death of Sisera, his own mother, who considers the victory of her enterprising son to be assured:

> Out of the window she peers,
> the mother of Sisera gazes through the lattice:
> Why is his chariot so long in coming?
> Why do the hoofbeats of his chariots tarry?
> The wisest of her ladies answers,
> and she repeats the words to herself:
> They are finding and dividing the spoil,
> a maiden or two for each man ... (Judg 5,28-29).

If this piece is ancient, maturity arrived early on. Centuries later we find the dramatic irony of the book of Tobit, brought about by the angel in disguise. A masterly piece of dramatic irony is the relationship between Judith and Holofernes in the book of Judith. Two late books of narrative prose.

Another variation of this irony is found when the author distances himself from his character and makes him do ridiculous things before the audience. This is to expose him to whistling derision. (The French and the Germans call it "persiflage"; and the Bible already knew the whistling of mockery: Jer 50,13; Job 27,23, etc.).

A short phrase may at times be enough, as when the prophet parodies the devout actions of those who fast: "bowing their heads like rushes" (Isa 58,5), where the comparison is both descriptive and expressive. More sustained is the description made in Isa 44,12-20 of the makers of idols; even though he makes no comment, the description alone is a piece of mockery:

> Half of it he burns in the fire; over that half he eats flesh, he roasts meat and is satisfied; also he warms himself and says, "Aha, I am warm, and I have light!" and the rest of it he makes into a god, his idol; and falls down to it and worships it; he prays to it and says, "Deliver me, for you are my god!" (Isa 44,16-17).

The scene was created by the writer for the entertainment and instruction of his readers.

In the book of Job three characters from different countries, each famed for his wisdom, take the stage. The author presents them as teachers with great expertise in tradition and learning. And sometimes he lets them seem ridiculous in their speeches. At the start Eliphaz may be worthy and respectable, but he is treated with irony when the author gives him the speech in chapter 18. Job says of the three "your counsels are proverbs of dust" (13,12), and the author allows the reader to sense this at the expense of the three "wise men". The verdict given by Job in 13,4, "you whitewash with lies, you are worthless physicians", will be shared finally by the reader.

The author of Jonah also treats his hero with some irony; the Israelite prophet, who ought to be the "good" character in the face of the "bad" pagans, both sailors and Ninevites, takes on the role of the bad character, and the others are presented as good. The irony is sustained and increasing until the point where the author laughs sarcastically at his character and makes him say (*Profetas*, pp. 1025, 1029):

> That is why I made haste to flee to Tarshish; for I knew that you are a gracious God and merciful, slow to anger, and abounding in steadfast love, and that you repent of evil (Jonah 4,2).

To say that a prophet cannot serve God because God is able to let him down by not punishing the guilty who have repented is the very limit!

We find narrative irony at the end of the second chapter of Daniel, when grand Nebuchadnezzar, the golden head of the statue in the dream, ends up by paying divine honours to his foreign employee who has interpreted his dream:

> Then King Nebuchadnezzar fell upon his face, and did homage to Daniel, and commanded that an offering and incense be offered up to him (Dan 2,46).

G. *Irony in Proverbs*

The one who pronounces a proverb both elevates and distances himself by making general statements. If this is accompanied by neutral laughter then he is using irony. There are not many proverbs of this type, and one of the favourite victims of them is the idler. I have cited some of these examples before, in another context, but it does no harm to repeat them:

> The idler says, "There is a lion in the road!
> There is a wild beast in the streets!"

> As a door turns on its hinges,
> so does an idler on his bed.

> The idler puts out his hand to the dish
> but is too tired to raise it to his mouth.

> The idler is wiser in his own eyes
> than seven men who reply with tact (Prov 26,13-16;
> *Proverbios*, pp. 464 f.).

The following is a short vignette, almost a wink at the reader:

> "No good, no good!" says the buyer;
> then he goes away, boasting of what he has bought
> (Prov 20,14).

This general statement is an amusing scene of day-to-day life:

> He who greets his neighbour with a loud voice early in the morning
> will be considered as cursing (Prov 27,14; *Proverbios*, p. 476).

All right to say hello, but to rouse him from his slumber...! Prov 23,29-33 is a lively description of the drunkard, developed with a touch of irony.

Perhaps we can put in this company riddles, especially if they are charged with double meaning. Judg 14,14.18 offer a demonstration. Poor Samson will end his days as a spectacle to entertain his enemies, and who will gain revenge for him upon them in tragic mockery?

E. W. Good, *Irony in the Old Testament* (BiLit; Sheffield ²1981),

J. G. Williams, "Comedy, Irony, Intercession: A Few Notes in Reply", *Semeia* 7 (1977) 135-145. This study concerns the Book of Job.

J. Hempel, "Pathos and Humor in der israelitischen Erziehung", in J. Hempel – L. Rost (edd.), *Von Ugarit nach Qumran. Beiträge zur alttestamentlichen und altorientalischen Forschung*. Otto Eissfeldt zum 1. September 1957 dargebracht ... (BZAW 77; Berlin 1958), pp. 63-81.

V. **Ellipsis, Hyperbole**

A. *Ellipsis and Concision*

a) It is sufficient that the comment on *ellipsis* be brief. We must define clearly what we mean by ellipsis as a figure of speech and point of style. Bullinger dedicates 130 pages to the subject and six more to the zeugma, giving an enormous quantity of cases and minutely classifying them. But the vast majority of cases from the OT that he gives are due rather to textual criticism, vocalisation, translation or to grammatical phenomena. Let me give an example. The transitive verb *'śh* = "to make" is also used intransitively to mean "to act". In such cases there is no ellipsis because no complement to the verb is needed. If *yākōl* is used to mean "to prevail" then there is no ellipsis, but simply a semantic fact.

Let us consider an English sentence and its translation into Spanish:

He rides   better   than I do.
Cabalga   mejor   que yo.

Seen with English eyes the Spanish form is elliptical; seen with Spanish eyes the English form is redundant; for a grammarian both are quite correct. Now, if a Hebrew says: "At one extreme a cherub, at one extreme a cherub", the English is not thereby elliptical. And let us remember too the verb *hāyâ* = "to be", which Hebrew grammar allows to disappear without any trouble.

Another "economical" grammatical phenomenon is to make two equal words or phrases depend on the same word: two complements of a verb, two verbs belonging to one subject, two nouns with one adjective. In English we can say "on the one hand ... on the other", without having to repeat "hand". This happens in many languages and is also part of Hebrew usage. In recent years the observation has been made that such a phenomenon can affect the second phrase of two parallel phrases. For example, a possessive suffix in one can be understood also for the other. Such grammatical ellipsis has been given the strange name of "double-duty". The name may not be very good, but the observation is quite right. But on only a few occasions is this part of stylistics.

And so, what is there left of ellipsis as a rhetorical figure of speech? The answer is "very little". Let me give two contrasting cases. Hos 1,2, translated word for word, reads as follows: "Go, take for yourself a prostitute wife and sons of prostitution"; before the "sons" we must understand the verb *yld* = "to beget", since *lqh*

= "take" is used for marriage, but not for paternity. This is a case of ellipsis. The second example is Ps 4,3, which literally reads: "Until when my honour to shame". Adding the copula *hyh*, we obtain the normal construction *hyh l-* = "to become, change into", and the phrase clearly means: "Until when will my honour be changed into shame?" Is this a case of ellipsis? Perhaps, but it is not certain, because in Hebrew the verb *hyh* is often not explicit.

b) I have been talking of ellipsis, which omits something which is necessary, since it will be understood anyway. It is quite different when the author omits something which is not necessary to create conciseness. *Concision* (which was called by the ancients brachylogy) is a quality that certain biblical authors develop. It is typical of the good proverb, whether this is isolated, in an anthology, or found in a more extensive piece; in the second instance the phrase may be amplified before or after:

> Injustice is a two-edged sword ....

> A man who builds his house with other people's money
> is like one who gathers stones for his burial mound.

> The knowledge of a wise man will increase like a flood ....

> A fool's story is a burden on a journey ....

> When a wicked man curses Satan,
> he curses himself (Sir 21,3.8.13.16.27).

These five examples are taken from the same chapter, at random. They would go well in an anthology.

Another phenomenon which is related to ellipsis and to concision is the distribution of elements in parallelism. Let us suppose we have two subjects, subject A and subject B, a positive predicate and a negative predicate; more specifically, we have a wise son / a foolish son, joy / sorrow, father and mother. The wise son is a joy for both his father and his mother, the foolish son is a sorrow for them both. But the poet economizes and says:

> A wise son, the joy of his father,
> a foolish son, the sorrow of his mother (Prov 10,1).

This technique is frequent in Hebrew poetry. Isa 2,3: "From Sion will come the law; from Jerusalem, the word of the Lord" = law and word will come from Sion, the mountain of Jerusalem. Isa 3,12: "Children oppress you, women rule over you" = children and women govern and oppress you. Compare this with an opposite case: "They will be a shade in the heat, and a refuge in the storm" (Isa 4,6).

More examples. Ephraim and Judah are different entities in Hos 5,12; the moth and the beetle are enemies attacking both, yet the prophet says: "I am a moth for Ephraim, a beetle to the house of Judah." Hos 8,14: "I will send fire upon his cities and it shall devour his strongholds" = I will send a fire which will devour both cities and strongholds. Joel 3,1: "Your old men will dream dreams, your young men will see visions"; from the context one may conclude that both charismatic, prophetic activities should be attributed to both categories. The opposite is the case in the following example: "Put in the sickle, for the harvest is ripe. Come and tread, for the wine press is full" (Joel 4,13). Job 4,20: "Between morning and evening they are destroyed; they perish for ever, without anyone noticing" = between morning and evening, without anyone noticing, they are destroyed and perish for ever.

W. G. E. Watson, *Classical Hebrew Poetry*, pp. 303-306.

B. *Hyperbole and Litotes*

a) *Hyperbole*, as a rhetorical figure of speech, is a kind of literary exaggeration. It is very common in day to day speech, especially in certain nations and individuals. Hebrew poetry tends more to hyperbole than to sobriety, underestimation. It is particularly frequent in comparisons; it is found also in descriptions and of course in the expression of feelings.

The quails were numerous "like dust, like the sand of the seas" (Ps 78,27); the descendants of Abraham would be "like the dust of the earth and like the stars" (Sir 44,21). Prosperity produces "streams flowing with honey and curds" (Job 20,17). The arrogant city "soars aloft like the eagle and places its nest among the stars" (Obad 4). In a storm at sea the sailors "mounted up to heaven, went down to the depths" (Ps 107,26). Enemies can be more numerous "than the hairs on the head" (Ps 69,5). Excessive praise is "extolling his talent to the clouds" (Sir 13,23). When he wishes to weep Jer 8,23 asks: "Who will give water to my head, and fountains of tears to my eyes". Hab 1,8 describes horsemen as "flying like an eagle swift to devour". Of the proud it is said: "they set their mouths against the heavens, and their tongue struts through the earth" (Ps 73,9).

When Job 40,18 describes Behemoth: "His bones are tubes of bronze, his limbs like bars of iron", the imaginative use of hyperbole can be explained by the fact that his hippopotamus is a symbol of super-human powers. The numerous hyperbolic images in Job can be explained by the deep emotion of the book. Similar, in another tonality, is the enthusiasm of Second Isaiah. Isaiah too, who seems so discreet, can say that the city "is left like a shed in a vineyard, a hovel in a melon field, a besieged city" (Isa 1,8).

b) The opposite figure of speech is *litotes*, which reduces the expression but allows the true value to be understood. It is easier to find in negative forms. "He does not let their cattle decrease" (Ps 107,38) is equivalent to making them abundant. Isa 10,7 says "not a few nations", indicating that they are numerous.

W. G. E. Watson, *Classical Hebrew Poetry*, pp. 316-321.
I. H. Eybers, "Some Examples of Hyperbole in Biblical Hebrew", *Semitics* 1 (1970) 38-49.

CHAPTER X

Dialogue and Monologue

Dialogue can be seen as a literary genre and as a technique of style. As a literary genre it quickly reached a developed stage in the works of Plato and later on flourished above all in the field of philosophical writings.

I. Dialogue as a Genre

As a genre dialogue is present in the Bible in its own particular way. The book of Job should be regarded as dialogue; but there turns out to be little true dialogue between the speakers. From the length of the interventions and their arrangement it seems more like a series of speeches, placed one after the other. Two parallel lines may continue for many miles without approaching each other; two lines which are not parallel, however, even if they are far apart, will eventually meet. The attitudes of the friends of Job and of Job himself are similar in the sense that they all are dealing with a traditional problem pondered over by wise men, but in spite of the length of their speeches no agreement is reached between them. God seems to take a different angle and to remain very distant, but he does reach Job. The book of Job is a superb work of literature, but not a very good example of literary dialogue.

The Song of Songs contains much more true dialogue. Of course this is so, since it contains love-songs exchanged between lovers. But there are also an enormous number of love-songs which are monologues, pronounced by one of the parties. The Song of Songs is in fact exemplary as a dialogue. Perhaps this is why some have considered it a piece of drama, a category which is hardly suitable.

Certain liturgical pieces could also be catalogued as dialogues, for example Ps 136. The mode of recital is more important here than the actual text. Antiphonal recitation turns a written text into a dialogue.

II. Dialogue as a Technique

As a technique of style, we encounter dialogue mostly in prophetic poetry. (I am of course not considering narrative prose here, where dialogue is always present.) Such dialogue may be real, or fictitious. When I call it real, I do not mean that it in fact happened and the poet recorded it. This is possible, but it will not always be the case. I want to distinguish two types of real dialogue, so that with fictitious dialogue we will have a three-fold division:

a) a dialogue or discussion in which two or more prophets speak; b) the poet quotes two or more characters in dialogue in his poem (even if the quotations are invented); c) the poet pretends that the hearers make an intervention, but in fact he alone speaks.

a) *Real dialogue*. When the prophet Jeremiah complains about how God has treated him, it is possible that he received a reply from God (how he received it is another question). Both complaint and reply are recorded in the poem and I would call this dialogue real. Compare the complaint without response in Jer 20,7-10.14-18 with the complaint in 15,10-21, where a response is given:

Jer 15,11: Truly, Lord, I have served you faithfully....
15: Lord, remember me and visit me....
16: I am called by your name, Lord, God of hosts....
18: You have become for me like a deceitful brook,
like waters that fail.
19: Then the Lord said to me:
– If you return, I will restore you and you shall stand before me.

Consultation by oracle is like a dialogue. Jer 42 gives an example. But the dialogue there belongs to the narrative; the oracle alone is poetry.

Let me now pass on to other examples where the prophet speaks with God and intercedes for the people in personal fashion. The vision of Isaiah is presented as a vision in which Isaiah dialogues with God. The actual words are in verse, set within a narrative prose framework. Something similar happens in the vocation of Jeremiah. We are beginning to see that it is difficult to separate the dialogue from the narrative.

Jeremiah is more daring (like another Moses): he reaches the point of struggling with God to make intercession, even though God forbids it. God has the last word, a word of condemnation. Without citing the whole passage (Jer 14,11 – 15,3) I will indicate here the changes of speaker. Those changes which are not explicit are given in brackets (*Profetas*, pp. 482-487):

Jer 14,11: The Lord said to me:

      13: Then I said:

      14: The Lord said to me: (citing the false prophets)

      17: Say this word to them (directed to these prophets)

      19: (Jeremiah addresses the Lord again in the second person)

   15,1: The Lord said to me:

       2: ... If they ask you ... tell them ....

This and other clear examples help us in dealing with other more difficult passages, which become clear immediately when they are read as dialogues. I am referring to pieces which are not set in a narrative framework and where the changes of speaker are not indicated. The Hebrews had no signs to indicate the change of speaker. I will use abbreviations to indicate the speakers in a complex passage from the book of Jeremiah, citing only a few sentences and inviting the reader to read the whole passage following these directions. The speakers are God, the people, and Jeremiah (*Profetas*, pp. 460-465):

God: When I would gather them, says the Lord, there are no grapes on the vine, nor figs on the fig tree ....

People: Why do we sit still? Let us gather together, let us go into the fortified cities and perish there; for the Lord our God has doomed us to perish ....

God: I am sending among you serpents, adders which cannot be charmed ....

Jeremiah: My grief is beyond healing,
my heart is sick within me ....
Is the Lord not in Sion?
Is her King not in her?

God: Why have they provoked me to anger with their graven images, with their foreign idols?

People: The harvest is passed, the summer is ended, and we are not saved.

Jeremiah: For the wound of the daughter of my people is my heart wounded ....
Who will give water to my head,
and fountains of tears to my eyes,
that I might weep day and night
for the slain of the daughter of my people!

God:	O that I had in the desert a wayfarers' lodging place, that I might leave my people and go away from them!
Jeremiah:	I will take up weeping and wailing on the mountains, and a lamentation in the pastures of the wilderness ...
God:	I will make Jerusalem a heap of ruins, a lair of jackals ...
Jeremiah:	Who is the man so wise that he can understand this? ... Why is the land ruined and Laid waste ...?
God:	And the Lord says: Because they have forsaken my law which I set before them ... (Jer 8,13-14.17-21.23; 9,1.9-12).

I must add a cautionary note. This passage is not a unified and coherent dialogue. It is possible and even probable that the text is a later composition which uses material from Jeremiah. This is the explanation given by many these days due to the difficulties and extent of the passage. This solution is quite probable; nevertheless one must not dismiss *a priori* the idea that it is a dialogue.

We go on and find another prophetic text in which contrary affirmations on a particular theme follow each other. Let us take the theme of future salvation: it is announced as imminent and it is expected in the distant future; it comes to Jerusalem the capital and to Bethlehem the village; it will be nationalistic and deal cruelly with the pagans, or kind and beneficent towards them; it will be forceful or benevolent, like a lion or like dew. I am referring to chapters 4–6 of Micah: if we read them as a dialogue or controversy between Micah and the false prophets, then the difficulties and contradictions of the text are solved and it reveals a certain dramatic power. The same book speaks in another passage too of the struggle of Micah against the false prophets. (See the explanation given in *Prophetas*, II [*Ezequiel. Doce profetas menores. Daniel. Baruc. Carta de Jeremías* (NBE; Madrid 1980)], pp. 1037f., 1053-1063.)

The texts cited in this section a) and other similar ones might be regarded as pure literary creation of the prophet to bring his preaching alive; a putting into language of the polemical and dramatic side of his message. If such an explanation were accepted these passages would belong in the next section, but would of course remain examples of literary dialogue.

b) The prophet cites in his speech a *dialogue between different characters*. For example, Isa 3,6-7: "A man takes hold of his brother in the house of his father and says: 'You have a mantle, you shall be our leader, and this heap of ruins shall be under your rule'. The other protests: 'I will not be a healer; in my house there is neither bread nor mantle; you shall not make me leader of the people'." By putting this short dialogue into his vision, the prophet presents in a lively fashion the full dimension of the catastrophe, for no-one can be found to take up the administration. The following comparison becomes more alive by the insertion of dialogue:

> The vision of all this has become for you
> like the words of a book that is sealed.
> When they give it to one who can read,
> saying, "Read this",
> he says, "I cannot, for it is sealed".
> And when they give it to one who cannot read,
> saying, "Read this",
> he says, "I cannot read" (Isa 29,11-12).

c) The most frequent cases are those in which the speaker, the prophet, *cites the words* of the hearers or of others *in order to refute them*. He may give the contents or the general meaning of what they say. It may be an objection which is already formulated, or it may anticipate an objection. The latter was called in classical rhetoric *praeoccupatio*. Sometimes the text will give a signal to identify the citation; on other occasions the reader must understand this on his own initiative. We may suppose that in the recitation voice changes were sufficient to identify certain words as citation. This matter is important for the interpretation; we must not take as words of the prophet — words of God, therefore — what are in fact objections of the listeners.

I must repeat that we must always be ready for possible fiction created by the poet, who puts on the lips of others his own words. The important thing is that he gives a true idea of what those others really feel. The first example comes from Ezekiel. The prophet had preached the imminent arrival of the end, the catastrophe, and the end had not come. Accordingly, the listeners invent and repeat a proverb, a mocking refrain, which the prophet reports in order to refute it with another:

> Son of man, what is this proverb that you are
> saying in the land of Israel: "Many days pass
> and every vision comes to nothing"?...
> Rather, say to them this new proverb:
> "The days are approaching, and every
> vision will come true" (Ezek 12,22-23).

Compare the two proverbs and see how the first proverb has a kind of boomerang effect on the ones who threw it:

People: "Many days pass and every vision comes to nothing."

God: "The days are approaching and every vision will come true."

Whether it is real or fictitious dialogue can be very effective, both as literature and as prophetic word. In the following passage an understanding, though demanding, God speaks to Baruch, the secretary of Jeremiah:

You say: 'Woe is me! for the Lord has added sorrow
to my pain ...!'
Thus says the Lord: 'Look,
what I have built I am breaking down,
and what I have planted I am plucking up;
and are you asking for miracles for yourself?' (Jer 45,3-5).

The citation of the complaint allows a dialogue to begin which leads poor Baruch to historical and theological understanding.

In the next example God addresses foreigners in a particular way, with the formula "let him not say". Forbidding certain statements is an implication that they are already being said and that they should cease, or that they are being felt. In the first case there is a clear refutation, and in the second the complaint is anticipated before it is made. Isa 56,3-7: "Let not the foreigner who has joined himself to the Lord say.... Let not the eunuch say.... For thus says the Lord to the eunuchs.... to the foreigners who join themselves to the Lord...".

Jer 2–3 contains elements of a lawsuit of the prophet against the people. During the accusation, as part of the proof of guilt, the guilty party's words are quoted: "Long ago you broke your yoke and burst your bonds, and you said: 'I will not serve'" (2,20). A little later on it is supposed that the accused protests and denies the accusation, and the prophet insists: "How can you dare to say 'I am not defiled, I have not gone after the Baals'? Look..." (2,23). And later on still the accused pretends to be the accuser, and the prophet replies: "Why do you complain against me, when you are all rebels?" (2,29).

In Isa 49,14-16 there are a few linguistic signs which indicate the presence of an objection which is taken up and refuted; this allows us to make up for the third linguistic sign which is omitted, and to interpret a verse as the third objection. Thus the layout is as follows:

Isa 49,14: Sion was saying: "The Lord has abandoned me ...".

     15: Can a mother forget her baby? ...

     21: But you say: "Who bore me these? ...

     22: Thus says the Lord: Look ....

     24: [you say]: "Can booty be seized from a hero?"

     25: Thus says the Lord: Yes, a hero can lose his prisoner ....

In Isa 58 the linguistic sign is lacking, but the dialogue is clear: objections are cited in order to be refuted. One could make it more explicit with "You say"; the reciter might change his voice; we might use punctuation marks. I will put the speakers on the left and present the text as it stands:

God: They ask of me righteous judgements, they delight to draw near to God.

People: Why do we fast, if you take no notice? ...

God: Look, in the day of your fast you seek your own interests ... (Isa 58,2-4).

When the linguistic signs are lacking the commentator may get the text completely wrong. This is why he has to be aware of the stylistic technique to discover where it lies submerged or disguised.

d) We have examined the three types indicated at the beginning of this section, but now I must add a final point. There are some cases in which the *dialogue is lacking*. Such a lack can take on a theological significance. This is a developed use of the technique, precisely by not using it. The Lord invites people to debate with him; he waits for their response. The gods of Babylon do not respond ... because they do not exist. The lack of response when the dialogue is scarcely begun reveals that the idols are nothing. This is one of the themes of the Second Isaiah.

Since this whole technique of using dialogue has scarcely been examined by scholars, I will present here a list of examples from prophetic and apocalyptic literature:

Isa 10,5-15: Citation of the words of Assyria. The Lord refutes them in v. 15.

Isa 21,1-10: A complex piece of dialogue. The Lord gives a command; the prophet replies that he has carried it out. The prophet repeats the announcement of the messengers and then addresses the people: vv. 6-8a.8b-9a.9b-10. (See the following chapter.)

Isa 28,7-13: Very ingenious. The mocking taunts of the leaders are turned against them by the prophet.

Isa 28,15-19: Citation and refutation.

Isa 30,16: A lively, rapid dialogue between the people and God.

Isa 37,21-29: Citation of the arrogant words of Sennacherib followed by God's reply.

Isa 40,27-31: Citation of the people's complaint and the Lord's reply.

Isa 51,9 – 52,6: Magnificent dialogue between Jerusalem and the Lord, with two lengthy interventions.

Isa 66,7-8: Announcement, wondering objection, explanation.

Jer 3,14 – 4,4: Composed in the form of a trial: act of accusation, final confession of the guilty party, invitation of the Lord.

Jer 4,10: The prophet interrupts the oracle.

Jer 12,1-5: Jeremiah discusses with the Lord: "Even though, Lord, you are always right when I discuss with you, I want to put a case to you". God replies *ad hominem*.

Jer 31,18-20: Complaints of Ephraim and God's reply.

Ezek 18: God cites the people's protest and refutes it.

Ezek 24,19-20: Dialogue of the people with Ezekiel incorporated into the story.

Hos 5,15 – 6,6 (a doubtful case): God begins by expecting conversion: "until they acknowledge their guilt and seek my face" (5,15); the people reply with a superficial conversion, based on false confidence (6,1-3); the Lord replies giving the terms for an authentic conversion (6,4-6).

Amos 7,1-9; 8,1-3: The prophet dialogues with God in various visions.

Zech 1–6: In these visions a mediator of God, an angel, intervenes as speaker on various occasions. This indicates a theological and literary development.

Malachi makes extensive use of the technique: an objection is taken up and refuted. He provides the relevant linguistic signs: "You object... you ask again... you ask why".

Daniel uses the device of the angel who interprets visions or dreams, with clearly indicated dialogue.

R. Lapointe, *Dialogues bibliques et dialectique interpersonelle. Étude stylistique et théologique sur le procédé dialogal tel qu'employé dans l'Ancien Testament* (RMont 1 Theologie; Paris–Tournai–Montreal 1971).

A. Graffy, *A Prophet Confronts His People. The Disputation Speech in the Prophets* (AnBib 104; Rome 1984).

III. **Interior Dialogue and Monologue**

a) *Interior dialogue* brings about an internal "doubling" of the individual. Monologue must be understood in its relationship to dialogue. Stylistically speaking, monologue is not one person speaking, but the breaking into a context of dialogue with a reflection directed to oneself. These are not easily distinguished from what are called monological functions of language, the internal, mental language with which we think out and clarify things, or express ourselves to ourselves.

When the Psalmist says "Bless the Lord, my soul", it is as if he "doubled" himself to encourage himself. In his mind, the "soul" hears the "I". I am interested in more complex cases. Even though they may be few in the Bible, they had to be mentioned here.

b) In Deut 32 we read the great poem of Moses, which according to fictitious tradition he left as an accusing testament to the Israelites. Moses speaks to the people reliving in poetic fashion the whole of their history. Suddenly God enters the poem, giving his interior thoughts aloud. Since it is personal thoughts, it is *monologue*; nevertheless it is intended to be heard. This contrast is basic to this point of style. Carrying on with his train of thought, God interrupts himself and corrects himself:

Deut 32,19: The Lord saw it and spurned them,
              because of the provocation of his sons and daughters.
      20: He thought: I will hide my face from them,
              I will see what their end will be ....
      26: I thought: I will scatter them,
              I will make the remembrance of them cease among men.
      27: But no; I fear the boasting of the enemy
              and the evil interpretation of the adversary.

Ps 42–43 is a dramatic text, which expresses the desolation of the Psalmist at the absence of God: a God who was the water which satisfied his thirst and has become the flood which brings destruction. His desolation is expressed in an aside in which the Psalmist no longer addresses God, but addresses himself. The poetic device of "doubling" expresses magnificently the internal tension which is brought about by his experience of God's absence and presence. This aside is the refrain of the poem:

Why are you cast down, my soul?
Why are you disturbed within me?
Hope in God, for you will again praise him:
"My salvation and my God" (Ps 42,6.12; 43,5; *Treinta Salmos*, pp. 158-159).

One might compare this with Ps 73, which has a different order. The Psalmist expresses his interior struggle without using the technique described. Then God gives him the solution to his problems and he immediately opens himself and directs himself to God. From a narrated monologue we move to speech directed to another speaker:

> When I thought how to understand this,
>   it seemed difficult to me;
>   until I went into the mystery of God,
>   and understood their destiny.
> Truly, you set them in slippery places,
>   you make them fall to ruin (Ps 73,16-18).

The theme of dialogue could bring us on to the phenomenon of changes of speaker and changes of person spoken to, with or without linguistic signs. But I prefer to conclude this chapter here.

CHAPTER XI

Development and Composition

Development and composition are two different activities
which may seem to coincide in the final result. Development means
starting with a simple element or idea and making it grow by
looking on it in a series of different ways. A simple idea like "the
return from exile to the native land" contains within it potentially
many different aspects which will be used in the development. It
may be compared to the title of a book, article, or poem. A musical
idea or theme is also developed perhaps into a sonata, a symphony,
or a fugue.

Composition on the other hand means starting with a number
of elements and placing them in such a way that they form a whole.
Through this composition the elements take on different
relationships between each other, which can be meaningful as well
as formal.

The final result placed before the reader or the critic is the
work. In the work development and composition are fused. From
the point of view of the one who is analyzing the work development
and composition may be two ways of looking at the same work, two
points of view 180 degrees apart. When he analyzes the way the
elements are placed together the critic will perhaps discover how an
initial or central idea has been developed. Discovering an idea, a
basic symbol in the development, he will uncover the wisdom of the
writer who put all the elements together in a harmonious whole.

Classical rhetoric distinguished three stages in the process of
production of the work: *inventio, dispositio, elocutio*. This may be
understood as: the finding of material and arguments; the making
of a precise plan as to how they should be put together; and finally
the redaction. We prefer to focus on the analysis of the work for
two principal reasons: because we do not really have any definite
knowledge about the production of the work: all we can guess
comes from an examination of the works themselves, which is all we
have; and because we are not trying to teach anyone how to write
biblical texts.

This being established, the distinction and separation of
development and composition has a didactic value here, it is a way

of explaining the production of the work. It will be unavoidable that during my presentation the two aspects will frequently be interwoven.

I. **Development**

A. *An Example*

We are going to pretend that there is an Israelite poet called *š^emaryāhû* or Semariah, or at least that this is the name of the one who bids him to write, or of a friend; or we might just say that this name, which means "the Lord guards", just occurs to him as a theme or idea for the writing of a prayer. His starting point is this statement about God which includes potentially within it many aspects: the theme must be developed in such a way as to demonstrate these aspects. Now to guard is the duty of the watchman, who watches by day or keeps vigil by night; if it is by night, he must not sleep; if he is guarding the gate, he watches who enters and who goes out; if he is the personal guard of some individual, he protects him from the sun so that he will not feel the heat, and from the darkness so that he will not stumble. This is what the Lord is like, only at a higher level: he does not need relief, he is always there; to indicate this superiority of the Lord, a contrast from the natural world will be used.

I have developed this theme in reflection, revealing its different aspects. Now is the time to order and redact the material. In the process I can use parallelism, merismus, polar expression, repetition, antithesis. Some of these have already appeared in the previous stage of development by reflection. I write, I make some corrections, and a short prayer like this one may be the result:

> I lift up my eyes to the mountains.
> From where will my help come?
> My help comes from the Lord,
> who made heaven and earth.
> He will not permit your foot to stumble,
> he who guards you does not sleep;
> he does not sleep nor rest,
> he who guards Israel.
> The Lord guards you in his shadow,
> he is at your right hand:
> By day the sun will not damage you,
> nor the moon by night.

The Lord guards you from every evil,
he guards your life;
the Lord guards your coming in and your going out
now and for ever (Ps 121; *Treinta Salmos*, pp. 344-347).

Let us now forget about all our initial suppositions about the
author, because in fact we know nothing about him, nor about the
production of the poem. Everything I know I have taken from an
analysis of the poem. It is not difficult to find the central theme,
when the root *šmr* = "to guard" is found five times and the name
of the Lord four times in this short poem.

Did the poet invent what he has written? No, for most of it is
taken from the tradition in which he lives and works. The reference
to the Lord "who made heaven and earth", the examples of
merismus "sun and moon", "coming in and going out", the very
idea of God who guards and protects. But the poem is original,
developed richly but with sobriety. It is well put together: the
beginning with its hesitant search and quick reply, the end which
opens out without limits "now and for ever".

The poet therefore develops the idea or theme using traditional
material, literary motifs, known forms and stylistic techniques; in
this way he makes his personal contribution. The Psalm in question
is very traditional, but it is also original. It is not easy to confuse
with others, we remember its shape. Now we must look separately
at the questions of material or theme, forms, and individual
contribution of the poet.

B. *Material Used: Themes, Motifs, "Topoi"*

When we speak of *material* we are speaking of content, even
though some material may be in an initial stage of organisation and
therefore have some kind of form. The *theme* is more generic, less
differentiated: God the protector, the weakness of man, enemy
threat. The *motif* is more specific, more clearly differentiated: a man
caught in the trap he has laid, dust returning to dust, the enemy
waiting in ambush. Motifs are often in the form of images.

When a literary motif achieves a certain regularity in the
tradition so that it becomes part of the tradition, we may call it a
topos (a Greek word which in Latin is "locus" and means "place").
If the motif or *topos* is overused we might begin to call it a cliché.
This is something like a lexicalised metaphor. A cliché may regain
its original impact through the skill of a poet.

Biblical poets use abundantly not only common and traditional
themes, but also literary motifs, like multiple threads of a tenacious

and persistent tradition. They are not too afraid of using clichés. The critic is able to establish the frequent presence of certain *topoi* without too much difficulty; what cannot be so easily established is a clear idea about the development in the use of such motifs.

L. Alonso Schökel, *Estudios de poética hebrea*, pp. 345-353.
A. Altmann (ed.), *Biblical Motifs. Origins and Transformation* (STLI 3; Cambridge, Massachusetts 1966).

Let us take the military levy, or recruitment, as an example. Recruitment can be done with visible signs like standards, banners, flags or gestures, or with audible signs with shouts and the blowing of trumpets. This military exercise is applied as an image to the Lord for summoning people for military or peaceful purposes. It can also appear in the literal sense, as part of a description of preparations for war. It is used in other contexts too, for there are other reasons for summoning people. I will give some examples now, following the order they appear in the Bible, but adding some comments on relative dating if I think them probable.

> He will raise a signal for a nation far off,
> he will whistle for it to the ends of the earth:
> look at them coming speedily and swiftly (Isa 5,26).

The Lord recruits the enemy to come against his people. Then their advance is described.

> The root of Jesse shall stand as an ensign to the peoples, the
> nations will seek it (Isa 11,10).

This is the beginning of a section added to 11,1-9 by Second Isaiah or a writer of his school and mentality. It is a peaceful summoning.

> On a bare mountain raise the signal,
> cry aloud to them, waving the hand ... (Isa 13,2).

This refers to the army the Lord recruits on the day of anger; it may be applied to the Medes coming against Babylon in the historical sense, or it may be seen as having eschatological meaning. This passage is probably late, and related to the eschatology of Isa 24-27.

> Inhabitants of the world, dwellers on the earth,
> when a signal is raised on the mountains, look!
> when a trumpet is blown, listen! (Isa 18,3).

The Lord calls people to witness his action against Nubia. They will witness battle and victory.

> His rock will escape in terror
> and his leaders desert the standard panic stricken (Isa 31,9).

There are difficulties about the syntax here. The "rock" is the Assyrian divinity. The standard — of the Lord? — alarms and scatters the men, rather than gathering them. This is an original use of a well-known motif.

> Look: with my hand I give a signal to the nations,
> I raise my standard for the peoples;
> they will bring your sons in their arms,
> your daughters will be carried on their shoulders (Isa 49,22).

This is not a military recruitment, but a peaceful one: the conquering peoples liberate their prisoners of war and bring them personally back to their land. The Lord has authority over the pagans too. This explains the multitude of Israelite "children" gathered around the "mother" Jerusalem.

> Announce it in Judah, proclaim it in Jerusalem,
> sound the trumpet in the land, shout with full voice:
> Assemble to march to the fortified city (Jer 4,5).

Under the threat of imminent invasion, the prophet summons the citizens in military fashion, not in order to attack, but to take refuge in a walled fortress.

> How long must I see the flag
> and hear the trumpet calling to arms? (Jer 4,21).

This is a merismus which sums up war. The prophet is tired of seeing and announcing imminent or present war.

> Set up a flag on the earth,
> sound the trumpet for the nations,
> summoning them to the holy war;
> recruit the kingdoms for war against her:
> Ararat, Minni and Ashkenaz;
> appoint a general against her (Jer 51,27).

The Lord conducts a general levy of allies against Babylon.

In the announcement or description of any great calamity the following topics may be found: an invitation to weeping, hands and knees made weak, anguish and terror like those of a woman giving birth. Against the background of a continuity of the tradition there are occasional cases where the topics regain their original force.

The expression "pangs and agonies will seize them, they will be in anguish like a woman in travail", or a variation on it, is frequent: Isa 13,8; 21,3; Jer 6,24; 22,23; 49,24; 50,43; Mic 4,9. Two special cases may be singled out:

> Ask and find out:
> Can a man bring a child to birth?
> But what do I see? Every man like a woman giving birth:
> their hands on their loins, their faces disturbed and livid
>   (Jer 30,6).

> For a long time I have held my peace,
> I was silent, I restrained myself;
> now I cry out like a woman giving birth,
> I gasp and pant (Isa 42,14).

In the example from Jeremiah the prophet sees something never seen: men acting like women giving birth. For they are dying of fear and anguish. The irony is without pity. The example from Isaiah is remarkable not only for the series of chosen verbs, but because the subject is the Lord, giving birth to history.

I think that this section on material used for development might also include a mention of *semantic fields*. The poet is usually well versed in his language, he uses it creatively. A lax and open structure of language is the series of words which belong to a particular field: the elements, dwelling places, crops, employments. These materials of language, kept together in the loose associations which we call semantic fields, are familiar to the poet and he uses them in the development of a theme. They will obviously be used for lists and series; but they are also useful for parallelism, antithesis and even for the organization of a complete poem.

C. *Forms*

The majority of the points of style we have studied are relevant here. They may be ways of repeating, dividing, articulating, or of positioning, before, after, in parallel, in chiasm.

What about Ps 148? The "universal praise of the Lord" is a theme. It can be developed by articulation or by listing. The universe is divided into heaven and earth, the elements of the former and the inhabitants of the latter are given, ordered in their various groups. Everything is organized with two numbers: the number seven for the heavens, the number twenty-two (letters of the alphabet) for the earth. Thus this is what results:

Heavens: angels//armies, sun and moon// stars
           spaces//higher waters

Earth: sea monsters, lightning/hail/snow/frost//wind
           mountains/hills, fruit trees/cedars
           wild beasts/cattle, reptiles/birds
           kings/peoples//princes/rulers,
           young men/ maidens, old men/children.

The psalm is almost finished. We have the theme, the development and the composition. All that remains is to redact it and present it. (See L. Alonso Schökel, *Treinta Salmos*, pp. 441-448).

During the development of the poem, or the redaction, the arrangement of the pieces of the poem is also achieved. The members or parts of a fourfold parallelism, of a series, or of a list have to be positioned in a suitable way. In parallelism, chiasm, in a series, etc. Sometimes the order has no effect on the mode of expression: the pieces have to be ordered in some particular way but it is of little significance. But on other occasions the order has a particular significance. The critic must be alert to this, and must be able to discern such cases.

I can mention here an anomalous positioning, which rhetoricians observed and called in Greek *hýsteron-próteron* = "later earlier", which is a kind of chronological inversion. E. Zurro gives the example of Zech 10,11:

> They shall pass through the narrow sea,
> the waves of the sea shall be smitten
> and all the depths of the Nile will be dried up.

At first it is said that they cross over the sea, and then that the waters dried up. The order of events should be inverted.

Cecilia Carniti has given me other examples:

> O God, our ears have heard,
> our fathers have told us (Ps 44,2).

> Your throne is established from of old
> and you exist from eternity (Ps 93,2).

> You are my son,
> today I have begotten you (Ps 2,7).

For this technique to work it is necessary that there be no link introducing an explanation; for if the second member is presented as the cause of explanation of the first, the order would be the regular syntactical order.

Common and easy ways of development are patterns like announcement – fulfilment, command – execution of command, sentence – motivation. Paraphrase, which is not always undesirable, can be another means of development since it can explain, confirm or prolong the idea. Dialogue in its various forms is another way of developing a theme.

But development is not always practised. Sometimes it is not desirable, sometimes it is minimal. Proverbs are better not developed. Who would dare to add anything to Prov 26,15:

> The idler puts out his hand to the dish
> but is too tired to raise it to his mouth.

Similarly, Prov 20,14, again in two stages:

> "No good, no good!" says the buyer;
> and he goes off boasting of what he has bought.

Many proverbs have been ruined by being developed with synonymous or antithetical parallelism, or with an explanation. Ps 117 seems to defy Ps 119: two verses against one hundred and seventy-six. Opposite the lengthy oracles of Ezekiel against pagan kings we can place tiny and effective pieces with scarcely a word of development. Isa 14,24-27; 21,11-12 (allusive and enigmatic); 21,13-15; 30,6-7.

D. *Individual Contribution*

The poet may also have something personal to contribute as he uses traditional material and forms, something which may provoke surprise, interest or satisfaction in the reader, at least for the good reader who is not in a hurry.

The house is built with stones, with skill. Jer 22,13 says: "Woe to him who constructs his house with injustice!" The injustice of leaders and governors is a repeated theme in the prophets; Jeremiah addresses Jehoiakim (translated rather literally):

> You do not have eyes nor heart except for dishonest gain,
> for innocent blood: for shedding it,
> for abuse and oppression: for practising them (Jer 22,17).

Isa 30,28 describes a theophany of the Lord who comes to sift the nations, to bridle them, but with no ordinary sieve and bridle:

> To sift the peoples
> with the sieve of destruction,
> to place on the jaws of the nations
> the bridle which leads astray.

The same technique appears in Isa 34,11:

> The Lord applies to it
> the measuring-line of chaos
> and the level of nothingness.

I have reached the point where development of a theme and redaction or writing may be confused. The continuity of the motifs allows us to enter into a tradition. Once we are in that tradition we must observe carefully the texture of the individual text.

E. *An Analysis of a Text*

I will conclude this section by repeating the operation with which I began, but in the opposite direction. I will not imagine the different stages of the production of the poem, but I receive it completed and preserved, and I begin to analyze it to discover how it has been developed and perhaps also how it has been composed. The text is Psalm 122:

> What happiness when they said to me:
> "Let us go to the house of the Lord"!
> And now our feet are standing
> within your gates, O Jerusalem.
> Jerusalem is built
> as a well-constructed city.
> There the tribes go up,
> the tribes of the Lord
> according to the custom of Israel,
> to give thanks to the name of the Lord.
> There are the tribunals of justice,
> in the palace of David.
> Desire peace for Jerusalem:
> "May those who love you live peacefully,
> may there be peace within your walls,
> tranquillity in your palaces".

In the name of my brothers and friends
I greet you with peace;
for the sake of the house of the Lord our God
I desire your good.

At the beginning we have the journey, in two stages: firstly, the announcement of a pilgrimage to the capital city; second, the arrival at the gates to the capital city. Once there, the speaker gazes at the city: its compact construction (not scattered houses), the arrival of different groups to celebrate the worship of the temple, the royal palace where justice is dispensed. Then come the greetings and invitations with the constant theme: peace. Thus, the journey is divided into departure and arrival; the contemplation of the city considers streets, temple and palace; and the third part is the repeated desire for peace. Thus the poem speaks of the city, and of peace. The city *'îr* is in assonance with *yᵉrû*. Peace is *šālôm*. The two together form Jerusalem, *yᵉrûšālēm*. So it seems that this psalm develops a name according to its two components, just as they sound to the author. (*Treinta Salmos*, pp. 350-365).

II. Composition

Now I must explain what makes a Hebrew poem a unified whole. I am not concerned here with the unity external to the text. In a liturgical service, for example, various heterogeneous texts may be used; the celebration unifies them by bringing them into the liturgical context. This produces certain relationships between the texts, though from an external point of view. The liturgical service will always be outside the text. It would be quite different when a celebration, whether cultic or profane, required the writing of a suitable text; in such a case the situation would enter into the writing of the text.

I must make a distinction between primary and secondary unity. A real artistic unity may be produced by different processes. It could be a chance event, as when different houses in a street have come together to form a beautiful and harmonious group of buildings. The opposite case is when the unity is planned beforehand: as with Pienza in Renaissance times or Brasilia in our own days. A later writer could take already completed pieces and bring them together skilfully to form a new and complex unity. What is important is the result, not the process, the stages of contemplation and analysis, not the actual production.

Now, in modern investigation of the Old Testament, especially of the prophets, there is a strong tendency to consider what we read now as the result of a build-up of successive layers of text, deposited in different centuries by later authors or schools, on an original base, which at times is very limited. There is some truth in this hypothesis, for it seems undeniable that certain oracles were reelaborated, adapted, brought up to date. It is true too that from the separate oracles the disciples of a prophet, or people intent on conserving the material, gathered together groups of oracles and, finally, books. However, I believe there are some exaggerations in applying this approach ("Of Methods and Models", VTS 36, pp. 3-13).

Few will deny that Isa 11,1-9 is a unit and that 11,10-16 is an addition, weakly dovetailed by the repetition of the words "root" and "Jesse". The perfectly rounded unity of Isa 1,21-26 receives an addition of two verses. The vocation of Jeremiah, his naming as a prophet and his mission, is interrupted by the wedge of the two visions. The remarkable complaint of Jer 20,7-18 has to suffer the violence of the triumphalist insertion in vv. 11-13. The initial vision of Ezekiel must tolerate notable additions, more or less theological, which confuse the image and violate the grammar. Ezek 3 is a collection of different pieces concerning the mission of the prophet but the grouping together is weak. And so on.

If we wish to analyze the poems as units, we must bear these issues in mind. On some occasions we will remove additions and insertions in order to rediscover the original poem; on other occasions we will simply recognise that the final unity was not part of the original plan, but that another poet has worked over material he has received. In any case, what we want to analyze and understand is the unity of the result, the work. My task now is to describe some of the methods of composition of Israelite poets, or, more precisely, some of the ways in which the actual poems are put together. We can agree with a great number of authors in calling this the structure of the work. I will divide the explanation into three parts: clear composition (the surface structure), patterns or schemas, individual structure.

A. *Obvious Composition — The Surface Structure*

Here I wish to deal with cases where the structure is clear from explicit linguistic signs, and is therefore neither hidden nor completely absent.

a) *Alphabetic* composition. This is both obvious and artificial. A Hebrew acrostic will use the twenty-two letters of the Hebrew alphabet. To each letter corresponds a hemistich (Ps 111; 112), a verse (Ps 25), two verses (Ps 37), three verses (Lam 1), or even eight verses (Ps 119).

The technique is so obvious that the Vulgate removed the letters from their words, preserved them in latinized forms and placed them at the beginning of each strophe of the Lamentations. Later on these letters were even put to music. The technique does not help the internal unity and coherence of the poem. It is sufficient for the poet to find words which begin with the required letter, and he goes on writing, developing, verse by verse (as may happen to a writer of verse who tries to complete the fourteen lines of a sonnet). However, it is also possible that this artificial alphabetical composition has a robust poetic structure which gives it a far deeper dimension. This is what happens in Ps 37; being an acrostic it has deceived many commentators who have been unaware of the other dimension of the unity of the poem (*Treinta Salmos*, pp. 409-415).

Acrostics of another type, based on a name or a text, have not yet been found in the Bible. (There was an attempt to find one in Ps 2.)

A weakened form of alphabetic composition consists in making a structure of 22 parts, corresponding to the alphabet.

Here is a list of examples: Ps 9–10; 25; 34; 37; 111; 112; 119; 145; Nah 1; Prov 31,10-31; Sir 51,13-20.

W. G. E. Watson, *Classical Hebrew Poetry*, pp. 190-195. Then there are studies dedicated to individual texts.

b) *Numerical* composition. Such compositions use as their basis certain numbers: four, seven, ten, twelve, twenty-two; or the schema "x plus one". The number may be explicit or implicit. If it is implicit it belongs to the next section, on underlying patterns and schemas.

Cf. L. Alonso Schökel, "Estructuras numericas en el Antiguo Testamento", *Hermenéutica de la Palabra*. II. *Interpretación literaria de textos bíblicos* (Madrid 1987), pp. 257-270.

c) *Inclusion*. I spoke about this in the chapter on repetition. The inclusion defines the limits of a poem and in this sense contains the poem and brings it together. In itself it is a weak structure, but it may happen that a word or phrase of the inclusion expresses the heart of the poem. In these cases it is the function of the inclusion to bring to the surface, to make perceptible, the essence of the poem. A good example is Isa 1,21-26: the repetition of "faithful city" and "righteousness" provides both the outline and the meaning of the poem.

An inclusion may help in defining the limits of a poem when they are in doubt. It may indicate the extent of a section, which has its own particular structure, as in Pss 90; 51.

The book of Isaiah is enclosed in a huge inclusion: about fifty words of chapter 1 are repeated in chapters 65–66. This means that the final author desired to edit the work as a book; it does not mean that the inclusion has brought about a unity of composition throughout the book (*Profetas*, pp. 383-385).

d) The *refrain* is a periodical repetition. It indicates the strophes and is a sign of the composition of the poem. Sometimes the refrain gives a concentrated expression of the theme or situation or central emotion of the poem, as is the case in Ps 42–43. Usually the refrain does not have simply formal value, but emphasises by repetition and makes more obvious the deeper structure of the poem.

e) A *concentric* structure is one where words are repeated in inverse order on both sides of a central point. This is also called symmetrical structure. Others see it as a kind of augmented chiasm. Such structures may be indicated thus: ABC X CBA, or ABCD DCBA.

The study of this technique has been intensive in the last thirty years and has yielded abundant results (even though proponents always find a few more examples than those which actually exist).

Concentric structure appears in short units, like Amos 5,4-6; in units of average size, like Isa 14; in parts of oracles, like Isa 13,11-17 (which might also be considered an inclusion); a later author could also use this technique to bring together some independent oracles into a higher unity, as in Isa 56–66 (according to P. Bonnard). Concentric structures are also found in narrative prose (for example, Jonah 1) and in rhetoric (for example, Deut 8).

f) *Key word/root.* I have spoken of this in the chapter on repetition. It is found in both prose and poetry. It does not require regular repetition, simply a reiteration which is easily perceived.

Isa 66,15-24 repeats the verb "come" six times, directing us to Mount Sion as the centre of the universe; furthermore the section's limits are defined by an inclusion of three repeated words. The word "loincloth" is found eight times in a prose text, which is symbolic action and explanation: Jer 13,1-11. Jer 14,11-16, found in a section of extensive dialogue (see the chapter on dialogue, pp. 170-179) repeats the noun "prophets" four times, the verb "prophesy" four times, and four times again the word-pair "sword and hunger". In Ezek 7,1-9 the key word "end" brings with it the resonance of "doom, time, day". Ezek 37,15-28 announces in prose the reunification of the people; the key word *'eḥād* = "one", is repeated seven times in the first part and three in the second part.

Tjhe verb *šûb* = "to return", with seven appearances, gives a secondary unity to Hos 5–11, though the effect is not noticeable in normal reading. Jer 14,2-9 is more complex, for it repeats the root *šwb* in various meanings: "return, backsliding, convert, apostasy". The "dies irae" of Zephaniah 1,14-18, hammering home the word "day", is well known.

When the poem is recited aloud the resounding repetition of the key word focuses the attention on the crucial point, concentrates the vision, and engraves the theme in the memory of the listener.

B. *Patterns or Schemas*

The pattern is a design that is placed on the cloth. The cloth is cut according to the shape and size of the pattern. But then the pattern is removed. Thus the pattern is a structure which provides the structure, but at the same time an absent structure. Others might say that it lies hidden below the surface, or that it is implicit. It may be compared to a mould, a model or a matrix. What is left of it in the finished work? Only the traces.

Patterns must somehow be known, and must be identifiable in the living tradition, ready for repeated uses. The pattern stylizes the material, brings heterogeneous elements into unity. It can even bring about a complete metaphorical transformation (see the chapter on images).

a) The patterns or schemas known as *literary genres* have become well known in biblical studies particularly since the time of Gunkel. In fifty years we have achieved a good list and significant descriptions of many: prophetic genres, wisdom genres, and the different types of psalms: the hymn, the lament, the thanksgiving, the song of trust, psalms of the kingship of the Lord, royal psalms, wisdom psalms. Any special introduction to the OT or to books or groups of books is bound to give information on this well-known literary theme. But our assurance in knowing the theory and description of literary genres should lead to two notes of caution. Firstly, there is no point in distinguishing and sub-distinguishing *ad infinitum*; and second, assigning a passage to a genre is not everything, and cannot dispense us from study of the individual text.

b) There is another kind of pattern which comes from historical *traditions* or from social *institutions*. A few decades ago there was a lot of talk of the "royal" pattern, and of sacral kingship.

The recognition of the pattern of the Exodus has had more luck and is better substantiated, articulated in the series: "departure from Egypt – journey through the desert – entry into the promised land". This pattern allows various possibilities: it can be applied with its three stages, it may be reduced to two, one stage can be developed further, it may be inverted (the antiexodus).

A. Spreafico, *Esodo, memoria e promessa* (Bologna 1985).

The judicial pattern is very frequent, especially in its bilateral version. Through the prophet the Lord takes issue with his people, he accuses them of failure to keep the covenant, he urges confession and conversion. This pattern presupposes two parties and the role of each, and it is developed in a series of basic stages. Variations are possible in the order of the stages and through the substitution of other elements. In some examples God presents himself as the judge to pronounce the sentence.

P. Bovati, *Ristabilire la giustizia. Procedure, vocabulario, orientamenti* (AnBib 110; Rome 1986).

The first chapter of Genesis uses the pattern of a week of six days followed by one day of rest.

This field has been studied little; so there is a great possibility of further studies which will help interpretation.

C. *Individual Composition*

Even the common patterns are subject to the work of the individual writer. It is true that there are some poems which are so conventional that they keep to the basic schema with no sign of personal effort by the writer. These poems are usually not the most interesting. There are many poems which follow their own path, even though they do not totally leave tradition to one side. Whatever the case, the final and most important task of the critic is to explain the individual poem, considering its own individual structure.

When the poem is an authentic unit, and not simply an amalgamation of bits, multiple relationships are set up between the various elements. In some cases these relationships may be of a purely formal nature, since the elements had to be put together somehow. But in the majority of cases the relationships have a bearing on the meaning. In other words, the poem says more by the internal relationships of its elements than by the sum of these elements.

a) The poet may place together two or three pictures, or compact blocks, he may create alternating sequences, he may want to proceed by waves which take up a motif again and take it further. I will begin by explaining a rather difficult and particular case, that of Isa 21,1-10.

A most important piece of international political news! Important in itself, for an empire has fallen; important for the victims of its imperialism too, the people "threshed and winnowed". The poem could have begun with the great news (thus it is with the version found in Rev 18,2). Thus it could have taken pleasure in the effects of the news on various peoples. Compare the oracle against Tyre in Isa 23. The great news could have been placed as a climax in the middle of the poem, with a build-up to the point of excitement and an ensuing relaxation of tension. But in this poem the news is kept until the end, creating a sense of tension, building up and titillating the curiosity. Nevertheless, the news dominates the poem from the very beginning and the game consists in saying that something serious has taken place without saying precisely what. The poem distributes the news in two stages, which are not simply parallel, but which follow each other dynamically: firstly, the prophet's vision; second, the prophet's announcement. The vision is confused and chilling: the poet only manages to trace separate, rapid lines and powerfully to express his anguish: it is clear there is something about war and we hear some names of assailants; their advance is swift, like the impetuous, burning desert wind. V. 5 possibly allows us to hear, without introductions, some words pronounced at a distance: the domineering and self-satisfied empire is planning banquets, the enemy is already oiling shields. The first picture concludes with these voices echoing through the air, almost without characters who pronounce them: a great wind, a war, Elamites, Medes, set against the destroyer to destroy him.

The second part gives the explanation, but not at once. The Lord speaks, but instead of giving the news himself he announces that a pair of horsemen will bring the news. A watchman must be stationed constantly to receive the news and pass it on immediately. The prophet takes on the watchman's role; he knows that the message of the riders is God's message. He sees them come from afar. As they approach, they shout out the news: "Babylon has fallen!" All that remains is for the poet to communicate the news from God, news of liberation of those who have been "threshed and winnowed".

The poem has its own structure which is powerful and dynamic. Thus the poet exploits to the maximum the transcendence of the historical event of the fall of the second Babylonian empire. It is clear that this poem is not from Isaiah, and that historically it belongs to the period in which Babylon is threatened with destruction. Here is the complete poem:

> Like whirlwinds coming from the Negeb,
> it comes from the desert, from a terrible land.
> A sinister vision has been shown to me:
> the traitor betrayed, the devastator devastated.
> — "Forward, Elamites! Lay siege, people of Media!
> And end to the cries!"
> — On seeing it, my loins are filled with anguish,
> pangs have seized me like those of a woman giving birth;
> hearing it overwhelms me,
> seeing it terrifies me;
> my mind reels, horror appals me;
> the evening I longed for has turned into trembling.
> — "Prepare the table, lay out the cloth,
> let us eat and drink!
> — On your feet, captains! Oil the shields!"
> — This the Lord has told me:
> Go and mount a guard; let him announce what he sees.
> If he sees people on horseback, a pair of riders,
> sitting on asses, or mounted on camels,
> let him heed, let him pay great attention,
> and let him cry: I can see!
> — As a watchman, Lord, I myself am here,
> ready waiting all the day,
> and at my post all the night.
> Attention! a rider is coming,
> a pair of riders, and they are shouting:
> Fallen, fallen is Babylon!
> The statues of her gods lie,
> shattered on the ground.
> My people, threshed and winnowed,
> what I have heard from the Lord of armies,
> the God of Israel, is what I announce to you (Isa 21,1-10).

Of course, there will be a different kind of analysis for each poem. One can only learn by practising such analysis.

b) Composition in *scenes* is easier to detect and more frequent. One may have a diptych, triptych, or even a set of several scenes or pictures. Ps 51 — omitting the addition in vv. 20-21 — is made up of two contrasting scenes: vv. 3-11 in the kingdom of sin, vv. 12-19 in the kingdom of grace. One word from each scene has escaped to the opposite side to serve as a link: "happiness" in v. 10 and "sin" in v. 15. There is neither bridge nor hinge between the two parts, but a violent break. A definite, categorical verb "Create!" introduces the kingdom of grace.

Zephaniah 1,1-6 places two small pictures together: in the first there is a great panorama of the multitudes which God annihilates; in the second the scene is close and more limited, the Jewish people alone. The relation between the two pictures states: what God does throughout the world will also be your fate, chosen people.

c) Another type of individual structure is based on a *semantic centre*, which is frequently an image or a symbol. The above-mentioned alphabetical Ps 37 is bound together strongly by the theological motif "possession of the land", together with its opposite "being excluded, exiled, exterminated"; possession of a piece of land is seen as part of God's design, beginning with law and history (Joshua); the promise is annulled due to injustice but restated by God. This vigorous deep structure to the psalm emerges to the surface at five points, like the periscope of a submarine, and spreads out in synonymous phrases. It is curious that commentators have missed it. This shows just how far behind this kind of analysis is and how necessary it is to understand poems correctly.

In Ps 102 time creates the semantic axis: the broken time of the disappointed sick man, the time of the destroyed city, the time of successive generations, cosmic time, the infinite time of God. Cutting across this is another semantic axis: the individual – the chosen people – pagan nations.

In Isa 62,1-9 the symbol of marriage provides various elements and unifies the poem.

This type of analysis can first be applied in texts the extent and unity of which are quite sure: psalms, wisdom instructions, oracles against pagan nations. In the rest of prophecy we must be prepared for possible later elaborations and secondary compositions. What we must not do with a prophetic oracle is to remove verses claiming that they are incoherent with the author or poem, without first examining whether they are coherent in poetical terms.

d) *Other examples.* Ps 4 has the psalmist facing two groups of people. The first group is hostile; he addresses them with seven imperatives, moving them to conversion, and finally trust in the Lord. The second group are dispirited friends, whom he desires to strengthen with his witness. The trust of the psalmist opens and closes the psalm with two symbols which harmonise with each other: space and rest (*Treinta Salmos*, pp. 39-47).

Ps 23 proceeds in two complementary pictures: the Lord as shepherd and as host. God guides his people through the desert as shepherd and welcomes them into the land offering his hospitality. The end of the psalm opens up into a new pilgrimage which symbolizes the life of the psalmist (*Treinta Salmos*, pp. 110-117).

Ps 8 has three anaphora-like expressions each beginning with the particle *mâ*. The first and the last, both statements of admiration, form an inclusion; the one in the middle, a question, emphasises the scope of the psalm. The whole psalm is marked by wonder and questioning concerning man and God. The central part of the psalm is a kind of rite of enthronement of man: his rank is "little less than God", he is crowned "with glory and majesty", he has power "over the works of your hands", he places his feet over "animals, birds and fish" (*Treinta Salmos*, pp. 111-118).

Ps 65 presents the temple as the centre of attraction for the people. From his temple the Lord of history and of the world rules, and is presented in short and intense descriptions. This universal Lord becomes *paterfamilias* of the country people, who feeds them in the land of pasture and cultivation. Seven verbs with the grateful land as subject correspond to seven others denoting God's actions as farmer (*Treinta Salmos*, pp. 257-264).

Chapter 9 of the book of Proverbs, leaving aside the central insertion, is a diptych of two similar but contrasting pictures. Lady Wisdom and Lady Foolishness invite guests: to the banquet of life, and to the stolen bread which brings death. The picture of Lady Wisdom may be seen as a prologue to chapters 10–22, where the food of the great banquet is laid out (*Proverbios*, pp. 245-249).

Qoh 1,3.4-11 is like an introduction which establishes the atmosphere and sums up the whole book. A cyclic vision, monotony and disillusion, gives a sorry picture of everything. The universe, an endless turning without sense; human history, an amorphous entity saved for the obstinate forgetfulness of human beings. Repeated words and formulas serve to obliterate any differences. If it is read slowly, the poem stupefies you and puts you to sleep; if it is read fast, it worries and confuses you. All that remains, the substance of it all is "vanity, mere breath".

Chapter 24 of Ben Sira is a fine construction with well-defined lines. Wisdom sings a hymn telling her history in four strophes or parts. Firstly, her birth, her travels and her dominion over the universe. Second, the historical establishment in a land and in a people, both chosen by God for her; there she dwells, there she ministers to God. Third, she is transformed poetically into a tree, which flourishes, gives a pleasant odour and fruit; like the new tree of paradise, which gathers together all the virtues of the best trees. Fourth, this is not the forbidden tree, but a tree offered to all that they may have success, a tree which communicates strength and liberates from sin. When Wisdom finishes speaking the wise man or teacher takes up the poem. In the fifth strophe he identifies her historically with the book of the covenant, and poetically with the six rivers of a new paradise, rivers which spread out with dimensions of the sea and the ocean, as in a repeat of the creation. In the sixth strophe the wise man talks of himself, with various images: he is a channel of this ocean source, he waters his orchard and lets his waters form a sea; then it is like a source of light which shines forth into the distance, and his teaching is like prophecy, like a testament for future ages. The last verses correspond with their waters to the waters of the first strophe, with their garden they correspond to the new tree of life of the third strophe; and the wise man, trained by Wisdom, offers his gifts to others just like that tree. Creation and paradise appear in this poem. Water and light and vegetation are the chief elements (fire and wind are absent). After the journey comes rest, but the rest here is marked by the disquiet of vegetation which must grow and give itself, and contribute to the growth of life with its fruit and its waters. The author has been inspired to write a poem which is clear and well-defined in its exterior, and enlivened internally by great traditional symbols. (We know this text only from a Greek translation.) (*Proverbios y Eclesiástico* [LLS; in collaboration with J. M. Valverde and J. Mateos; Madrid 1968], pp. 227-232).

Job 28 is a poem in honour of Wisdom, a kind of restful interlude at the end of three cycles of the dialogue. Various external signs mark the division of the poem into three strophes or parts and lead us to recognize significant relationships within the poem. Vv. 12 and 20 each bring to a close a stage of human striving, and in vv. 14 and 22 we find two superhuman forces, those of Sea and Ocean, and Death and the Abyss. The strophes are linked dynamically with each other. First strophe: *homo faber* is portrayed as triumphing in the great feat of mining; but he fails in not being able to find the dwelling place of Wisdom. Second strophe: we turn to the *homo oeconomicus* who is ready to offer treasures in order to buy Wisdom; but he fails because Wisdom cannot be bought, it has no price. Third strophe: man's double failure directs us to God as the Lord of Wisdom, who uses wisdom in his work of creation and is prepared to give wisdom as a gift to the one who fears him, the *homo religiosus*.

It is my opinion that the analysis of the composition of Hebrew poems is one of the most important, most difficult and least practised of tasks. Rules and classifications are not of much use in learning how it should be done; the most fruitful approach is to see how clear-sighted and experienced experts analyze poems and learn by imitation.

R. G. Moulton, *The Literary Study of the Bible*, pp. 90 ff. He speaks of simple unity, of contrast, of transition, accumulation, circumstances extrinsic to the poem.

N. W. Lund, "The Presence of Chiasmus in the Old Testament", *AJSL* 46 (1929-1930) 104-126.

N. W. Lund, "Chiasmus in the Psalms", *AJSL* 49 (1932-1933) 281-312. He applies the term chiasmus to what today we call concentric structure.

L. Alonso Schökel, *Estudios de poética hebrea*, pp. 309-361.

Many articles dedicated to particular texts and entitled "The literary structure of..." refer to superficial structure. I must also issue a warning against the desire to find always and show by diagrams any kind of relationship within a poem. Even though these relationships may be multiple and complex the diagram should always be simple and never confused.

Abbreviations

Books of the Bible

Am	Amos	Lev	Leviticus
Bar	Baruch	Mac	Maccabees
Cant	Canticle of Canticles	Mal	Malachi
	[Song of Songs]	Mic	Micah
Chr	Chronicles	Nah	Nahum
Cor	Corinthians	NT	New Testament
Dan	Daniel	Num	Numbers
Deut	Deuteronomy	Obad	Obadiah
Exod	Exodus	OT	Old Testament
Ezek	Ezekiel	Prov	Proverbs
Gen	Genesis	Ps	Psalms
Hab	Habakkuk	Qoh	Qoheleth
Hos	Hosea		[Ecclesiastes]
Isa	Isaiah	Rev	Revelation
Jer	Jeremiah		[Apocalypse]
Jdt	Judith	Sam	Samuel
Jon	Jonah	Sir	Sirach [Ben Sira]
Josh	Joshua		[Ecclesiasticus]
Judg	Judges	Zech	Zechariah
Kgs	Kings	Zeph	Zephaniah
Lam	Lamentations		

Periodicals, Series, Encyclopaedias

AcCh Academia Christiana. Madrid.
AJSL *American Journal of Semitic Languages and Literatures.* Chicago.
AnBib Analecta Biblica. Rome.
AnOr Analecta Orientalia. Rome.
ATANT Abhandlungen zur Theologie des Alten und Neuen Testaments. Zürich and elsewhere.
BAC Biblioteca de autores cristianos. Madrid.
BEFAR Bibliothèque des écoles françaises d'Athènes et de Rome. Paris.
BH Bibliothèque historique. Bruxelles and elsewhere.
BHSGS Beiträge zur literarischen Syntax der griechischen Sprache.
Bib *Biblica.* Rome.
BiBe Biblische Beiträge. Einsiedeln and elsewhere.
BibOr Biblica et Orientalia. Rome.
BiL Biblia y lenguaje. Madrid.
BiLit Bible and Literature. Sheffield.

BZAW	Beihefte zur Zeitschrift für die alttestamentliche Wissenschaft. Berlin and elsewhere.
BZfr	Biblische Zeitfragen gemeinverständlich erörtert. Münster.
DBS	*Dictionnaire de la bible.* Supplément. Paris.
DN.ST	Dissertationes Neerlandicae, Series Theologica. 's-Gravenhage.
EHPhR	Études d'histoire et de philosophie religieuses. Paris and elsewhere.
EE	*Estudios ecclesiásticos.* Madrid.
CEA	Collection d'études anciennes. Paris.
FOTL	The Forms of Old Testament Literature. Grand Rapids.
HK	Handkommentar zum Alten Testament. Göttingen.
HLW	Handbuch der Literaturwissenschaft. Potsdam.
HUCA	*Hebrew Union College Annual.* Cincinnati.
IDB	*Interpreter's Dictionary of the Bible.* New York and elsewhere.
IluCle	*Ilustración del clero.* Madrid.
Inter	*Interpretation.* Richmond.
ISJ	Institución San Jeronimo. Valencia.
ISJ.EAT	Institución San Jeronimo: Estudios de Antiguo Testamento. Valencia.
JBL	*Journal of Biblical Literature.* Philadelphia.
JJS	*Journal of Jewish Studies.* London.
JPOS	*Journal of the Palestine Oriental Society.* Jerusalem and elsewhere.
JSOT.SS	Journal for the Study of the Old Testament. Supplementary Series. Sheffield.
JTS	*Journal of Theological Studies.* Oxford and elsewhere.
KBANT	Kommentare und Beiträge zum Alten und Neuen Testament. Düsseldorf.
KGw	Kultur und Gegenwart. Berlin and elsewhere.
LBs	Library of Biblical Studies. New York.
LLS	Los Libros Sagrados. Madrid.
OrPh	L'ordre philosophique. Paris.
OTL	Old Testament Library. London.
OTSeries	Old Testament Series. Philadelphia.
NBE	Nueva Biblia Español. Madrid.
RB	*Revue biblique.* Paris.
REJ	*Revue des études juives.* Paris.
RMont. Théologie	Recherches. Théologie. Collection dirigée par la Faculté de la Compagnie de Jésus à Montréal. Paris and elsewhere.
RevSR	*Revue des sciences religieuses.* Strasbourg.
RHPhilRel	*Revue d'histoire et de philosophie religieuses.* Strasbourg and elsewhere.
RiProp	Ricerche o Proposte. Turin.
RivBib	*Rivista biblica italiana.* Rome and elsewhere.
RPS	Religious Perspectives Series. London and elsewhere.

SAOC	Studies in Ancient Oriental Civilization. Chicago.
SAT	Schriften des Alten Testaments in Auswahl. Göttingen.
ScrHie	Scripta Hierosolymitana. Jerusalem.
Sef	*Sefarad*. Madrid.
Semeia	*Semeia*. Missoula and elsewhere.
Semitics	*Semitics*. Muckleneuk.
SGV	Sammlung gemeinverständlicher Vorträge und Schriften aus dem Gebiet der Theologie und Religionsgeschichte. Tübingen.
SP.SM	Studia Pohl. Series Maior. Rome.
STLI	Studies and Texts. Philip W. Lown Institute of Advanced Judaic Studies. Braideis University. Cambridge, Massachusetts.
Théol(P)	Théologie. Paris.
TQ	*Theologische Quartalschrift*. Tübingen and elsewhere.
TB	Theologische Bücherei. Münich.
TRu	*Theologische Rundschau*. Tübingen.
VD	*Verbum Domini*. Rome.
VTS	Vetus Testamentum. Supplements. Leiden.
WiB	Wissenschaft und Bildung. Leipzig.
ZS	*Zeitschrift für Semitistik und verwandte Gebiete*. Leipzig.

Books on Biblical Themes by Luis Alonso Schökel, S. J.

Viaje al país del Antiguo Testamento (Santander 1956). English language edition: *Journey through the Bible Lands*. Translated by J. Drury (Milwaukee 1964).

El hombre de hoy ante la Biblia (Barcelona 1959; ²1964). English language edition: *Understanding Biblical Research*. Translated by P. J. McCord (New York 1963). German language edition: Düsseldorf 1961, ²1966; Italian language edition: Brescia 1963; Chinese language edition: Taipeh 1982.

Estudios de poética hebrea (Barcelona 1963). German language edition: Cologne 1971.

La palabra inspirada. La Biblia a la luz de la ciencia del lenguaje (Barcelona 1966, ²1969, ³1986). English language edition: *The Inspired Word. Scripture in the Light of Language and Literature*. Translated by F. Martin (New York 1965). Italian language edition: Brescia 1967, ²1987. French language edition: Paris 1971. Polish language edition: Cracow 1983.

Doce Profetas Menores: Oseas, Joel, Amós, Abdías, Miqueas, Nahum, Habacuc, Sofonías, Ageo, Zacarías, Malaquías. Traducción, introducciones, notas (LLS; Madrid 1966). [In collaboration.]

Salmos (LLS; Madrid 1966, ²1968, ³1972, ⁴1977, ⁵1982, ⁶1985, ⁷1988). [In collaboration.] Italian language edition: Casale Monferrato 1982. Portuguese language edition: São Paulo 1982, ²1987.

Jeremías (LLS; Madrid 1967). [In collaboration.]

Isaías (LLS; Madrid 1968). [In collaboration.]

Proverbios y Eclesiástico (LLS; Madrid 1968). [In collaboration.]

Concilio Vaticano II. Comentarios a la constitución "Dei Verbum" sobre la divina revelación (BAC 284; Madrid 1969). [In collaboration.] Italian language edition: Brescia 1970.

El Cantar de los Cantares (LLS; Madrid 1969). [In collaboration.]

Pentateuco I. Génesis. Exodo (LLS; Madrid 1970). [In collaboration.]

Pentateuco II. Levítico. Números. Deuteronomio (LLS; Madrid 1970). [In collaboration.]

Job (LLS; Madrid 1971). [In collaboration.]

Ezequiel (LLS; Madrid 1971). [In collaboration.]

Josué y Jueces (LLS; Madrid 1973). [In collaboration.]

Samuel (LLS; Madrid 1973). [In collaboration.]

Reyes (LLS; Madrid 1973). [In collaboration.]

Rut. Tobías. Judit. Ester (LLS; Madrid 1973). [In collaboration.]

Eclesiastés y Sabiduría (LLS; Madrid 1974). [In collaboration.]

Nueva Biblia Española (Madrid 1975). [In collaboration.]

Nueva Biblia Española. Edición latinoamericana (Madrid 1976). [In collaboration.]

Crónicas. Esdras. Nehemías (LLS; Madrid 1976). [In collaboration.]

Macabeos (LLS; Madrid 1976). [In collaboration.]

Daniel. Baruc. Carta de Jeremías. Lamentaciones (LLS; Madrid 1976). [In collaboration.]

La traducción bíblica: lingüística y estilística (BiL 3; Madrid 1977). [In collaboration.]

Primera lectura de la Biblia. Selección, introducciones y comentarios (NBE; Madrid 1977, ²1981). [In collaboration.]

Profetas. Introducción y comentarios. I. Isaías. Jeremías. II. Ezequiel. Doce Profetas Minores. Daniel. Baruc. Carta de Jeremías (NBE; Madrid 1980, ²1986). [In collaboration.] Italian language edition: Rome 1984.

La Bibbia, Parola di Dio scritta per noi. I. Antico Testamento, Libri storici. II. Antico Testamento, Libri sapienziali e profetici. III. Nuovo Testamento (Turin 1980). [In collaboration.]

Diccionario terminológico de la ciencia bíblica (Madrid–Valencia 1979). [In collaboration.] Italian language edition: Rome 1981. French language edition: Paris 1982.

Treinta Salmos: poesía y oración (ISJ.EAT 2; Madrid 1981, ²1986). Italian language edition: Bologna 1982.

Job. Comentario teológico y literario (NBE; Madrid 1983). [In collaboration.] Italian language edition: Rome 1985.

¿Dónde está tu hermano? Textos de fraternidad en el libro del Génesis (ISJ 19; Valencia 1985, ²1988). Italian language edition: Brescia 1987.

Sapienciales. I. Proverbios (NBE; Madrid 1984). [In collaboration.] Italian language edition: Rome 1988.

Hermenéutica de la Palabra. I. Hermenéutica bíblica (AcCh 37; Madrid 1986).

Hermenéutica de la Palabra. II. Interpretación literaria de textos bíblicos (AcCh 38; Madrid 1987).

Hermenéutica de la Palabra. III. Interpretación teológica de textos bíblicos (AcCh 39; Madrid 1988).

Index of Biblical Texts

Index of Authors

Boldface type indicates full bibliographical information.

Index of Subjects